Mapping Hispaniola

New World Studies

J. Michael Dash, Editor

Frank Moya Pons and
Sandra Pouchet Paquet,
Associate Editors

Mapping Hispaniola

Third Space in Dominican and Haitian Literature

Megan Jeanette Myers

University of Virginia Press
Charlottesville and London

Partial support for the publication of this work was contributed by the Iowa State University Publication Endowment, ISU Foundation.

University of Virginia Press
© 2019 by the Rector and Visitors of the University of Virginia
All rights reserved
Printed in the United States of America on acid-free paper

First published 2019

9 8 7 6 5 4 3 2 1

Library of Congress Cataloging-in-Publication Data

Names: Myers, Megan Jeanette, author.
Title: Mapping Hispaniola : third space in Dominican and Haitian literature / Megan Jeanette Myers.
Description: Charlottesville : University of Virginia Press, 2019. | Series: New World studies | Includes bibliographical references and index.
Identifiers: LCCN 2018056067 (print) | LCCN 2019013506 (ebook) | ISBN 9780813943091 (ebook) | ISBN 9780813943077 | ISBN 9780813943077 (cloth : alk. paper) | ISBN 9780813943084 (paperback : alk. paper)
Subjects: LCSH: Dominican literature—History and criticism. | Haitian literature—History and criticism. | Hispaniola—In literature. | Haiti—In literature. | Dominican Republic—In literature.
Classification: LCC PQ7400.5 (ebook) | LCC PQ 7400.5 . M94 2019 (print) | DDC 860.9/97293—dc23
LC record available at https://lccn.loc.gov/2018056067

Cover art: La Hispaniola postcard project, Scherezade Garcia, 2015. (Used by permission of the artist)

*For Marialíz, Marisol, Marcela, Holly Dolores,
and my great-grandfather Thomas Steel,
whose autobiography, detailing his life
in Santo Domingo as a young man,
first interested me in the Dominican Republic*

Contents

	Acknowledgments	ix
	Introduction	1
1.	Haitian and Dominican Third Space and the *Trujillato* (1930–1961)	21
2.	A Disappearing Act: Marcio Veloz Maggiolo's *Línea*	64
3.	"Here We Are the Haitians": Seeing Haiti from the Diaspora	99
4.	Multiple Haitis	125
	Conclusion	163
	Notes	171
	Bibliography	189
	Index	205

Acknowledgments

Mapping Hispaniola began years ago, and countless thank-yous are due to those who have helped, encouraged, challenged, and mentored me along the way.

In the academic sphere, I first need to thank my mentors and colleagues at Vanderbilt, where the roots of this project first took hold. I thank Benigno Trigo, Lorraine Lopez, and Ruth Hill for their helpful comments on this manuscript in the earliest stages. Special thanks are due to my adviser and continuing mentor, William Luis, for encouraging me throughout this process and offering feedback and advice beyond my time at Vanderbilt. I am also grateful to Rosie Seagraves for her editing skills and friendship and to Ben Galina for his support. I am particularly grateful for a FLAS grant that allowed me to spend the summer of 2013 studying Haitian Kreyòl at Florida International University and in Cap-Haïtien, Haiti. *Mèsi anpil* to Nicolas André and Liesel Picard for making that experience so formative. I also want to credit the journal *Confluencia* for allowing me to reprint part of an analysis that appeared in a 2013 article (vol. 32, no. 1) in chapters 3 and 4. For help in the final stages, I am grateful to the knowledgeable staff at the University of Virginia Press for their guidance and professionalism, in particular Eric Brandt, J. Michael Dash, Helen Chandler, and Ellen Satrom. I also thank Joanne Allen for her expert copyediting. In addition, a sincere thank-you to the two anonymous peer reviewers, whose readings of the manuscript helped me to shape my argument and produce a much-improved end product.

At my current home institution, Iowa State University, I am fortunate to be a part of the collegial and supportive Department of World Languages and Cultures. My colleagues in the Spanish Section in particular have cheered me on both formally and informally. *Gracias* to Chad Gasta (department chair extraordinaire), Julia Domínguez, Eugenio Matibag,

Charles Nagle, Lucía Suárez, Cristina Pardo Ballester, and Rachel Haywood Ferreira, many of whom have read portions of this book or hashed out ideas with me over coffee or in hallway chats. Special thanks go to Elisa Rizo for supporting me as my formal mentor at Iowa State and to the ever-helpful Carly Johansen and Amanda Runyan. Also a shout-out to the Straw Dawgz writing group and my friends Rachel Meyers and Charlie Nagle for reading portions of this book and for the many conversations about not just work and writing but also life. I am also grateful to my wonderful students at Iowa State for encouraging me and keeping me energized and excited. At the institutional level, financial support in the form of LAS small grants, foreign-travel grants, and a Center for Excellence in Arts and the Humanities (CEAH) grant enabled me to finish this project and embark on related travels. In addition, Bailey Hanson and the Essentials of ArcGIS Workshop at Iowa State, the Iowa State GIS Research Lab and Josh Obrecht, as well as the 2017 Digital Humanities Summer Institute at the University of Victoria, enhanced my digital-mapping skills.

I am also grateful for conversations with colleagues about aspects of this book at numerous conferences over the past few years. I benefited as well from my work as the assistant editor of the *Afro-Hispanic Review* in 2012, in particular helping to organize an issue focused on transnational Hispaniola. Some of the individuals who contributed to the *Afro-Hispanic Review* 32.2 and/or engaged in conversation with me at conferences or via email include John T. Maddox, John Ribó, Raj Chetty, Elena Machado Saez, Nathan Dize, Edouard Duval-Carrié, Silvio Torres-Saillant, Edwidge Danticat, Davide Sala, Scherezade García, Chiqui Vicioso, Polibio Díaz, Jacques Pierre, Èvelyne Trouillot, Juan Carlos González Díaz, Walter Thompson-Hernández, Deisy Toussaint, and countless others. A heartfelt thank-you to Scherezade for permission to use her amazing artwork on the cover of this book.

As I note in the following introduction, Border of Lights (BOL) is a community of activists, artists, writers, academics, and others who meet at the Haitian-Dominican border each October on the anniversary of the 1937 Haitian Massacre to pay tribute to the lives lost and to recognize the solidarity between Hispaniola's border communities. For me, over the past six years the BOL organizers have become much more than colleagues or an extended network: they have become my BOL *familia*. Cynthia Carrión, Edward Paulino, Rana Dotson, DeAndra Beard, Erika Martínez, Michele Wucker, Sady Díaz, Bill Eichner, and Julia Alvarez—¡qué equipo! It has been a true pleasure to collaborate over the years with these individuals and with Hispaniola-based organizations such as Centro Montalvo,

Reconoci.do, MUDHA, the DREAM Project, and the Mariposa Foundation. Thanks also to Mario Serrano, Padre Regino, and the staff at Hotel Raydan for supporting BOL from the outset. I also want to thank those who welcomed me into their homes in the Dominican Republic. To my *madre dominicana* Dolores, Silbano, *mis compadres* Gladys and Bichan, Carolina y Romero, Don José y Doña Nati Cruz, and countless others in Jarabacoa and surrounding communities, thank-you from the bottom of my heart. I am grateful as well for a continued relationship with the Mariposa Foundation in Cabarete, where I have spent summers teaching literature classes. I thank Patricia Suriel, Amanda Bucci, and their lovely families for continually welcoming my own family with open arms and for tirelessly advocating for the education of girls in the Dominican Republic and worldwide. *Sí que son la fuerza más potente para cambiar el mundo.*

Lastly, I am grateful to my network of family and friends who have encouraged me and believed in me as an academic, a writer, a teacher, a mom, a partner, a *comadre*, a friend, a runner. Over the course of writing and revising this book I have run literally thousands of miles. Thanks to Sandra Looft, Jenn Baumgartner, Julie Gould, and Valentina Salotti for accompanying me on many of those miles and for being willing to wake up before sunrise to get our runs in before most people (especially our kids) were awake. Sandra, thanks for being a sounding board for this book from start to finish and such a great friend. Thanks also to Glen Myers for his coaching and bike-along expertise. I could not have completed this book, or more than ten pages, without amazing childcare. Thanks to the many stellar teachers at Eagle's Loft in Ames, Iowa, and student nanny McKenzie Theisen for loving and caring for my girls. Special thanks are due to Shelley Mishler and Amy Myers for stepping up time and time again; thanks to them I was able to attend conferences and continue an active research agenda over the last five years. I will be forever grateful to you both for your many trips to Tennessee and Iowa to support my family. Thanks are also in order to John Mishler, who read and edited an earlier version of this book in its entirety; to Ellen Mishler for her constant encouragement and fashion tips; and to Ron Mishler for his unending support and advice. Last but most certainly not least, I thank my partner, Chris/Peach(es), for always believing in me and for embracing the chaos with love and laughter; and our sweet girls, Marcela and Holly Dolores, for bringing endless joy into our lives. This book, and everything I do, is for you.

Mapping Hispaniola

Introduction

> Now let them say that we have no borders.
> —Rafael Leónidas Trujillo

In October 2017, on the eightieth anniversary of the 1937 massacre of Haitians and Dominicans of Haitian descent, members of the border communities of Dajabón and Ouanaminthe, alongside international allies, erected the first permanent memorial commemorating the massacre.[1] The existence of the memorial prompts the following questions: What does it mean to memorialize a massacre, an ethnic genocide? What is the significance of remembering a moment in history that some community members have consciously elected to forget? Who has the responsibility or right to memorialize? In this case, Border of Lights, an organization seeking to commemorate the 1937 Haitian Massacre and to encourage the recognition of collaboration and solidarity between Haiti and the Dominican Republic, funded the 2017 monument. Founded in 2012, Border of Lights celebrates the physical and metaphorical intersections of the border as third space, a unique and porous zone of contact between two countries. Each October in Dajabón, Dominican Republic, and Ouanaminthe, Haiti, the Border of Lights collective organizes a two-day meeting on the Haitian-Dominican border. The collaborative works with community members to organize events, from public art installations to documentary screenings and park clean-ups, that aspire to unite rather than divide the two nations that meet at the Massacre River.

Border of Lights is an ideal starting point from which to critically approach the physical and metaphorical spaces that define Haitian-Dominican relations. Set both on and off the geopolitical border, Dominican and Dominican American literature envisions the contact zone between the two countries of Hispaniola as neither Haitian nor Dominican but as intermediary third space. In this book I consider how certain literary texts offer an alternative to the dominant and at times exaggerated Dominican anti-Haitian ideology and I endeavor to reposition Haiti on the literary map of the Dominican Republic and beyond, challenging the physical space of the border and its history of blurred lines. This book builds on the growing interdisciplinary study of literary geography and localizes a representation of *entre-deux,* or in-between, spaces within a broad understanding of Hispaniola and the Dominican and Haitian US diasporas. This holistic view not only considers Dominican, Haitian, Dominican American, and Haitian American border representations in literature but expands to include a Puerto Rican American's text in an effort to recognize the interethnic communities of the US Latino/a diaspora. Analyzing the work of numerous writers who at times depict the border as ambiguous and/or anonymous, this project challenges what a fluid border looks like in literature and considers to which discourse(s) it responds. The demarcation of the Dominican-Haitian border loses significance as narratives with an interest in portraying Dominican-Haitian relations both on and off the border produce a cultural politics of diversity and inclusion, forging a literary geography of Hispaniola that softens or diminishes the historical rendering of the border. As Roberto Cassá et al. signal, the idea that Dominicans are superior to Haitians has been "magnified to frightening proportions" (60) and suggesting that such *antihaitianismo* is a pillar of Dominican national thought is inaccurate. In a similar vein, Dixa Ramírez avouches, largely in reference to a patterned narrative of black denial and anti-Haitianism, that "Dominicans have expressed their dissatisfaction with how they have been described in dominant discourses" (4). *Mapping Hispaniola* deemphasizes the antipodal portrayal of the two nations of Hispaniola by focusing on representations of the Haitian-Dominican dynamic that veer from the dominant history, disrupting and challenging the "magnification" and repetition of a Dominican anti-Haitian narrative.

An increasing number of scholars have alluded to the border dividing Haiti and the Dominican Republic as porous and undefined, and the physical border spaces are fittingly described by what the historian Anne Eller refers to as "center-island" areas (47).[2] The use of this term highlights the autonomy of border regions in response to and at times in refutation of constant domestic land disputes and imperial conquests. Although Eller places the term historically in the nineteenth century, leading up to the independence of the Dominican Republic and following Spanish annexation in 1861, its success in labeling the Dominican-Haitian border regions as stateless and freestanding makes it useful in discussions of contemporary relations between the two countries. Moreover, the erasure of national identification when referring to the Haitian-Dominican border also exists in earlier publications of the Haitian geographer Jean Marie Théodat, who emphasizes the "oneness" of Haiti and the Dominican Republic, referring to the geopolitical reality of the two countries sharing one island as "insular twinness" in *Haïti-République Dominicaine: Une île pour deux, 1804–1916* (2003; Haiti–Dominican Republic: An island for two, 1804–1916).

Théodat's approach to transnational relations between Haiti and the Dominican Republic, in addition to other postcolonial theories that epitomize zones of cultural contact, helps to guide the spatial pulse and organization of *Mapping Hispaniola* by emphasizing that both physical *and* ideological borders double as site(s) of disruption, spaces that constantly challenge constructions of identity. In the case of Hispaniola, the border is where Dominicanness/*dominicanidad* and Haitianness/*haitianidad* break down; it is the site of reconstruction and reevaluation of identity. As Judith Butler articulates in *Bodies That Matter,* the border can be read as the "constitutive outside" that troubles or "haunts" identity formation, the space creating "the persistent possibility" of "disruption and rearticulation" (8). This book considers various theoretical approaches to this "rearticulation" of the border, namely, Chicana Gloria Anzaldúa's ideological border construct and her understanding of *nepantla,* Michel Foucault's heterotopia, and Homi K. Bhabha's third space. While the various approaches of these postcolonial thinkers all examine disjunctive understandings of place, devoted to zones of contact and intersection, I frame Anzaldúa's borderlands and Foucault's heterotopia within a broader conceptualization of third space. I utilize Anzaldúa's and Foucault's articulations of borders as unique strategies to examine third space in literature, thus approaching third space as related to Bhabha's definition of the term but also as a distinctive, singular third space that pertains exclusively to the border between the Dominican Republic and Haiti. This motion toward situating close readings of Haiti in Dominican and Dominican American literature within a theoretical lens centered on third terms, or "thirding," provides an avenue for approaching space(s) like the Haitian-Dominican border, historically portrayed as binary. Anzaldúa's, Foucault's, and Bhabha's spatial theories critique binary thinking by portraying both real and imagined spaces as intersectional and synergistic.

As this project assesses documented periods of peace and examples of interdependency and camaraderie between Haiti and the Dominican Republic in literature, it also builds on recent interdisciplinary scholarship on transnational Hispaniola that similarly posits relations between Haiti and the Dominican Republic as collaborative.[3] Alaí Reyes-Santos dissects the relationship as a narrative of national kinship, focusing on textual, political, and cultural evidence of "solidarity and intercultural connections" (21). Other contestations to and refutations of an incessant history of antipodal relations between Haiti and the Dominican Republic that are grounded in literary criticism include Ramón Antonio Victoriano-Martínez's *Rayanos y Dominicanyorks: La dominicanidad del siglo XXI* (2014; *Rayanos* and Dominicanyorks: Twenty-first century Dominicanness), Maja Horn's *Masculinity after Trujillo: The Politics of Gender in Dominican Literature* (2014), Maria Cristina Fumagalli's *On the Edge: Writing the Border between Haiti and the Dominican Republic* (2015), Lorgia García-Peña's *The Borders of Dominicanidad: Race, Nation, and Archives of Contradiction* (2016), and Dixa Ramírez's *Colonial Phantoms: Belonging and Refusal in the Dominican Americas, from the 19th Century to the Present* (2018). In particular, both García-Peña and Fumagalli approach Dominican and Haitian relations vis-à-vis their borders. These studies offer an alternate vision of the intertwined history of the two countries, rejecting the vision of Haiti and the Dominican Republic as tragic twins, instead focusing on important yet overlooked aspects of the relationship between the two, namely, their reciprocal influence and interdependence.

Much as the aforementioned scholars attribute different meanings to the international border that divides Haiti and the Dominican Republic, Anzaldúa recognizes the border as both cultural signifier and analytic tool in her borderlands theory.[4] While the majority of border theory produced in the United States, including Anzaldúa's work, is concerned primarily with the US-Mexican border, the geographical and ideological dimensions of these studies apply to the Dominican-Haitian border as well. For Anzaldúa, ideological borders exist anywhere. She distinguishes between ideological and geographical borders in her writing by marking geographical borders with a lowercase *b* and ideological ones with an uppercase *B*. This less visible border materializes in literature in off-border narratives that reframe the Haitian-Dominican dynamic. An ideological, or "soft," Border also allows for a metaphorical understanding of borderlands that builds on a flexible understanding of the geopolitical Dominican-Haitian border that produces other borders—social, racial, religious, and cultural. I use Anzaldúa's border theory, centered on the ideological Border, to refocus the representation of Haiti in Dominican and Dominican American literature and to decipher how texts set both on and off border and written from both on- and off-border spaces reenvision Hispaniola's history and resist the dominant, patriarchal, anti-Haitian discourses surrounding Dominican culture and identity.

Foucault's heterotopia, on the other hand, conceptualizes space by attempting to define and categorize "other" spaces. Heterotopias, in ways similar to the Dominican Pedro Henríquez Ureña's (1884–1946) understanding of Latin America as utopia (addressed in chapter 4), describe identifiable geographical spaces. Foucault's concept of heterotopia, first introduced in a 1967 lecture and posthumously published in an essay titled "Of Other Spaces: Utopias and Heterotopias," reflects a broad interpretation of social and cultural space.[5] A discussion centered on heterotopias, in opposition to utopias, circles interdisciplinary fields from architecture to geography and in some cases has transferred to border studies. In an effort to conceptualize space and to analyze the fluidity of the Haitian-Dominican border in contemporary literature, I propose Hispaniola—as well as the island's growing diaspora—as heterotopic in nature. Keeping Hispaniola's alignment with heterotopia in mind, this book analyzes through Foucault's heterotopic lens the shifts in Dominican-Haitian relations and the delineation of an increasingly porous border in Dominican and Dominican American literature.

Foucault's "Of Other Spaces" serves as a useful theoretical base from which to explore both geographical and ideological borders and to address on- and off-border spaces in Dominican and Dominican American literature.[6] A Foucauldian understanding of broadly conceived borders informs the connection(s) between the Dominican-Haitian frontier and political power structures. Hispaniola constitutes a heterotopic entity in the sense that it represents a space where Otherness prevails, a space that functions in relation to other spaces, most specifically Haiti and the Dominican Republic but also the Caribbean, Latin America, and the broader African diaspora. In reference to Foucault's traits of a heterotopia, the notion that such a space has multiple layers of meaning helps to illustrate why many writers, even those outside Hispaniola, are drawn to the island and its unique history. Moreover, the ability of heterotopias to exist "without geographical markers" (25) speaks to Hispaniola's border; this line appears erased or blurred as Dominican, Dominican American, Haitian, Haitian American, and other authors elect to rewrite and reenvision the island's history and the relationship between Haiti and the Dominican Republic and Hispaniola and the world. In this way, the island of Hispaniola, too, constitutes a space that exists and thrives "without geographical markers."

Expressions such as Eller's "center-island" and Paulino's "backlands" (5) or "zones of contact" (5) strive to encapsulate the reality of the Dominican-Haitian frontier as an indefinite region.[7] Similarly, my use of *third space* to approach on- and off-border literature as related to the Haitian-Dominican dynamic articulates an international boundary zone functioning without set limits. The recurring reference to on- and off-border texts in this project is an attempt to distinguish between literature set on and off the physical border. Additionally, the juxtaposition of *on-* and *off-border* also distinguishes between authors writing from either on or off the border (or either on the island or from the diaspora). Prior to the 1930s and Trujillo's border negotiations, local-level border controls were "practically nonexistent" (Paulino 3), and the twentieth- and twenty-first-century literature analyzed in the following chapters blurs politically imposed boundary lines by writing the border as fluid and semiautonomous. The emerging pattern of third space in literature, bolstered by an understanding of Anzaldúa's ideological Borders and Foucault's heterotopia, connects the multigenre works at the center of *Mapping Hispaniola*.

In his 1994 book *The Location of Culture,* Bhabha imagines third space as a sociolinguistic theory and a tool with which to approach cultural hybridity in postcolonial discourse. Hybridity, for Bhabha, creates an in-between space that is on the "cutting edge of translation and negotiation" (*Location of Culture* 38). This liminal space, by definition "hybrid" and intermediary, does not exist without a fluid conceptualization of space created by hybridity. "For me," asserts Bhabha, "the importance of hybridity is not to be able to trace two original moments from which the third emerges, rather hybridity to me is the 'third space' which enables other positions to emerge. This third space displaces the histories that constitute it, and sets up new structures of authority, new political initiatives" ("Third Space" 211). This notion that third space does not constitute the collision or combination of two existing spaces but instead exists as a politics of inclusion and the initiation of "new signs of identity, and innovative sites of collaboration, and contestation" proves key (Bhabha, *Location of Culture* 1–2). Within a third space, defined by opportunities for innovation and collaboration, new identities coalesce and essentialisms or the existence of an original or dominant culture give way to new possibilities, new forms of cultural meaning and production. While other theorists, including Anzaldúa, who uses the term *third country* to define border culture in *Borderlands/La Frontera,* utilize what Chela Sandoval refers to as "third-term" nomenclature, flexibility and a "coalitional consciousness" routinely define these spaces (Sandoval 71).

Geographers, too, have elaborated on Bhabha's third space. The political geographer Edward W. Soja's *Thirdspace: Journeys to Los Angeles and Other Real-and-Imagined Places* (1996) builds on the spatiotemporal theories of not just Bhabha but also Foucault, Anzaldúa, bells hooks,

Henri Lefebvre, and others. Soja traces the critical strategy of "thirding-as-othering" (5) and specifically addresses physical spaces that stand for sites of "critical exchange" and "openness" (5). For Soja, "Thirdspace is a meeting point, a hybrid place, where one can move beyond the existing borders" ("Thirdspace" 56). Intersections of third space and Soja's "Thirdspace" are material, physical, ideological, and virtual, and the idea that these contact zones exist as both location and praxis guides *Mapping Hispaniola*. I approach third space not only as a physical, mappable border but also as a space of rhetorical, metaphorical contestation. The works analyzed in chapters 1 through 4 create, through fiction and other mediums, multiple renderings of third space. However, these references to the border are not always physical or geopolitical in nature. In addition to contemplating third space as a geographical "zone of contact," they also—in the case of Dominican American writers envisioning Dominican-Haitian relations as fluid—posit third space as off border. Similarly, chapter 4 offers a close reading of a Haitian American–authored novel and a Haitian-authored play that both contest and corroborate Dominican and Dominican American portrayals of third space. The chapter also increases this study's scope by exploring a Puerto Rican American novel that details diasporic dynamic beyond that of solely Haitian and Dominicans. While *Mapping Hispaniola* builds on Bhabha's inherently discursive third space and Soja's reconstructive physical Thirdspace, it also moves beyond them to imagine a Haitian-Dominican third space in literature, a unique space that is both real and imagined, both on and off border.

Border of Lights and Third Space

I elected to begin this introduction by referencing Border of Lights to underscore a diasporic and international interest in Dominican-Haitian relations and to outwardly address parallels between physical memorials to historical events like the 1937 Haitian Massacre and memorials or overt references to the history of Hispaniola in literature. The initial inspiration behind Border of Lights, spearheaded by conversations following the premature death of the Haitian human-rights activist Sonia Pierre between the Dominican American author Julia Alvarez and the journalist Michele Wucker, centered on the idea of "lighting up the border" in an act of solidarity and as a visual means to pay tribute to lives lost in the 1937 Massacre. Border of Lights, beyond organizing a candlelit vigil along the Haitian-Dominican border, recognizes and honors decades of collaboration between Hispaniola's border communities and works closely with community partners, including Reconoci.do, MUDHA (Movimiento de Mujeres Dominico-Haitianas, or Movement of Dominican-Haitian Women), Yspaniola, and Centro Montalvo (formerly Solidaridad Fronteriza, or Border Solidarity). Border of Lights began in 2012 to commemorate the seventy-fifth anniversary of the massacre.[8] This first border meeting, uniting Dominican Americans, Haitian Americans, residents of both the Dominican Republic and Haiti, and other members of the international community, included an interactive art exhibit in the central park of Dajabón, a dedicatory mass in both Dajabón and Ouanaminthe on the anniversary of the massacre, a candlelit vigil along the banks of the Massacre River with groups from both the Dominican and Haitian sides in attendance, and a clean-up of Ouanaminthe's municipal park. The park clean-up extended to the Massacre River, and more than two hundred Haitian and Dominican volunteers from the Ouanaminthe and Dajabón communities supported and attended these events. In addition, three bay trees were planted on the grounds of the Ouanaminthe municipal park to honor victims of the massacre. Beginning with Border of Light's second year in 2013, the organization has also connected with a digital Hispaniola diasporic population and other international supporters of its mission by hosting a virtual vigil. This virtual vigil, taking place the Saturday after the candlelit vigil on the physical border, unites social-media forums, including Twitter, Instagram, and Facebook, with a common hashtag. The online forum hosts digital question-and-answer sessions with authors, scholars, and activists on the Border of Lights Facebook page.[9]

From its inception following Pierre's death in 2011, Border of Lights has been a testament to the "in-between." The event that gives the collaborative its name, a candlelit border vigil, takes place within the physical third space, the most visible and mappable site of intersection between the communities of Ouanaminthe and Dajabón. Following the candlelit processional, members of the border community line both sides of the Massacre River, which is a natural border between the two nations. Metaphorically, Border of Lights is synonymous with collaboration and community, encouraging the peaceful coming together of not only Haitian and Dominican border communities but also members of the Haitian and Dominican diaspora. In its role as a physical meeting place and a cultural collaborative, Border of Lights has sparked a "creative outpour" (Wucker) that succeeds in uniting voices from the island as well as Haitian and Dominican diasporic communities. The artistic endeavors inspired or funded by Border of Lights since 2012, from public murals to art workshops with local youth, exist largely as temporary installments. A mural painted in 2017, however, offers an interesting example of disparate community responses to public art. Located outside Dajabón's central park, the mural reads "Amor, Arte, Respeto" alongside the symbol "Ø + ACRE" ("no más + "acre," or "no masacre/massacre"). In December of 2017 this mural was vandalized, buckets of hot black oil thrown on the artwork. While the act of public vandalism speaks to the vestiges of anti-Haitianism in the Dominican Republic today, the swift response of community members who cleaned and restored the mural exemplifies the too-often-suppressed border narrative, one of solidarity and camaraderie. Also in 2017, Border of Lights and community partners erected the first physical memorial to the massacre. The secure location of the permanent memorial, bolted to the outside wall of the Jesuit church in Dajabón, Dominican Republic, serves as a safe haven from both natural elements and vandalism. The English portion of the trilingual-text placard reads:

> In memory of the nearly 15,000 black Haitian and black Dominicans that were brutally murdered by orders of the tyrant Rafael Leonidas Trujillo during the final months of 1937. And in homage to the brave Dominicans who resisted this genocide by collaborating clandestinely in the rescue and protection of their neighbors and who continue in contributing to improve relations between the Dominican Republic and Haiti. And to the unwavering commitment that neither this act nor any other human rights violations be repeated in any way between these two nations.
> —September 29, 2017, (80th) anniversary of the massacre

In an interview with the Haitian American writer Edwidge Danticat by Myriam J. A. Chancy prior to 2017, the two women recognize the lack of memorials to the 1937 Massacre. Danticat speaks to the "historical echoes" that carry into each century and form part of the "living memory" of Haitians: "There are no actual memorials to those who died in the 1937 massacre, we must have these living memorials in our hearts" ("Recovering History" 111). The fact that no official memorials existed before the eightieth anniversary of the massacre reflects, in part, the imprecise reporting on the event and the historical inaccuracy of the numbers. The Dominican *Acento* columnist Juan Tomás Tavares writes in his 2017 article on the discrepancies in reporting on the massacre: "When the autocratic state insists on not reporting a terrible event or in erasing its tracks, as a result there are no traces of the occurrence in official documentation. The reconstruction of the event, then, largely depends on circumstantial evidence, above all the testimonies of living participants and observers" (my translation).

Although the 2017 plaque, because of the lack of official documentation, offers an approximate number of lives lost as a result of the 1937 Massacre, the mere existence of the placard and the act of paying homage to not only those killed but also those who resisted the genocide constitutes progress in responsibly remembering and memorializing the ethnic genocide. Moreover, the fact that no physical memorial existed prior to 2017 signals the role of literature as a model for Danticat's "living memory" and underscores the ability of literature to create and sustain "a chain of memory" ("Recovering History" 110). Literature, too, memorializes. Beyond serving as cultural memory and signifier in reference to literary historiography, literature can partly fill the void of physical memorials as important mediums of memory that interpret historical events in myriad ways. As is the case with the numerous literary texts analyzed herein—ranging in genre from novel to memoir, short story, and theater—authors write from Hispaniola and its diasporic reaches to depict the physical Haitian-Dominican border as well as metaphorical borders, thus illuminating the cultural, political, and religious contact of Haitian and Dominican culture in border and nonborder zones. This book considers how a diverse, transnational group of authors remodels fictional third space(s) and thus imagines these interstitial sites in various ways. Some writers elect to vaguely and ambiguously craft cartographic space in their texts—renaming towns or neglecting to mention or include certain communities—while others attempt to more accurately merge geographical coordinates and markers in fiction with the geohistorical record. The multifarious ways that the authors examined in *Mapping Hispaniola* portray on- and off-border spaces on the island or in the diaspora offer an alternate approach to Haitian and Dominican relations.

Furthermore, in reference to the 2013 Tribunal Court ruling TC/0168/13, a consideration of metaphorical borders relates to discussions about the present reality for Dominicans of Haitian descent living in the Dominican Republic. With this ruling, the Dominican Tribunal Court stripped the citizenship of Haitian Dominicans registered legally in the country. The *sentencia* revokes the citizenship of all Dominicans born to undocumented parents after 1929. As the average life expectancy is seventy-three in the Dominican Republic, compared with forty-nine in Haiti, the sentence does not "grandfather out" many individuals, if any at all. The 2013 ruling rendered an estimated two hundred thousand Dominicans of Haitian descent stateless.[10]

Figure 1. The plaque commemorating the 1937 Massacre, in Spanish, Kreyòl, and English, sits below a mural started in 2012 and finished in 2017, funded by Border of Lights and painted by Daniel Ramos. The plaque and mural are on the outward-facing wall of the Parroquia Nuestra Señora del Rosario in Dajabón, Dominican Republic. (Photo from author's personal collection)

The On- and Off-Border Literature of Hispaniola

While the organization of *Mapping Hispaniola* is not chronological, several historical moments that are central to a complete understanding of Hispaniola today are explored in numerous texts. Such historical moments that have shifted the Dominican-Haitian border and (re)defined the relationship between Hispaniola's neighbors include the events of the Haitian Revolution (1791–1804), the Trujillo Era (1930–61), the US military interventions in the Dominican Republic (1916–30 and 1965), and the aforementioned 2013 Dominican Tribunal Court ruling. These four historical moments, among others, resurface in each of the chapters, but (third) space guides the organizational framework. Chapters 1 and 2, which focus specifically on Dominican literature written on the island, center on both the physical border between Haiti and the Dominican Republic and Haitian-Dominican relations removed from the physical border. Chapters 3 and 4 turn to novels and memoirs by Latino/a writers as well as Haitian and Haitian American writers. Not only do these individuals write from a space that is geographically off border and off island but they envision metaphorical third spaces in diasporic spheres. I also consider how these "off-border" authors approach the physical border or envision it differently. In her extensively researched study *Tropics of Haiti* (2015), Marlene Daut explores earlier literary representations of Haiti, in particular of the Haitian Revolution, present in "off-border" eighteenth- and nineteenth-century French, British, and American works. Daut suggests that literary portrayals of the Haitian Revolution routinely become dominated by what she refers to as the "mulatto/a vengeance narrative" (4). A representation of third space remains the constant for the various primary works analyzed in the following chapters, and the varied descriptions of porous "zones of contact" and autonomous "center-island" spaces lead to a rich understanding not only of how Dominican authors have written Haiti and Haitians in the twentieth and twenty-first centuries but also of how those writing from spaces increasingly removed from the border envision the relationship between two neighboring nations. Likewise, the literary analyses included herein not only use Dominican texts as an entry point to discussing and problematizing the alternate representations of the Haitian-Dominican dynamic but move beyond this Dominicanist perspective to also explore how Haitian and Haitian American works and one Puerto Rican American text envision Hispaniola's borders both on and off the island.

The genre-spanning works analyzed in this book are unique in the ways they render state-sponsored distinctions between Haiti and the Dominican Republic less visible. As these texts—some of which have been examined in numerous literary analyses, while others have been little studied—either are written from or envision spaces that function as heterotopias, a unique Dominican-Haitian model of third space in literature emerges. Not only do these literary texts refuse to promulgate history as one-sided and biased toward power structures but they offer readers new ways of understanding what many believe can only be gleaned from historical texts, in this way challenging the dominant narrative. An analysis of the selected works lends new meaning to the Haitian subject as historically defined in the Dominican Republic and Dominican diaspora and, in many cases, creates or describes a space that blurs previously existing dividing lines. *Mapping Hispaniola* challenges both a metaphorical and a physical map of Hispaniola and offers a textual and geographical understanding of the island that deemphasizes the border as a cultural, racial, ethnic, and spiritual signifier—a line of demarcation between "us" and "them"—instead focusing on points of contact, camaraderie, and fluidity between the two sister countries.

Although acknowledgment of an alternate, at times eclipsed history of Hispaniola in literature allows for the recognition of a Haitian-Dominican relationship defined by interdependence and sometimes camaraderie, that is not to say that animosity between the two countries does not exist; the works of the Dominican nationalists Joaquín Balaguer and Manuel Arturo Peña Batlle, among others, provide evidence of such *antihaitianismo*. Anti-Haitian sentiment also surfaces in texts written by Dominicans such as Ramón Marrero Aristy and Freddy Prestol Castillo.[11] The first chapter begins with an understanding of "the complex weave of mutual fascination and repulsion, attraction and dislike, respect and fear" in which Haiti and the Dominican Republic are bound (S. Martínez 84) in order to confirm the twentieth-century complexity of the Haitian-Dominican relationship, exaggerated by Rafael Leónidas Trujillo and the stronghold of *trujillato* ideology following the general's assassination in 1961. Maja Horn not only verifies Trujillo's modulation of "Dominican national identity and anti-Haitian prejudices in incisive ways that imply a break with previous historical periods" (16) but also explores how the *trujillato* reconfigured societal understandings of gender in the Dominican Republic and manipulated the discourse of masculinity. While Horn reads the consequences of Trujillo's shifting of the gender paradigm through an analysis of Dominican social practices and globalizing forces such as tourism and mass migration, the reverberations of nationalist, racist Dominican thought fostered during the Trujillo regime also surfaced in contemporary Dominican society with the recent Dominican Tribunal Court ruling. A modern-day signpost for the racist vestiges of the Trujillo Era is the recent reporting of Dominican migration authorities requesting dark-skinned Dominicans and Dominicans of Haitian descent to "Diga perejil" (Say parsley), believing that only native Spanish speakers, not Kreyòl speakers, can correctly pronounce the Spanish *r* or *j*.[12] Dominican soldiers in 1937 made the same demand during the ethnic genocide of approximately fifteen thousand Haitians, Dominicans, and Dominicans of Haitian descent.

I am not interested in categorizing the literary works examined here as altruistic for the ways in which they represent Haiti and Haitians, nor do I desire to enter into a philosophical or religious debate regarding the significance behind certain positive approaches to the western half of Hispaniola in such texts. Instead, I hope to show that the representation of Haitians in Dominican and Dominican American literature is increasingly varied, especially as literary works anchored in the past attempt to illustrate how political powers throughout the history of Hispaniola have deformed, restrained, and suppressed the Haitian subject. Dominican American authors, for example, are influenced by various factors that help to explain their yearning to reenvision Hispaniola and position Haitians as more than the racial Other. Such factors include US politics and equality laws; a geographical distance from the homeland that allows them to form different perspectives on historical events; and a desire to forge a distinctive identity as "hyphenated" subjects, as Gustavo Pérez Firmat suggests in *Life on the Hyphen*.

Mapping Hispaniola clarifies that despite the often unmitigated negrophobia and anti-Haitianism in the Dominican Republic, one can encounter a balanced representation of Haiti in Dominican and Dominican American literature. Literature not only reflects the dominant discourse and hegemonic power structures but also provides readers with a counterdiscourse. Counterdiscourses, such as those acknowledging the linkages of the past and present between two neighboring countries, problematize dominant ideologies and lead readers toward an alternate understanding of Hispaniola and Haitian-Dominican relations. The Dominican and Dominican American writers examined in the following chapters write against a dominant anti-Haitian national ideology. They reenvision Hispaniola, its history, and the relationship between the two countries that make up the Caribbean isle, writing against the past to give voice to the forgotten actors and events in an often one-sided transnational history. The Dominican and Dominican American narratives of which I offer close readings, despite the silences imposed by the government-supported national ideology in which the Dominican national self appears defined by its division and distance from the Haitian foreign Other, give retrospective significance to the spectrum of views of Haiti and Haitians both on and off the border and the island. Chapters 1 and 2, for example, each consider two novels written by Dominican authors. One novel in each chapter is set on the geopolitical border, while the other writes the Dominican-Haitian relationship from metaphorical third space such as the sugar plantation, allowing for an exploration of plantation novels, or *novelas de cañaveral* (Costa), and their modification of Dominican land and its national boundaries.

More specifically, chapter 1 focuses on Dominican works written during the thirty-one years of the Trujillo dictatorship and positions the 1937 Massacre as the pivotal event on which these texts fixate. The chapter pays special attention to the unabashed anti-Haitian sentiment that appeared in the first half of the twentieth century, undeniably linked to the *trujillato* and supported by authors such as Peña Batlle and Joaquín Balaguer, both of whom were considered members of Trujillo's intellectual inner circle. The chapter begins by outlining the importance of the *trujillato* in Dominican history and showing how Trujillo's reign dramatically shaped Dominican-Haitian relations, while at the same time building on anti-Haitian sentiment present in earlier time periods. *El Generalísimo*, as many addressed Trujillo, not only was involved in politics but also marked his territory within the Dominican intellectual realm. Chapter 1 examines the works of two important twentieth-century Dominican intellectuals: Ramón Marrero Aristy and Freddy Prestol Castillo. Marrero Aristy's *Over* subtly creates a narrative context in which Dominican characters sympathize and commiserate with the Haitian subject, at the same time carefully evading a "pro-afro" discourse or signs of "changes that would ruffle the feathers of the old Trujillo guard and their ideological offspring" (Torres-Saillant, "Dominican Blackness" 282). My analysis of Prestol Castillo's *El Masacre se pasa a pie* includes a map created by me of the place names that the author bolds within the text, questioning his decision to emphasize certain geographical locations and revealing a spatial interpretation of the novel that both compliments and further develops previous analyses of the work. I include the map in order to closely examine "geospace"—the real or geopolitical space that textual space utilizes as a geographical referent—in Dominican narratives. I utilize the map not as an end-all or as a concrete analysis of Prestol Castillo's text but instead to probe the work for its complex relation to Hispaniola's geography. As Franco Moretti asserts in *Graphs, Maps, Trees,* literary maps do not serve to provide an explanation but instead are meant to show "that there is something *that needs to be explained*" (39, emphasis in original).

Chapter 2 looks at the stronghold of Dominican-Haitian counternarrative in post-Trujillo Dominican literature, with a specific focus on the US invasion in 1965 and the earlier US Marine intervention from 1916 through 1924. The end of the dictatorship's censorship on literature and the arts had a profound impact on salient themes in national literature, including those related to Haiti and the Haitian tradition. Marcio Veloz Maggiolo's novels form the nucleus of this second chapter. His work, often focused on an ancestral world in which the notion of time is nonexistent, transcends cultural, social, and geographical borders to reveal the social and political realities of the Dominican Republic. Haiti is integral to Veloz Maggiolo's imagining of the Dominican Republic, and the author constantly intertwines the histories of both nations to signal the interplay between them. In *El hombre del acordeón,* a novel set on the ambiguous Haitian-Dominican border, Veloz Maggiolo reflects upon the irreversible damage done by Trujillo's thirty-one-year reign, but he also portrays a broader history, tracing the ancestral line of a spiritual border community deviating from a single nationality. Chapter 2 also considers Veloz Maggiolo's literary chronicle of the first US occupation of the Dominican Republic in 1916 in *La vida no tiene nombre*. The novel boasts a Dominican Haitian protagonist navigating the first US Marine intervention from the off-border space of El Seibo in the Dominican Republic.

Chapters 3 and 4 examine works by Dominican American authors, and one Puerto Rican American author. These writers are geographically distanced from Hispaniola but portray Haitian-Dominican third space and US diasporic third space in general as both physical and ideological representations of the border. Given that these authors write from the diaspora—a physical, visible "off-border" space—the primary literary texts analyzed in these two chapters approach Hispaniola, as well as Haitian-Dominican relations, from the outside looking in. These works, written by Latino/a authors, curate visions of Haitian-Dominican third space both on the island of Hispaniola and from the US diaspora. Chapter 3 focuses on contemporary US diasporic representations of Haitianness as perceived by Dominican American women in memoir. The chapter also comments on the off-island response to the 2013 Dominican Tribunal Court ruling both in literature and from nonprofits and other organizations founded by Dominican Americans, such as We Are All Dominican. I consider two relatively recent and seldom critiqued works, Raquel Cepeda's memoir *Bird of Paradise* and Julia Alvarez's *A Wedding in Haiti,* to address what part the particular space of the United States plays when the writer revisits the history of his or her country of origin. The approach is complemented by a visual map referencing New York census data and the spatial proximity of Dominicans and Haitians in the diaspora and also showing the setting of the analyzed novels. This visualization of the pan-ethnic communities in Hispaniola's New York diaspora sets the stage for a broader, more holistic discussion in chapter 4 of the diversity of Caribbean immigrant communities that includes an analysis of the less-studied Puerto Rican–Haitian dynamic.

Chapter 4 builds on chapter 3 vis-à-vis an analysis of Latino/a works highlighting the longevity of the nebulous and intricate literary representations of occidental Quisqueya.[13] The Puerto Rican American Daniel José Older's *Shadowshaper* and the Dominican American Junot Díaz's short story "Monstro" uniquely and distinctively position Haiti as dystopic in nature. As Michel-Rolph Trouillot notes, "The more Haiti appears weird, the easier it is to forget that it represents the longest neocolonial experiment in the history of the West" ("Odd and the Ordinary" 5). Writing Haiti and Haitians as the center or nexus of dystopic third space permits an examination of how Latino/a authors write "weird" and why Haiti stands for peculiarity for these authors. A discussion spearheaded by the consistent referral to Haiti as multiple by writers like Gina Athena Ulysse, Ada Ferrer, and others elicits a final analysis in this chapter of the Haitian Évelyne Trouillot's play *The Blue of the Island* and the Haitian American Edwidge Danticat's novel *The Farming of Bones*. Haiti and the Haitian-Dominican border, for Trouillot and Danticat, are no longer "peculiar" but instead approached with new complexities and intricacies in mind. The final pages of chapter 4 highlight texts that nuance Dominican literary representations of Hispaniola's shared history. The vast majority of works explored herein are Dominican and Dominican American in large part because writers from the Dominican Republic and the Dominican diaspora have published more frequently about historical events that have played an important role in defining the modern border between Haiti and the Dominican Republic. My inclusion of a Haitian and a Haitian American work recognizes literature representative of Haitian voices and acknowledges the need for a more in-depth study of the exploration of the Haitian-Dominican border in Haitian and Haitian American literature. Moreover, my analysis of a Puerto Rican American text in this final chapter signals the diverse, transcultural and transnational communities that destabilize notions of social, cultural, racial, and ethnic borders in diasporic spaces. I include Haitian American–and Puerto Rican American–authored texts following a discussion of Dominican American literature to further the dialogue on *Latinidad(es)* and the Latino/a diasporic experience in order to examine the intermingling of diverse, interethnic and interracial groups of Latinos/as and other national groups in the space of the United States. I consider where Haitians fit within the intersections of what Frances R. Aparicio calls "horizontal hierarchies" when referring to the "horizontal scope of power differences, conflicts, tensions, and affinities between and among Latinas/os of diverse national identities" (116). Elaborating on the notion of horizontal hierarchies as a theoretical construct by bringing the Haitian US diaspora into the conversation is essential to an understanding of Hispaniola's literary third spaces.

Caribbean theoretical and historical models like those of Antonio Benítez Rojo and Édouard Glissant point to an extension of Caribbean cultural influence beyond national and political boundaries. The conception of figuratively flexible borders articulated by Benítez Rojo's "repeating island" framework, for example, foreshadows a similar idea with respect to Haitian-Dominican relations. His Caribbean conceptualization facilitates the connectivity of Hispaniola with other Caribbean countries in the sense that he advocates for an essential Caribbean character, embodying the diverse histories, peoples, and languages existing in different Caribbean spheres. Also departing from a transoceanic perspective, Yolanda Martínez-San Miguel locates her study *Coloniality of Diasporas* (2014) within a Pan-Caribbean context by considering intracolonial migrations to find common points between translingual literatures of the Caribbean diaspora. Martínez-San Miguel evades a compartmentalization of the Caribbean into national or regional spaces, instead looking at Caribbean islands and their literatures through a postcolonial theoretical lens. Multivocal explorations of literature such as Martínez-San Miguel's comparative study serve as ideal models of postcolonial and sociohistorical literary criticism for engaging Dominican and Dominican American literature in a historical context.

In spite of the more recent tendency of critics such as Paul Gilroy in *The Black Atlantic* to overlook Haiti's historical and cultural significance, situating Haiti in a historical context is important because it emphasizes the country's unique position as the first and only country to boast a successful revolt of black African slaves. The revolt of 1791 led to the abolition of slavery in the French colony of Saint Domingue and the formation of the first black republic on January 1, 1804. Likewise, as García-Peña signals in *The Borders of Dominicanidad,* the Dominican Republic is often left out of historical anthologies of the Caribbean or Latin America. Thus, not only does a multifaceted view of Haiti commonly go unmentioned in Dominican texts but in contrast to other Caribbean countries the Dominican Republic itself, for political and historical reasons, is often relegated to the margins in anthologies and histories. I want to show that the events both past and present in the Dominican Republic, and on Hispaniola as a whole, are as important as those elsewhere in the Caribbean and Latin America. The distinct revolutionary history of Haiti is indeed key to the present project, but so too is the unique history of the Dominican Republic. Santo Domingo, the first official colony of the Americas, is also a land of firsts: it was the first official colony in the New World; the first colony to import slaves from Africa, in 1502; the site of the first rebellion of black slaves, in 1522; and the first country to open a university, in 1538.

This book transgresses literary borders by venturing beyond the often one-sided, anti-Haitian national imagery in Dominican literature. Analyzing the alternate and nuanced representations of Haiti in Dominican literature—beyond the negative, stereotypical literary conception linked to Dominican negrophobia and anti-Haitianism—allows us to understand how Dominican and Dominican American writers today are reenvisioning their complex racial and ethnic identities and, by extension, Dominican-Haitian relations. This book uncovers literary evidence of Dominicans and Dominican Americans alternatively representing Hispaniola and the Haitian-Dominican dynamic across time and geographic limits and takes into account how Haitian and Haitian American authors portray the Dominican Republic and, by extension, Hispaniola. In this varied, less antagonistic Dominican national chronicle of a traditionally oppressed neighbor, the significance of a physical border weakens, and a unique third space—as envisioned in the texts examined herein—allows for a totality and wholeness to draw the two countries together instead of pushing them apart. Trujillo's words "Now let them say that we have no borders," in overt reference to his plan for the Dominicanization of the border region, gain new meaning when examining how literature offers an alternate understanding of the relationship between the two countries and problematizes a fixed understanding of Hispaniola's borders that leads to an alternative metaphorical, conceptual mapping of the Caribbean isle.

1 Haitian and Dominican Third Space and the *Trujillato* (1930–1961)

¡Tú mismo ya no eres de aquí!
—Ramón Marrero Aristy, *Over*

Trujillo's "Re-evaluation and Reconstitution" of the Dominican Republic

The anti-Haitian sentiment prevalent in the Dominican Republic during the first half of the twentieth century was undeniably linked to the thirty-one-year dictatorship of Rafael Leónidas Trujillo Molina. Trujillo's conversion of the island nation into his puppet, through which he realized his desire for racial purity and emphasis on Hispanism, or *hispanicismo*,[1] met no limits. The tyrant manipulated an oppressive social and cultural atmosphere not by his bloodstained hands alone, but also with the backing of his intellectual army, or *los trujillistas teóricos*, as I will refer to the group in the following pages.[2] Examining Trujillo's intellectual elites, who were largely responsible for the ideological roots of Dominican prejudice against Haitians, this chapter takes a closer look at the Trujillo Era and the increasing stronghold of anti-Haitian ideology in the twentieth century. Following an exploration of scholarly culture both prior to and during Trujillo's reign is an analysis of the works of two twentieth-century Dominican authors, Ramón Marrero Aristy's *Over* (1939) and Freddy Prestol Castillo's *El Masacre se pasa a pie* (1973; The Massacre is crossed on foot). Both texts are set in the Dominican Republic and center on markedly multinational populations, comprising not only Haitians and Dominicans but also *cocolos*[3] and other members of the sugar-plantation workforce. *Over* portrays off-border third space, and *El Masacre* details the geophysical border. In both works the sugar plantation manifests as a unique zone of cultural collision and a means by which the authors navigate alternate literary representations of Haitians. *Over* and *El Masacre se pasa a pie* are also unique for the ways they juxtapose an overt interest in and emphasis on geography to geographical anonymity or ambiguity; *Over* is set on an anonymous sugar plantation, and *El Masacre* opens with vague references to the Dominican border region. I propose that Marrero Aristy's and Prestol Castillo's narrative conceptualizations of geographic spaces as unspecified and ambiguous enable a representation of these communities as transnational and cross-border. A brief analysis of Dominican Manuel Rueda's *Bienvenida y la noche: Crónicas de Montecristi* (1994; Bienvenida and the night: chronicles of Montecristi) accompanies my close readings of Marrero Aristy's and Prestol Castillo's texts; Rueda's novel offers a premassacre portrayal of Trujillo as well as a comprehensive, firsthand description of the border and port town Monte Cristi in the early twentieth century.

The acceptance of anti-Haitianism as state ideology in the Dominican Republic was not spontaneous, and the underpinnings of the race-based doctrine can be traced as far back as colonial times. These early origins connect to racial prejudices of Spanish colonizers in the New World's first official colony, Santo Domingo. Santo Domingo represented an epicenter of colonial power during the fifteenth century; the land marks Christopher Columbus's claim to fame, the site of the first *mestizos* (offspring of Spanish and Taíno Indians) and later the first European colony to import African slaves for the cultivation of sugarcane. While Santo Domingo was a frontrunner of colonial growth and success, the French colony Saint-Domingue, representing the western third of the island, boasted a rapidly growing economy during the seventeenth and eighteenth centuries. Those on the eastern side of the island strived to distinguish themselves from their successful French neighbors, especially in the wake of two unifications of Hispaniola. As a direct consequence of the Treaty of Basilea, Spain ceded its colonial domain, Santo Domingo, to the French in 1795. When Haiti declared political independence in 1804, Haitian troops attempted to take full control of Santo Domingo, but they returned to Haiti in 1805 under the false pretense of a European naval attack on Port-au-Prince. Less than two decades later, in 1822, the Haitian general Jean-Pierre Boyer led the efforts to unify both sides of the island under Haitian rule; the unification lasted until 1844.[4] Although many Dominicans welcomed Boyer's rule and believed the unification would reinvigorate economic prospects for the eastern side of the island, the end of the twenty-two-year unification in the mid-nineteenth century ushered in a competitive intra-island environment in which the newly founded Dominican Republic routinely fought to repel Haitian armies. According to Paulino, "The Dominican Republic's attempts to express separateness from Haiti were intended to assert its place in the international community, which considered Haiti isolated. This assertiveness was also directed toward a rising and racialist United States expanding its influence in the region" (27). As a consequence of the nineteenth-century unifications of the island as well as the international community's ideological understanding of blacks as both culturally and racially inferior, some Dominicans have historically sought to define themselves as non-Haitian.

In addition to the two periods of unification, other significant events also contributed to the spread of anti-Haitian sentiment in the Dominican Republic, including the US occupation of the Dominican Republic from 1916 to 1924. Horn insists that more scholarly attention should be paid to the imperialist presence of the United States in the Dominican Republic and its influence on configurations of national identity, including anti-Haitian prejudices. She confirms that few scholarly studies have centered on "how national configurations also cannot be understood without taking into account the imperialist presence of the United States in the country from the mid- to late nineteenth century" (16). Recent scholarship on Hispaniola does agree, however, that Trujillo's reign marked the peak of anti-Haitian sentiment in Dominican society and culture.[5] Paulino argues that anti-Haitianism crystalized with the 1937 Haitian Massacre and Trujillo's plan for Dominicanization, or *dominicanización,* of the Haitian-Dominican border, a state-building campaign that aimed to reclaim control of the border regions. "Under Trujillo," he notes, "an entire history was erected on the premise that Dominicanidad and the country's development rested on an eternal opposition to a black Haiti" (33).

Addressing Trujillo's relationship with anti-Haitian sentiment in the Dominican Republic is not enough; we also need to consider the dictator's own heritage and background. Widely known yet inconspicuously erased from Trujillo's memory of his family tree is the fact his maternal grandmother was Haitian.[6] This familial "stain" was an impetus for the tyrant's obsession with race and his constant desire to cover up his racial and ethnic heritage. This "cover-up" was both literal and figurative: Trujillo used cosmetic powders to whiten his face and commissioned biographies stating his descent from both a French marquis and a Spanish officer (Howard 9). Trujillo's outward obsession with his European roots ultimately led to events such as the 1937 Massacre. His false claims to a white, non-negro, and non-mulatto lineage greatly influenced his rendering of Haiti into the racial Other and served as the foundation for the fomentation of a Dominican nationalism that excludes Haitians and Dominicans of Haitian descent.

Pre–Trujillo Era historical events heavily influenced the relations between the two colonies of Hispaniola. These moments set the stage for the conflicts between today's Haiti and the Dominican Republic and also provided Trujillo with an initial base from which to pronounce Haitians as non-Dominican. One of the early differences between the two colonies related to the number of African slaves exported to the French territory of Saint-Domingue, compared with the smaller number of slaves sent to Santo Domingo, to support the burgeoning plantation economy of the eighteenth century. In 1739, for example, there were 117,000 slaves in Saint-Domingue, while less than a century later, in 1791 (the year of the uprising that led to the creation of the first black republic), the number had more than quadrupled, to 480,000 (Fennema and Loewenthal 17). The large number of African slaves brought to Saint-Domingue in the late seventeenth century and throughout the eighteenth century by French colonists to sustain the plantation economy and the production of sugar, coffee, and cotton led to an early colonial and elitist perception of Haiti and Haitian as synonymous with backwardness, uncleanliness, and poverty. Furthermore, the reverberations of the monumental event at the end of the eighteenth century—the Haitian Revolution (which began with the first slave rebellions in 1791 and ended with Haitian independence in 1804)—were felt strongly on the Dominican side of the island and contributed to the Dominican perception of the Haitian subject. As Eller notes, the Haitian Revolution "swept the *whole island* and region into pitched battles for freedom" (2, my emphasis). As mentioned previously, the Haitian occupation of the Dominican Republic in 1822–44, following the revolution, also played a role in widening the gap between Dominicans and Haitians. The occupation, although initially supported by many Dominican nationals, positioned Haiti as the perennial enemy of the Dominican Republic, and the Dominican nation came to see the neighboring country as a constant threat, eager to control the eastern side of the island. Largely owing to the racial realities of the early plantation economy and the aftermath of events such as the Haitian Revolution and the Haitian Occupation, the Dominican national identity came to be associated with a three-tiered "perfecta" defined by whiteness, Catholicism, and Hispanic heritage (Moya Pons, *El pasado dominicano* 238). Trujillo championed this three-part harmony, painting Dominicans as proud, modest campesinos of Taíno and European descent and Haitians as superstitious, backward Africans. Trujillo ideology went to great lengths to emphasize the underpinnings of the Dominican nation as white, Hispanic, and Catholic, a dominant conception that led to a "re-evaluation and reconstitution of the Dominican nation" (Howard 31).

The pervasiveness of antiblack and anti-Haitian sentiment in the Dominican Republic, bolstered during the *trujillato*, permeates the literature published during the time and sanctioned by the Trujillo regime. Yet an alternative view of Haitians characterizes both *El Masacre se pasa a pie* and *Over*. The texts of Prestol Castillo and Marrero Aristy, who were most productive during the 1930–61 period and influenced by the cultural politics of their time, can be read as products of the Trujillo Era, specifically in relation to the burgeoning sugar industry. In particular, the surge of Haitian migrants to the Dominican Republic during the first half of the twentieth century followed as a consequence of a decline in sugar prices during the 1920s. Because of fluctuations in international-market prices for sugar, migrant Haitian laborers—who worked for the lowest wages—filled the positions of the *cocolo/a* labor force on the sugar plantations. The term *cocolo* in the Dominican Republic typically refers to plantation workers from Caribbean islands as opposed to seasonal laborers from neighboring Haiti, and the transition from a largely *cocolo* workforce to a Haitian one during this time frame is key. This labor shift was a consequence of the low price of sugar in the 1920s as a result of an excess supply and a rise in competition from European producers of beet sugar.[7] Despite price vacilations in the global market, cane sugar remained the most important export for both Haiti and the Dominican Republic. Because the Haitian labor force is at the center of both *Over* and *El Masacre,* an assessment of the sugar industry in the Dominican Republic is essential to understanding the geographical spaces and labor populations shaped by the lucrative trade. In the analyses to follow, I consider *Over* a plantation novel, or *novela de cañaveral* (Costa 68),[8] because of the work's overt concern with the influence of the sugar industry in social, political, religious, or other contexts that extend beyond the immediate sphere of the plantation itself. In *El Masacre,* too, the sugar industry shapes Dominican geography and also directly influences the targeted populations during the October 1937 Massacre. The Haitian migratory population and its complex link to the exploitative Dominican sugar industry in the twentieth century heavily influenced Marrero Aristy's and Prestol Castillo's curations of Haitian-Dominican third space in their respective on- and off-border narratives.

Marrero Aristy and Prestol Castillo: *¿Trujillistas teóricos?*

Before considering Marrero Aristy's and Prestol Castillo's connection to the Trujillo regime and its literary production, it is important to understand the intellectuals preceding them. For such early intellectuals, the notion of *dominicanidad* was not synonymous with antiblack and/or anti-Haitian.

Instead, these early interpretations of a Dominican racial imaginary were variations of the anti-Haitian discourse beginning as early as the eighteenth century with Antonio Sánchez-Valverde's (1729–1791) *Idea del valor de la Isla Española y utilidades que de ella puede sacar su monarquía* (1785; An idea of Hispaniola's value and how it benefits the monarchy). The Spanish author's audience comprised mainly Madrilenian authorities, his goal being to update them on the economic potential of the colony of Santo Domingo. Such reports no doubt compared the western colony with its eastern neighbor, Saint-Domingue. For Sánchez-Valverde, the French colony's economic project represented a model for success, and he attributed the triumphs of Saint-Domingue to "the *Negroes,* whose arms are the prime movers of so much productivity" (168, emphasis in original). However, Sánchez-Valverde represented the racial makeup of Santo Domingo as *non*black, electing to use the term *Indo-Hispanic.* This racial marker denotes mixture between the indigenous population and the Spanish. Pedro San Miguel argues that the majority of Dominican elites from the eighteenth century defined mixing as a racial synthesis between these two groups, and "thus the true origin of mestizaje in Santo Domingo is concealed, and the demographically dominant black presence is ignored" (43).

Pedro Francisco Bonó (1828–1906) was a sociologist writing in the wake of the Haitian occupation of the Dominican Republic that ended in 1844 and forced Dominican intellectuals to confront and construct a Dominican national identity. His view on the ethnoracial composition of the Dominican Republic opposes that of Sánchez-Villaverde. Bonó emphasized the imprint left by the Spanish conquest on Dominican society, firmly stressing the nonexistence or extinction of the indigenous Taíno population. In Bonó's work, owing to his entrenchment in the period of Haitian domination and Dominican independence that followed, the result of Jean-Pierre Boyer's short-lived attempt to unite the island was "a fundamental, indestructible antagonism between the two people" (*Papeles* 343–44, my translation). Bonó stressed the specific colonial experience in the Dominican Republic, as opposed to that in Haiti, as the root of racial difference and favored "mulatoism." Under this ideology, "by distancing itself racially from its neighbor, Santo Domingo moves closer to Europe" (San Miguel 50). This turn away from Haiti and differentiation from all things French also highlights emphasis on a (mythical) Hispanism key to the Dominican national consciousness. While on the surface it appears that Bonó's work aligns with the underpinnings of anti-Haitian sentiment, he also recognized common interests between the two countries and did not view racial difference as an impediment to Haitian-Dominican relations.

The anti-Haitian xenophobia promulgated by the Trujillo regime found its epicenter in the writings of the nationalist intellectuals Manuel Arturo Peña Batlle (1902–1954) and Joaquín Balaguer (1906–2002). These educated, upper-class government officials expanded on the earlier ideas of Sánchez-Valverde, Bonó, and other Latin American intellectuals who espoused views championing *blanqueamiento,* or a whitening of national populations, to spearhead an ideological campaign that equated Haiti as the perennial enemy of the Dominican people. Peña Batlle, for example, attributes all failures of the Dominican state to Haiti. He identifies Haiti's Afro population as a persistent threat to the Spanish descendants who called the Dominican Republic home: "El haitiano que nos molesta y nos pone sobreaviso es el que forma la última expresión social de allende la frontera. Ese tipo es francamente indeseable" (67). For Peña Batlle, Haiti engendered the antithesis to Spanish values, and it was the Trujillo regime that rendered possible a return to a Dominican nationality untainted by the events and repercussions of the Haitian Revolution and the Haitian occupation of Santo Domingo.[9] Much like Peña Batlle, Balaguer equates race with nation in his attempt to distance Dominicans from Haitians, claiming that the two groups belong to different nations *and* races, an ideology expressed in *La isla al revés: Haití y el destino dominicano* (1983; The island upside down: Haiti and Dominican destiny).[10] Balaguer bolsters his argument through the supposed fundamental whiteness of the Dominican people, a "whiteness" stained by the black presence stemming from Haiti. His four-part solution to the "border problem"—economic, moral, political, and racial—claims that "la raza etiópica acabaría por absorber a la blanca" (97).

Although Peña Batlle and Balaguer fostered a tradition of antiblack and anti-Haitian thought in the Dominican Republic that has continued into the twenty-first century, many other intellectuals writing during the Trujillo Era, including Marrero Aristy and Prestol Castillo, did not subscribe wholeheartedly to the dominant, state-sponsored anti-Haitian ideology. The works of these latter two authors refute the regime's encouragement of anti-Haitian ideology by offering alternatives and reimagining the relationship between Haitians and Dominicans. Just as the negrophobic nationalism of Peña Batlle and Balaguer manipulated racism to garner political power and oppress the nation's lower classes, Marrero Aristy and Prestol Castillo maneuvered the dominant discourse regarding the Haitian subject and succeeded in producing texts with a conflicted, alternate representation of their western neighbors during and after the *trujillato*.

Manuel Rueda: Montecristi and Trujillo before the Massacre

The Dominican poet Manuel Rueda's *Las metamorfosis de Makandal* (1998; Makandal's metamorphoses) and *Imágenes del dominicano* (1998; Images of the Dominican) look at the Haitian-Dominican border primarily during the Trujillo Era. Numerous poems contained in both collections reflect the author's nostalgia for the Dominican border towns before the massacre and offer a picture of his carefree childhood in the capital of the northwestern border region of the Dominican Republic, in the Monte Cristi province. Rueda's literary corpus is a product of his time and a reflection of his geographical proximity to the border. Located in the coastal lowlands, Monte Cristi's proximity to the border and its prime location on the Atlantic Ocean make it unique. "Towns like Monte Cristi," writes Paulino, "were shaped by the Haitian-Dominican frontier as well as a maritime culture that linked it with other ports like Cap Haïtien and Puerto Plata on Hispaniola and North American ports as far north as Pennsylvania" (19). Rueda's work prior to *Las metamorfosis* also reflects a keen interest in the history of the Dominican Republic as related to Monte Cristi. His novel *Bienvenida y la noche: Crónicas de Montecristi* ranks as Trujillo narrative and confirms the author's motivation to reassess his country's history, developing within the novel a fictional Trujillo *before* his thirty-one-year reign commenced in 1930.[11] The novel details then *coronel* Trujillo's marriage to Bienvenida Ricardo in 1927. *Bienvenida y la noche* relies on the collective memory of the inhabitants of the town in which the wedding took place to narrate the nuptials. The novel is geographically linked to the Dominican "border capital" by the subtitle alone, *Crónicas de Montecristi*. Like *Las metamorfosis*, Rueda's *Bienvenida y la noche* draws heavily from the author's own experience and recollections of past events, though he was a curious six-year-old when the wedding took place. The use of the term *crónica* in the subtitle emphasizes Rueda's role in recounting the occasion. His grandmother and aunts, especially his aunt Luisita, Bienvenida's best childhood friend, also were important contributors to the narrative.[12] As Fumagalli writes in *On the Edge*, the labeling of the work as chronicle "signposts his [Rueda's] attempt at a faithful transposition of events" (138).

While on the surface the novel narrates the minutiae of wedding preparations, from the design of the decorative crepe paper on the terrace to the multilayer wedding cake, it also comments on Trujillo's early character. While Colonel Trujillo initially appears to *montecristianos* as "un tipo elegante" and "un buen mozo" (49), the young political figure is later described as "un advenedizo" (65) with "una inconmesurable vanidad" (147). Toward the novel's end, Luisita expresses fear for Bienvenida's future, telling her mother that Trujillo scares her. Doña Emiliana's response reveals her concern for the Montecristi-born newlywed: "¡Pobre Bienvenida!" (132). Moreover, the novel subtly addresses the racial-ethnic divide in Monte Cristi owing to its proximity to the border. There are four separate references to an anonymous Haitian girl who accompanies the betrothed Bienvenida, the young Haitian always buried under shopping bags. This purposeful inclusion links the seemingly simple narrative of a wedding between two young Dominicans to a broader narrative that hints at the large and growing population of Haitians and Dominicans of Haitian descent living in Monte Cristi in the early twentieth century. The unnamed girl is first mentioned on page 61: "La seguía una sirvienta negra que perdía el equilibrio por la cantidad de paquetes que cargaba" (61). The second mention is the most revelatory, marking the *haitianita* as "la negrita a quien no le alcanzaban las energías para continuar *su duelo a muerte* con los paquetes" (66, my emphasis). Here the young girl is presented as a living corpse, the boxes she carries nearly suffocating her, her domestic task deemed a "duel to the death."[13]

Montecristi, a main port for ships arriving from North America in the early twentieth century, namely those originating from Philadelphia, Massachusetts, and New York, recorded an influx of Haitian residents from the late nineteenth century on (Herrera Rodríguez 39). According to the 1919 census, of the 577 foreign residents in Montecristi, 405 were Haitian. As Rafael Darío Herrera Rodríguez notes, "En Montecristi, probablemente como resultado de la prosperidad de sus habitantes entre 1870 y 1930, aproximadamente, una gran proporción de hogares empleaban mujeres haitianas en el servicio doméstico" (73–74). While the inclusion of "la haitiana de los paquetes" in *Bienvenida y la noche* is a clear reflection of the growing Haitian population in Montecristi and the common occupation of Haitian women as domestic servants during the time period, the coupling of the girl to a "duelo a muerte," referencing a kill-or-be-killed mentality, can also be read as a precursor to Trujillo's anti-Haitian politics and the 1937 Haitian Massacre. The influx of Haitians in Monte Cristi palpable in Rueda's novel reflects not only the town's proximity to the border but also the aftermath of the US occupation of the Dominican Republic (1916–24), ending just two years prior to Trujillo's Monte Cristi nuptials. The eight-year occupation shaped the economic and racial structure of the Dominican plantations, frequently managed by North Americans and powered by US migration policies that favored the cheap labor of the neighboring Haitians.

In *Las metamorfosis de Makandal* Rueda returns to a characterization of Trujillo. The collection deals with a wide range of historical events related to the island of Hispaniola, both explicitly and implicitly, including the 1937 Haitian Massacre, the two US military invasions in the Dominican Republic in the twentieth century, and the corrupt, imperialist US-dominated Dominican sugar industry. As a metaphor directly referencing the two US interventions, Rueda inserts "las ratas" (the rats) into *Las metamorfosis*. Figuratively associated with filth and trickery, Trujillo and Balaguer are Rueda's national rats *per excelencia*, in particular, "rata ciega" (Balaguer) and "rata de bicornio" (Trujillo) (93). The rats are also posed as "Ratas condecoradas / que discursean en Washington" (93). The word *condecoradas* has multiple meanings; it can mean "awardee" in the sense of highly decorated with metals, but it can also mean "stain" or "mess." If understood as referring to a championed individual, perhaps *condecoradas* alludes here to Trujillo's nickname "Chapitas" (Bottlecaps), for the profuse number of medals he wore on his uniform. Rueda describes so many "rats," in fact, that the poem "El gran desfile" ends with a clear depiction of the innumerable throng of scavenger-commensals: "Oye el ejército de patas minuciosas que infectan / la ciudad" (97). This imaginary army of life-taking disease carriers forms the central trope of the poem. Through the rat metaphor, Rueda criticizes the US influence on the Dominican economy during the first military occupation. Of interest is the rats' clear connection to US imperialism. Sugarcane crops, widely susceptible to rat damage on a global scale, serve as cover from predators and a primary food source. In both *Bienvenida y la noche* and *Las metamorfosis* Rueda subtly comments on the sugarcane industry and construes Trujillo as *la rata* who meddles with the United States and increases Haitian labor. Marrero Aristy's *Over*, however, explicitly frames the North American usurper within the Dominican sugar industry and criticizes US imperialism. Marrero Aristy's novel, unlike Rueda's *Bienvenida y la noche* or *Las metamorfosis de Makandal*, posits the sugar plantation as a unique third space in order to describe an "in-between" site that elicits new forms of cultural meaning and blurs pre-established categories of identity.

"Un batey sin nombre": Ramón Marrero Aristy's *Over*

The Dominican Ramón Marrero Aristy's (1914–1959) novel *Over* is an example of a text written and published during the *trujillato* that provides an alternate to *antihaitianismo* ideology. The Dominican scholar Silvio Torres-Saillant identifies the work as "easily the most frequently read and highly regarded Dominican fiction work from the first half of the century" (*Introduction* 19), and the myriad analyses of the canonical text confirm its position as what Doris Sommer categorizes as one of Latin America's "foundational fictions." Although some critics, including Reyes-Santos, problematize the novel's parallel to other national romances categorized as "foundational" by focusing on the text's inability to unify national and transnational subjects, *Over*'s place as one of the Dominican Republic's most widely read novels of the twentieth century proves difficult to refute. My analysis of the prize text focuses on the sugar-plantation landscape—the sole setting of the novel—as anonymous off-border space. I analyze this unidentified plantation alongside Marrero Aristy's representation of the Haitian laborers. My analysis considers how the sugarcane cutters are transformed into essential characters in the novel, capable of rendering the unspecified geographical location identifiable, and how the text provides an alternate to Dominican-Haitian relations espoused by the Trujillo regime in the twentieth century. The fictional setting of anonymous off-border space—"un batey sin nombre" (30)—engenders the desired cultural and racial collisions indicative of the consequences of the US occupation and the race-based hierarchies and economic inequalities it left behind. *Over* further exposes the unequal, harsh treatment of Haitians and other foreign laborers on US-owned and US-operated sugar plantations in the Dominican Republic and, in doing so, reenvisions the state-sponsored anti-Haitian narrative.

Marrero Aristy, a loyal supporter of Trujillo from a young age, also published works praising the dictator's confrontation of the "border problem" that mirrored the typical anti-Haitian discourse of the mid-twentieth-century Dominican Republic. He dedicated his three-volume work singing the dictator's praises, *La República Dominicana: Origen y destino del pueblo cristiano más antiguo de América* (1957–58; The Dominican Republic: Origin and destiny of America's oldest Christian town), to Trujillo. This tripartite work re-creates historical rebellions of black slaves in the Dominican Republic, siding completely with the lighter-skinned Dominican slaveholders. Going hand in hand with Marrero Aristy's positive portrayal of the country's progress under Trujillo is the fact that the author was employed by the Trujillo government. As García-Peña asserts, "All writers who did not manage to go into exile had to write *within* Trujillismo" (102). In *Over*, Marrero Aristy, who remained in the Dominican Republic during the *trujillato*, until he was assassinated by the regime in 1959, managed to do more than critique the US imperialistic practices that had a stronghold on the nation's sugar industry. The novel also intricately deconstructs and problematizes the reality for foreign, nonwhite laborers within the racial and economic hierarchies of the Dominican sugar plantations.

In the following pages, I focus primarily on the representation of Haitians in *Over* to illustrate how Marrero Aristy succeeded—albeit under the censorship of the Trujillo regime—in reimagining an insular community where Haitians and Dominicans coexist. My close reading of the novel emphasizes a clear focus on Haitians, as opposed to other foreign laborers, in order to illuminate the text's alternative representation of the Haitian subject within an off-border third space. I also highlight the outwardly sympathetic stance of the protagonist, Daniel, concerning the Haitian customers who kept his store in business. Prior to an analysis of *Over*, I underscore Marrero Aristy's biography and his early alignment with the Trujillo regime.

Marrero Aristy was the son of a cattle rancher. His family lived comfortably until they were forced to flee the Dominican Republic for economic reasons at the onset of the first US military intervention in the Dominican Republic, from 1916 to 1924. After spending nearly a decade in Venezuela, Colombia, and Aruba, the author returned to his native Dominican Republic in 1922 (*Over* 5). As an adolescent, Marrero Aristy helped his father rebuild the family business while also completing primary and secondary school. Notably, he worked alongside his family as a shopkeeper on a sugar plantation in the Dominican province of La Romana (Graciano 57). At the age of fourteen he worked as a correspondent to both *El Diario* and *El Nuevo Diario*.[14] From an early age Marrero Aristy's writing merited attention. The young writer's *crónicas* "se advertía el conocimiento profundo que tenía el autor de la vida, miserias y sacrificios de los peones y de los capataces, con los que desde casi un niño había convivido" (*Over* 5). While he began working for the regime in 1930, at the age of seventeen, and held various illustrious posts, of particular significance is Marrero Aristy's post as the director of the National Salary Committee during the 1940s, when many strikes in the sugar industry took place.[15] In this role, Marrero Aristy responded to public outcries resulting from the sugar strikes taking place on and around various Dominican plantations.

Moreover, Marrero Aristy was a mulatto, and Torres-Saillant definitively marks him as "the black Dominican intellectual" (*Introduction* 39). In Marrero Aristy's fictional re-creation of a 1522 rebellion of black slaves on a Dominican sugar plantation—included in volume 2 of his *La República Dominicana* (1958)—he elects to side with the planters instead of with the black rebels, whose phenotypical traits he had inherited. It is essential to note that Marrero Aristy's offering of support to the white planters aligned with the culture of the period and with the dominant Trujillo discourse. The mulatto author shows compassion for the white victims of the black slave population, demonstrating, according to Torres-Saillant, his "inability to see his ancestry in the rebellious slaves rather than in the white planters, despite the phenotypical evidence to the contrary" (*Introduction* 40). Had the author's text encouraged the black rebels, it would have been a red flag, marking him as a Trujillo dissident. The Dominican writer Diógenes Céspedes, in his *Antología del cuento dominicano,* comments on the pro-Trujillo nature of Marrero Aristy's work, asserting that his national and racial ideologies served to align the author with the Dominican elite but contrasted with his internal compass. Céspedes notes: "En su fuero interno, era enemigo del régimen de Trujillo" (103).[16] Céspedes excuses Marrero Aristy's publications that overtly support the Trujillo regime because everyone who elected to stay in the country, especially intellectuals, "had to collaborate with the dictatorship" (103, my translation). *Over,* in many ways, emerges as an ironic prelude to Marrero Aristy's position as director of the National Salary Committee in the forties, shortly following the novel's publication in 1939. While the novel reflects the author's experiences working with his father, an overseer, as a young boy, it also precedes his own career-driven involvement with the nation's sugarcane production.

Like Marrero Aristy's 1957 tripartite publication commending Trujillo and his policies, *Over* is a product of its historical moment. Published a mere two years after the Haitian Massacre, during the first decade of Trujillo's reign and in the midst of an important period for the sugar industry in the Dominican Republic, *Over,* in its interest in Haitian laborers on Dominican sugar plantations, reflects this reality. According to Catherine C. Legrand, "From 1910 on, sugar accounted for more than 50 percent of Dominican export revenues" (559). Legrand continues, "The demands of sugar production created the first large concentration of wage workers in Dominican history" (559). While the 1920s witnessed a drop in sugar prices that resulted in changes to the workforce and to hourly wages, the early international interest in the Caribbean sugar industry should also be acknowledged, given that North American investment in the Dominican plantation economy is pertinent to the historical context of *Over*. Notably, Dominican laws passed during the dictatorship of General Ulises "Lilís" Heureaux (1888–99) can be linked to the foreign managerial presence on Dominican sugar plantations. General Lilís not only allowed foreign companies to import machinery used on the plantations tax free; he also passed numerous other laws that incentivized large-scale agricultural production. As Mayes asserts, it was easier for US citizens to buy land for the cultivation of sugarcane in the Dominican Republic than in Puerto Rico or Cuba (37–39).[17]

Not surprisingly, the politics of the time favored the growth of this industry, especially in economic terms. The monetary success of the sugar industry in the Dominican Republic, however, proved to be irreversibly linked to foreign labor. Reyes-Santos notes that "while Haitian labor produced profit, Trujillo espoused an official state anti-Haitian and anti-black nationalism" (84), attempting to inscribe whiteness as an essential component of his conception of *dominicanidad*. In 1936, just before the 1939 publication of *Over* (written primarily in 1938, after the publication of the author's collection of short stories, *Balsié*, earlier that year), Trujillo solidified a new border agreement. This agreement, the Trujillo-Vincent Treaty, established Dominican dominance in the areas of the Dominican territory that were previously nondescript, unclaimed spaces between the two countries sharing Hispaniola. These zones were in large part populated by *rayanos,* individuals of mixed Dominican and Haitian descent. The Trujillo-Vincent Treaty is an important historical marker of the antipathy Trujillo harbored toward the growing influence of the Haitian culture in Dominican territory. This 1936 agreement set the stage for Trujillo's plan for Dominicanization of the border region, a plan not only firmly defined by policies and this modern border agreement but also violently internalized with the 1937 Haitian Massacre.

The 1937 Massacre was a flagrant action confirming the Trujillo Era's anti-Haitian discourse. It was a horrific border event that, as Torres-Saillant notes, "made it incumbent upon the scribes of the regime to produce an ample scholarship directed to demonizing Haitians and, thereby, justifying the unspeakable act" (*Introduction* 29). Marrero Aristy formed part of this Trujillo "scholarship," the intellectual project of the all-powerful regime; his participation in this group defines the author as an individual who negated his possible role as a literary champion for Afro-Dominican writers in the mid-twentieth century.[18] The author's negation of blackness in favor of whiteness and Eurocentric values confirms Jean Price-Mar's claim in *La República de Haití y la República Dominicana* (1953; The Republic of Haiti and the Dominican Republic) that "nadie quiso ser negro y hoy mismo—salvo en la literatura—nadie se hace pasar por negro, ni siquiera aquellos cuya piel dice a las claras lo que son" (30). Price-Mar's insistence that "only in literature" might an individual claim blackness aligns with Marrero Aristy's decision to alternatively portray the Haitian subject in *Over*, a portrayal that was likely part of the reason why the bestseller was printed only once during the *trujillato*. Another likely corollary to the one-time print run of the novel during the Trujillo Era is Trujillo's monopoly of the country's sugar plantations in the 1940s: any critique of the industry could be interpreted as a critique of the Trujillo regime.[19] The Dominican critic Berta Graciano, however, posits that *Over* was not well known until the second edition, with a preface by Juan Bosch, was released following Trujillo's assassination (59).[20] While the year 1963 marks the second and perhaps more successful edition of *Over*, the success of the novel's debut in 1939 was due to its erasure of the Dominican father figure, Trujillo. Instead of pointing the finger at Trujillo Era policies for the social, cultural, and racial hierarchies of Dominican sugar plantations, Marrero Aristy instead blames the North American overseer.[21]

When the setting is not specified, to approach a text with a specific geography in mind proves difficult, regardless of a possible strategic symbolism explaining such geographical anonymity. The sugar plantation on which the action of *Over* is set has no name. The first-person narrator, Daniel Comprés, who is the plantation's newest *bodeguero*, refers to the location simply as "un batey sin nombre" (30). According to Daniel, it is nameless because "los fundadores de este central, en su afán de abreviar tiempo y depersonalizar tanto a las gentes, a los sitios como a las cosas, lo han numerado todo" (30). Another twentieth-century Dominican *novela de la caña*, Francisco Eugenio Moscoso Puello's *Cañas y bueyes* (1936; Sugarcane and oxen), locates the sugar plantation geographically from the very first sentence.[22] The novel begins in third person, "Al norte de la provincia de Macorís . . ." (5). The supervisors of the *central* in *Over* depersonalize not only places and things but also people; the laborers, too, are dehumanized, viewed as a collective mass that comes and goes with the passing of seasons. Even though all laborers on the "batey sin nombre" initially appear as a conglomerate, an unidentified mass, the anonymity inherent in this observation unravels when the plantation workers of one nationality—Haitian workers—garner more attention than the others as the novel progresses.

While the Haitian laborers on the farm emerge as integral not only to the plantation's success but also in their interactions with the narrator, in this way overcoming the supposed anonymity of workers on the plantation, the location of the farm itself remains unidentified. The reader gleans from contextual clues that the farm is *not* located in the Cibao region, which is "muchos kilómetros" from Daniel (10),[23] but never becomes privy to information regarding where the farm *is* located. Although the anonymity of the plantation itself proves significant and also speaks to Foucault's heterotopia and the functioning of space(s) "without geographical markers" (25), the aforementioned detailed focus on the range of characters in *Over* solidifies the power structure on which the plantation thrives. Marrero Aristy's "no-name" approach to the plantation suggests that the farm could be located anywhere, on any island in the Caribbean. The Caribbean theoreticians Édouard Glissant and Antonio Benítez Rojo promulgate this same Caribbean unity. Benítez Rojo's understanding of an essential Caribbean character, as defined by a basic pattern shared by the region, leads to his conclusion that Caribbean people act "in a certain kind of way," a decidedly "Caribbean way" that defines the geographical region and melds together Caribbean society. Much like the Caribbean, Marrero Aristy's plantation has complex, multinational roots. Benítez Rojo borrows from Deleuze and Guattari's machine metaphor to explain the historical links between different Caribbean cultures, stating that "every machine is a conjunction of machines coupled together, and each one of these interrupts the flow of the previous one; it will be said rightly that one can picture any machine alternatively in terms of flow and interruption" (6). This same machine metaphor can be utilized to better understand the workings of the anonymous plantation in *Over*, "a conjunction of machines coupled together," the roots of the *finca* extending far beyond the Dominican Republic, and its trans-Caribbean and intra-island ownership and workforce lend themselves to Benítez Rojo's conception of the Caribbean.

Marrero Aristy's farm, however, is not entirely anonymous. His careful, pointed focus on the influx of workers, pinpointing the Haitians from within the group of *cocolos*,[24] unmistakably links the location of the farm to the Dominican Republic. The author neglects to name the country outright, though, instead offering names of Dominican regions and provinces. To illuminate the representation of the Haitian subject in *Over*, I will first focus on Marrero Aristy's "singling out" of the Haitian workforce. This clear identification of Haitian laborers juxtaposes the anonymous location and other no-name features of the sugarcane plantation. Then, I will turn to the novel's protagonist and narrator, Daniel, to analyze the sympathetic rendering of the Haitian workers that his character makes possible.

Daniel describes the anonymous farm as he first arrives at the "gran cañaveral" (29). His very first observation, a comment on the view of the *batey* from the car window, sets the stage for the novel's focus: "Los haitianos con quienes tropezamos se lanzan asustados entre la caña" (29). The sugarcane provides the Haitians refuge from the car barreling down the narrow road. Ironically, the very plant that ties them to the oppressive, hierarchical economic system of the plantation comforts and protects them as much as it brings them pain and suffering. While this first mention of the plantation laborers only includes Haitians, it becomes clear in the following pages that the group is more diverse. The workforce comes from not only Haiti but also "las islas inglesas" (165). Later, the apparent diversity of the laborers is mentioned again, this time as the "tromba humana que llegó de Haití y de las islas inglesas" (75). In the relatively few mentions of the Haitian workers *and* those from neighboring islands, the Haitians are almost always mentioned first; the only inversion appears when the narrator refers to the workers as "cocolos y haitianos" (75).[25]

In a novel that prioritizes a numbering system, the apparent "ranking," or hierarchical positions, of foreign laborers is significant. The managers' organizational strategy of numbering on the plantation, a tactic aimed at dehumanizing and depersonalizing laborers, relates to the plantation's processing of new laborers. In this process the workers were not only assigned numbers but also given fake, temporary names, ones that Dominicans and English-speaking owners and managers from the United States could more easily pronounce: "A cada hombre, se le ata en la pretina, en la pechera de la camisa o en el harapo que haga sus veces, el número que le servirá de identificación. Ya podrá llamarse Joseph Luis, Miguel Pie, Joe Brown, Peter Wilis o como mejor desee" (76–77). The narrator's elaboration of this "receiving" process, which was much like picking teams for a sporting event, also demonstrates how the *mayordomos* and *contratistas* often verbalized their preference for either *cocolos* or *haitianos* (77).

The distinction between *cocolos* (understood as those from the "islas inglesas" in the novel) and *haitianos* suggests that the seasonal laborers breathing life into the plantation each harvest were not only from neighboring Haiti. Nevertheless, the narrative focus turns repetitively toward Haitians, as opposed to the workforce as a whole, as those that suffered most at the hands of both Dominican and foreign usurpers. Every individualized transaction recounted by Daniel is between himself and a Haitian, with the *islas inglesas* never specified nor workers from this region considered as individual entities. In fact, the laborers from the English islands are only singled out when the narrator and protagonist, Daniel, defines the term *abogado*. Within the plantation context, *abogado* refers to literate members of the sugar mill's workforce. The equation of certain workers from the *islas inglesas* with *abogados* permits the reader to infer the rarity of a Haitian who could both read and write arriving to work the *zafra* (77). Regardless of the clear signaling of Haitian illiteracy, the *bodeguero* narrator and protagonist communicates relatively easily with the Haitians visiting his storefront despite possible language barriers and allusions to Haitians' (lack of) education. While the narrator admits to focusing intently on his work—"pongo todos mis sentidos en el trabajo, para sacar el mayor beneficio. Oigo pedidos en tres idiomas" (83)—there is no mention of verbal misunderstandings in the numerous re-creations in the text of conversations between Daniel and Haitians. In Daniel's capacity as shopkeeper, he is singularly attentive to the Haitians in the workforce. Daniel remembers his customers as, simply, "[los] haitianos que venían a comprar" (34). The narrator describes his interactions with the customers as transactional, with a clear understanding of the power structure at play: "Los negros obedecen temerosos, con una sonrisa servil que solicita disculpa" (35). Daniel even excuses himself, *solicitando disculpa*, for the treatment of the helpless, hungry, and overworked Haitians, and he openly admits that the plantation system's unfair treatment of seasonal laborers weighs on his conscience: "¡Gran trabajo me ha costado dominar mis nervios y acallar mi conciencia!" (47).

The inversion of the representation of Haitians as thieves is one of the more established alternate portrayals of Haitians in *Over*. Balaguer, among other *trujillistas teóricos,* was especially preoccupied with Haitians' affinity for stealing. He paints Haitians not only as cattle thieves but also as silent thieves of Dominican jobs: "La fuerza de trabajo haitiana que emigra clandestinamente a nuestro país hace, por otra parte, una competencia desleal a la clase trabajadora dominicana" (156). In *Over,* however, the opposite transpires: A Haitian labels Daniel "ladrón." The narrator recalls:

> Cierto día un haitiano, a quien le vendí una libra de arroz, me dijo ladrón. Al instante salté fuera de la tienda, machete en mano, dispuesto a ajustarle cuentas.
> —¡Vuelve a decirlo!—le gritaba furioso—. ¡Vuelve a decirlo!
> El viejo, que estaba por allí, me atajó:

Haitian and Dominican Third Space and the Trujillato 39

>   —No haga esto, bodeguero. ¡No haga eso!
>   Y aunque me veía encolerizado y dispuesto a herir, hablaba con calma, como quién está seguro de que será obedecido.
>   —¡Pero ese haitiano me ha dicho ladrón, y yo no tolero que nadie me insulte!—fue mi alegato.
>   Sin dar importancia a mis palabras, como no se les da a las de un niño, el viejo respondió:
>   —Déjese de pendejá y aprenda a vivir en la finca. ¿Que le dijo ladrón? ¡J'a, carajo! ¿Y cómo se llama usté?
>   Fue entonces cuando le dije mi nombre por primera vez. Me respondió con despreocupación:
>   —Bueno, pué olvide su nombre. Aquí pa los dominicanos usté se llama ladrón, y pa lo s'aitiano volé. Ese e s'el nombre que nos dan a to lo s'empleado de la compañía. ¡No le haga caso a esa gente! (40–41)

Despite Daniel's initial outrage—jumping over the storefront with machete in hand—he is easily calmed; in the following paragraph he reflects on the incident in an overwhelmingly understanding, sympathetic tone. He excuses the outburst of the Haitian and instead recognizes the reality on the plantation for *all* Haitians: "Ellos hablan sin ningún sentimiento de rencor o de maldad. Viven tan indefensos, han sido tan exprimidos, que ya no tienen energías" (41). He goes as far as to embrace the label, proclaiming that "en la finca tó son ladrón" (41).

Recognizing stealing as unavoidable on the plantation, Daniel turns his attention to the root of the problem, identifying the biggest, baddest *ladrón* of them all: "Yo ta creyendo que la má ladrón de toitico son el blanco que juye en su carro" (41). This statement, transferring the label of "thief" away from the Haitian and onto the white plantation owners, serves as a rebuttal to dominant, primitivist tropes of anti-Haitian sentiment in the early twentieth century implying that "Haitians are animals, Haitians are cannibals, Haitians are savages, Haitians are violent, Haitians are thieves, Haitians are close to nature, and Haitians are promiscuous and prolific" (Valerio-Holguín, "Primitive Borders" 76). The "blancos"—such as Mr. Robinson and Mr. Lilo in *Over*—are the only ones able to escape the harsh realities of the sugar plantation, and they have built the plantation on a shaky foundation of distrust and thievery. If everyone on the *finca* is a thief, it becomes plausible to read the plantation as a microcosm of the country as a whole, or by extension the island as a whole, and the *ladrón* classification proves inescapable. This all-encompassing classification, then, stands for a reflection of the Trujillo regime and the North American interest in the Dominican sugar industry and the effect(s) and influence they exercised on the nation at large. In the same sense, distinguishing both Dominicans *and* Haitians as thieves produces an equalizing effect. This inversion of the "thief" stereotype and, later, the recognition that no one on the *finca* or in the country escapes the classification, goes against David Howard's perception of the Haitian role in the Dominican Republic: "Haitians exist as an internal colony, marginalized individuals in a society that demands their labor, but refuses to accept their presence beyond that as units of labor" (30). The Haitian presence in *Over* extends beyond one of mere units of labor.

What at first appears as an anonymous labor force—working on a nameless plantation—later expands through the singling out of Haitians from among those of other neighboring Caribbean nations. Although members of the Haitian workforce are only sometimes referred to on an individual level, the honing in on the group as a whole grants the workers a more human face. If the author's generalization and depersonalization of the laborers appears at first unintended, his repeated focus on one specific group is far from accidental. Marrero Aristy's purposeful decision to pinpoint the Haitian workers on the plantation highlights the suffering and oppression of this specific group on Dominican terrain. The following paragraphs more closely examine the narrator and protagonist of *Over*. Through Daniel's interactions with the sugarcane cutters Marrero Aristy defends this specifically identified collective within the novel and represents the struggle of Haitian laborers in a novel capable of passing the Trujillo censorship.

Daniel, as the protagonist of *Over*, serves as the work's moral compass.[26] It is a distorted morality, shifting throughout the two hundred pages of Marrero Aristy's text as Daniel struggles with the reality of his shopkeeper position and the suffering that his own monetary success as shopkeeper causes others. Daniel's arrival on the plantation, his employment as the new *bodeguero*, and, later, his dramatic departure from the farm, unemployed and disillusioned, frame the novel. The title of the work draws attention not only to the foreign forces behind the plantation economy because it is an English word, a word that also represents widely used plantation jargon, but also to Daniel's plight. Despite his position above the seasonal laborers, Daniel also proves to be a victim of the oppressive plantation system as he finds himself a prisoner of this very "over," an objective created by the foreign managers of the plantation to avoid deficits. This term refers to the surplus of funds the Dominican workers on the farm stole from the laborers. A prime example of "over" is the shop owners' surcharge of food items. The North American company forced this "policy" on the shopkeepers until they became convinced that they were not committing an injustice. Daniel's comrade and fellow *bodeguero* persuades himself upon addressing the "over": "La compañía así lo exige, y además, yo no robo" (45). Sommer confirms the presence and significance of the term *over* in Marrero Aristy's novel: "The word refers to the North American Usurper, to be sure, but the reference is specifically to economic exploitation, that is, to a systemic injustice in the industry, and it thus goes farther than a merely nationalist objection. Trujillo didn't plan to reform sugar production, but simply to own it" ("Populism" 263). Daniel is consumed by the fear of the always pending inventory of the supervisors, an anxiety that intensifies since he proves unable to follow through with the collection of this "over" and thus incapable of robing the throngs of miserable workers—his customers—who inhabit the *batey*. The narrator asks, "Este maldito *over*, ¿quién lo inventaría? ¿Dónde halló esta gente tan diabólica forma de exprimir?" (47). The only answer Daniel offers reads as a disconsolate observation: "¡El hombre hambriento vende hasta el alma!" On the following page, the "hombre hambriento" is equated more specifically with the Haitians, implying that this population may be hungrier than others: "Los haitianos ... mastican su hambre, como bueyes que se echaran tranquilamente a rumiar" (48).

Hunger materializes in the novel as a trope, constantly alluded to in both a figurative and a metaphorical sense. An endless, desperate hunger for food, change, and rebellion, among other things, permeates *Over*. Daniel describes an almost motionless, overworked Haitian in this way: "Su mirada, su cara, todo ¡todo él! decía claramente: HAMBRE" (101). The capitalization here, reproduced from the novel, stresses the importance of the word and its meaning in the text; the hunger felt by those oppressed by the plantation economy surpasses the physical and extends to a spiritual, emotional level.

While a defense on the part of the Haitian population is palpable in the novel and Veloz Maggiolo's definition of *literatura compadecida* constitutes a plausible approach to reading the text, the dominant discourse mirroring the *antihaitianismo* of Balaguer and Peña Batlle also emerges in *Over*. Veloz Maggiolo's "Tipología del tema haitiano" (1972; Typology of the Haitian subject) defines *la literatura del haitiano compadecido* as any work that accepts the Haitian subject as "un ser explotado; la narrativa lo albergó como la víctima total de las intrigas y del azar" (28). At times, Marrero Aristy's novel paints *lo haitiano* as a helpless and oppressed laborer, pinned down by the exploitative churning of Benítez Rojo's *maquina*. In doing so, however, *Over* also regurgitates the anti-Haitian ideology typical of the era. Marrero Aristy renders the fictional Haitian workers "weak" (García-Peña 109) and describes the laborers lowest on the plantation's race-based hierarchy as "apathetic and uninterested" (Reyes-Santos 85); in this way the author mirrors the national anti-Haitian and anti-immigrant policies. The racist undertone, however, parallels the perilous plight of the foreign laborers on Dominican sugar plantations, in particular Haitian laborers, and forces the reader to identify with the nonwhite workforce, blaming North American owners and managers for the unjust plantation structure. This representation of Haitians as displaced farmers who unjustly become the target of racial and ethnic prejudice, alongside a description of these same workers that aligns with the Dominican Republic's racist regime, allowed Marrero Aristy to avoid ruffling "the feathers of the old Trujillo guard and their ideological offspring" (Torres-Saillant, "Dominican Blackness" 282).

Marrero Aristy evaded censorship during the controlling *trujillato* by electing to mirror the discourse of Trujillo's intellectuals, consciously aligning his work with a primitivistic representation of the Dominican Republic's western neighbors. In direct reference to the singling out of the Haitian population compared with those from other islands arriving en masse to work *la zafra, los haitianos* are also pejoratively identified as "negros," "negrazos" (45), and "colorados teutones" (50). Often, these racially scored descriptions follow the same pattern as common twentieth-century Haitian stereotypes. The Haitian woman Daniel hires to clean his house, for example, proves inept at her job according to the narrator: "La negra y grajosa mujer no sabía cocinar, ni tenía costumbres, ni la más leve noción de lo que significaba limpieza" (175). Furthermore, in his initial description of the Haitians upon his arrival at the farm the *bodeguero* likens the population to deformed, useless, repugnant beings: "Veo sus caras sucias, erizadas de barbas, grasientas; sus narizotas deformes, sus bocas generalmente llenas de raíces podridas y de sus ojos desorbitados" (49).

While primitivistic jargon typical of the era permeates descriptions of the Haitian subject in the novel, Haitians are not the only group associated with negative or stereotypical characteristics. Marrero Aristy describes the North American *manager,* Mr. Robinson, a man who is as grossly malicious as he is large, as having "ojos tan azules y desconfiados" and "un humor del diablo" (22). Although both Mr. Robinson and the Haitian workers are described in negative terms, the Haitians do not have control over their own lives or their behavior or cleanliness; their existence on the plantation is tied irreversibly to the company that exploits them. Mr. Robinson, however, does have control over his own behavior and appearance. Daniel also critiques the racism of the North American administrators in a way that circles back to the racist language he employs when describing the Haitian workers. Micah Wright confirms that with the ushering in of US officials, whiteness was reinforced and "a significant portion of the laboring class—those whose wages declined due to Haitian immigration—came to share creole elites' understanding of blackness as a foreign threat to the nation" (25).

It is essential to note that although Daniel sympathizes with the Haitians on the *finca* even as he describes them in racist language, this sympathy does not pair with action. While the narrator overtly excuses the Haitians from any possible chance of revolt—they are only temporary workers who "no pueden pensar en reformas" (65)—excusing himself from taking action is more difficult. Daniel proves unable to shift the exploitative nature of the *central,* as his frustrations lead him to insult an assistant manager, which results in his dismissal. Exiled from the plantation, Daniel departs completely disillusioned, admitting that after the loss of his job and the downward spiral that followed, "viví borracho" (208). The novel's attack on the foreign usurpers takes the place of the potential plot for a plan to come to the defense of the ultimately defenseless plantation laborers. The foreigners investing in and controlling the Dominican plantation economy are culpable for the oppressive plantation system—a narrative focus that removes Trujillo from the position of primary target. The novel's indictment of foreign capitalists succeeds in redefining the villain. Casting North American managerial forces, rather than Trujillo, as the villain was key to the novel's successful publication in 1939, allowing it to slip past the censors, who were eager to indict any foreign presence and exonerate Trujillo. To some degree, however, Trujillo, who was trained by US Marine forces during the first occupation, also aligns with this adversarial North American presence. Marrero Aristy's critique of racism in *Over* is complicated and convoluted; Daniel's description of the Haitian workers often mirrors Trujillo policy and ideology, but his pronounced mistrust of whites and outwardly empathetic stance toward Haitians confound this regurgitation of anti-Haitian racism.

I believe that one of the primary reasons why the novel's critique of US imperialism and exploitation dominates the narrative and overshadows the anti-immigrant language relates to the novel's portrayal of anonymous plantation space and its conscious singling out of the Haitian laborers indispensable to the landscape. Moreover, Marrero Aristy's (un)marking of the plantation as an unspecified location speaks to the importance of the personalization of the anonymous *batey* in the text as opposed to a specific point on the map. This unnamed space has a personality and defining characteristics, highlighting the geographer and literary critic Marc Brosseau's view that literature is important because it shows the "personality of a place in intimate ways" (29). By establishing unspecified plantation space as key to the novel and to the early twentieth-century Dominican socioeconomic climate, Marrero Aristy succeeds in converting his "batey sin nombre" into a synecdochic representation of Dominican sugar plantations. The novel's description of the *central*'s exploitation of the foreign laborers, in particular the Haitians, as well as Daniel's interactions with Haitian workers are set against the nameless plantation. Daniel works in opposition to the plantation administration's impulse to "abreviar tiempo y depersonalizar tanto a las gentes" (30) by refusing to reduce Haitians to an anonymous collective; instead he gives them names and feelings and exposes their suffering at the hands of the race-based system of economic inequality.

Marrero Aristy's careful curation of an anonymous sugarcane *batey*, coupled with a pointed representation of the individuals exploited at the hands of the *central*, positions the twentieth-century Dominican sugar plantation as shared third space. The setting of *Over*, via Daniel's sympathy for his Haitian counterparts, stands for an off-border *batey* in which new identities coalesce, a hybrid and diverse space that contests previous or national understandings of identity. When Daniel flees from the farm and his occupation as *bodeguero* at the novel's end, he removes himself both ideologically and physically from the sugar industry: "No te apegues a esto que ya no es tuyo. ¡Tú mismo ya no eres de aquí!" (213). *Aquí* (here) becomes both nowhere and everywhere; just like the Haitian cane cutters and other foreign laborers, Daniel recognizes his status as implant on the plantation. Unsubscribing completely from US imperialism and its exploitation of foreign labor, Daniel disassociates himself from the anonymous plantation, a stark contrast to the narrator's first description of his surroundings as "todo esto tan familiar" (9). Much like Foucault's heterotopia, what at first appears familiar is also the inverse of the "familiar site," as heterotopic spaces both represent and invert the site that contain them. Daniel's lived reality on the plantation dissolves the real, representational space that the protagonist-narrator thought he knew so well. Foucault describes this "joint experience" of heterotopias in relation to the functionality of mirrors: "It makes this place that I occupy at the moment when I look at myself in the glass at once absolutely real, connected with all the space that surrounds it, and absolutely unreal" (22). The plantation, for Daniel, exists precisely in what Foucault refers to as an epoch of "simultaneity" and "juxtaposition" (22); his "batey sin nombre" represents what is most familiar to him and a place in which he no longer belongs.

Mapping the Massacre: Freddy Prestol Castillo's *El Masacre se pasa a pie*

Although *El Masacre se pasa a pie* was published in 1973, twelve years after Trujillo's assassination, Prestol Castillo composed the work in the wake of the 1937 Massacre and buried it in his mother's backyard until he deemed it safe to "unearth" the manuscript.[27] Despite the work's publication date, I have elected to include an analysis of this text in a chapter focused on the *trujillato* in order to illuminate the political climate during the time when the work was written rather than when it was published. A true product of the Trujillo Era and an eyewitness account of the general's most atrocious, large-scale crime, *El Masacre* can be examined for both its deviation from and its occasional alignment with Trujillo ideology. I also briefly consider a collection of short essays written by Prestol Castillo, *Paisajes y meditaciones de una frontera* (1943; Landscapes and border musings), as it not only fills the thirty-six-year gap between the production and publication of *El Masacre*, but also offers a palpable focus on border space for the ways it highlights the author's travels along the Dominican-Haitian border after the massacre.[28]

Each chapter of *El Masacre* uncovers a particular aspect of the massacre, and the bounty of characters—Dominican, Haitian, and those of both nationalities—lends multiple perspectives to the horrific event. The fragmented stories outlined in each chapter can be read as anecdotal, individual testimonies recounting *el corte*. The 1937 Massacre has many nicknames: *el corte*, *kout kouto-a* ("the stabbing" in Kreyòl), and *la masacre del perejil* (the Parsley Massacre), among others. The name *la masacre del perejil* is derived from the fact that Dominican soldiers asked those of African descent in the border towns to verbally identify the parsley plant. As explained in the introduction, since the Spanish *r* and *j* are difficult for French and Kreyòl speakers to pronounce, any individual unable to pronounce *perejil* correctly was deemed Haitian and therefore killed.[29] Each fragmented story narrated in the text reads as an individual testimony, and this anecdotal framework gives way to the question of whether *El Mascare* belongs to the genre of novel or testimony. Similar to *Over*, the work is one of the most profitable Dominican texts of the twentieth century, with more than twenty thousand copies sold following its first publication; its genre, however, is a common point of contestation.

Earlier analyses of the work highlight the testimonial pulse of *El Masacre*. Sommer praises the "accessibility of Prestol's writing—as opposed to the more self-consciously literary styles of other narrators—and the social significance of his testimony" (*One Master* 162). She also signals Prestol Castillo's insistence on honesty and his disuse of invention as reasons to label the book as testimony (89). Likewise, the Dominican historian Bernardo Vega writes that the work is best described as testimony given the author's status as witness and the fact that it was written shortly after the massacre (*Trujillo* 326). More recently, García-Peña has stipulated that the text's value is inherent in its testimonial "intellectual reaction to the violence" of the massacre (110). Describing *El Masacre* as an "intellectual reaction" and at the same time labeling the text as testimony suggests a possible positioning alongside publications of *los trujillistas teóricos* and signals the work's alignment with Trujillo policies, namely, anti-Haitianism and Hispanism. García-Peña further asserts: "To write a Dominican nationalist text in the context of the Trujillo regime is to write an anti-Haitian text" (111). While *El Masacre* indeed bears characteristics of Trujillo Era anti-Haitianism, explored in the analysis to follow, accepting Marrero Aristy's text as nationalist conflates the production of the text with its publication; *El Masacre* was written in the wake of the 1937 Massacre but published nearly four decades later. This gap between writing and publication—the work published more than a decade after Trujillo's assassination—positions Prestol Castillo's *El Masacre* instead as an antinationalist text or at the very least a work that questions and problematizes Trujillo's Dominicanization of the border region. However, even if Sommer is correct in her assertion that Prestol Castillo's recollection of the event was an "honest" one, even honest accounts have their flaws. As Iván Grullón asserts, the "libro representa con *relativa* exactitud los acontecimientos" (39, my emphasis). With the author's "relative" certainty in mind, I refer to *El Masacre* in the following pages as novel, just as the Dominican literary canon and the author, on the first page of the text's first edition, recognize the work. Notably, Prestol Castillo himself revisited the genre of his text following its initial publication. In an interview with Sommer, the author referred to the work as "simply my book," evading any generic tag: "Había aquí un debate sobre el género de mi libro, si era novela o no. Yo lo puse novela al terminarlo, pero lo considero simplemente mi libro" (*One Master* 161). Prestol Castillo's decision to label the text "novel" in 1973 and his later neglect to categorize the work were likely strategic. If *El Masacre* represents pure "invention," then Trujillo is not at fault, since the author classifies such border atrocities as figments of his own imagination. Despite Trujillo's assassination more than ten years before the publication of *El Masacre,* even in 1973 the dictator's contemporaries, such as Joaquín Balaguer, still held positions of power in the country, and challenges to the government were still dangerous.

The fact that *El Masacre* does not fit within the parameters of the Latin American testimonial novel as described by John Beverley also supports my decision to identify *El Masacre* as novel; the work does not span the author's entire life or even a significant portion, and that it is purely autobiographical is debatable.[30] Beverley's voice, however, is not the only one to define the Latin American *testimonio,* and one of his faults is his failure to pay tribute to the importance and existence of *two* voices in the creation of numerous foundational testimonies, such as in the case of Miguel Barnet and Esteban Montejo's *Biografía de un cimarrón* (1966). *El Masacre,* too, can be read as a text with two voices when considering Prestol Castillo's original "notes" (written directly following the massacre and buried in his mother's backyard) as distinct from his revision of those notes more than two decades later. It is true, however, that *El Masacre* shares commonalities with Latin American *testimonios* such as the aforementioned *Biografía de un cimarrón,* a testimonial narrative that also is "subject to the strategies of memory" (Luis, *Literary Bondage* 203). *Biografía de un cimarrón,* however, juxtaposes narration to historical texts, while the events recounted in *El Masacre* are difficult to compare with historical annals written during the Trujillo Era given the censorship during the dictatorship. Contestation of the work's genre aside, I believe that Prestol Castillo's re-creation of the massacre is the Dominican text that offers the most precise and unmoderated vision of this history, influenced by the fact that the author himself was stationed at the border as a government-paid lawyer (holding the position of magistrate of Dajabón), arriving at the *aldea* just as the infamous event occurred.[31] Prestol Castillo's representation allows readers to perceive Haitians—and the history of this particular event, one often written out of the historical annals of "genocide"—in a different and increasingly complex light.

My analysis of *El Masacre* focuses on its value as a denouncement of the Trujillo regime and of the 1937 Massacre. My approach to the work also opposes that of critics and historians who too often liken the book to Trujillo propaganda and signal the examples of primitivism in the text without adequately addressing Prestol Castillo's failure to align himself completely with Trujillo and the dominant discourse.[32] In ways similar to Marrero Aristy's delineation of "un batey sin nombre," Prestol Castillo's bestseller also presents space, specifically geographical border space, as ambiguous. Following the prologue, *El Masacre* opens with a brief vignette that exposes the author-narrator's premassacre unfamiliarity with the border region. In this vignette, the author-narrator remembers his "Geografía Patria" course and his first, ill-informed introduction to "una aldea lejana," Dajabón (15). Prestol Castillo critiques his former teacher and reveals his inadequacy: "El maestro hablaba rutinariamente. No conocía su país." The author mocks his teacher, noting his small lips and frustrated appearance, recalling his privileged remark about the border towns despite never having traveled there himself: "Esos pueblos *deben ser* insoportables" (15, my emphasis). While it is apparent from his sarcastic tone that the author takes offense at the *maestro*'s sorry attempt at accurately describing the "frontera," the naïveté of both the teacher and the author-narrator in this moment should not be overlooked. Before the author-narrator was sent as magistrate to Dajabón, he—just like his teacher—"era extranjerizado en sus preferencias" (15). Returning to the statement that "esos pueblos *deben ser* insoportables," it is the "should be" (deben ser) that demands critical attention. Prestol Castillo's recollection of his childhood teacher's remark, including these two words, prepares the reader for the author's own response and challenge concerning just what these towns "should be," challenging the elitist assumptions of his childhood teacher.

This start to the novel, signaling the importance of border space, while also underscoring the author-narrator's apparent unfamiliarity with the border region, sets the stage for the text's description of Haitian-Dominican third space in Dajabón. The analysis to follow recognizes and emphasizes how Prestol Castillo maneuvers and manipulates border space in *El Masacre* and, briefly, in *Paisajes y meditaciones*. Shifting to a structural analysis of *El Masacre,* it is noteworthy that the names of places—cities, countries, street names, and so on—are at times bolded.[33] Prestol Castillo's highlighting of certain words in this way is selective, as only certain places, along with the occasional title or person name, are singled out. This stressing of specific place names relates to the geographer Barbara Piatti's compartmentalized understanding of the geography of literature. Piatti identifies spatial entities that compose geographical space in a fictional text and classifies "markers" as locations that are only mentioned in the text and offer no significance to the story but simply indicate the geographical range of the text. Some of the locations bolded

Haitian and Dominican Third Space and the Trujillato   49

Figure 2. Selective bolding in *El Masacre se pasa a pie*

in *El Masacre* carry no weight in the narrative; many of these locations function as markers and exist solely to confirm the author-narrator's newfound familiarity with the border region. While *El Masacre* opens with an uninformed understanding of Haitian-Dominican border communities as "una aldea lejana," the author-narrator later asserts himself in the position of guide—an authority in the region with an apparent firm grasp on Dominican-Haitian border communities—vis-à-vis these geographical "markers." In the analysis to follow, I consider how these literary markers also function as a strategy on the author's part to highlight the solidarity and camaraderie of the transnational border region.

Figure 2 illustrates the various place names bolded in *El Masacre*. The size of the dot on the map is increased for each time it is bolded (as opposed to mentioned) in the text. Notably, the bolding and/or textual emphasis on certain place names succeeds in narrowing the reader's focus to specific locations, but the adverse effect of this selective bolding is the suspicious omissions also highlighted by the map. While literary critics such as García-Peña have commented on the omissions, largely historical, of *El Masacre* (110), a focus instead on the geographical erasures and gaps in the 1973 text allows for an alternate understanding of the author's convoluted attempt at denouncing the 1937 Massacre.

While there are twenty-four instances where a place name or geographical marker (such as the Massacre River) appears bolded, the most commonly bolded location (bolded in the text six times) is Dajabón, the novel's geographical pulse. There are, however, instances when a geographical location is referenced by another name within the pages of *El Masacre*. Dajabón, for example, appears as "provincia" (36) in references to the border town. Likewise, Santo Domingo is charted on the map for instances in which specific geographical markers located inside the capital city are mentioned. While there seems to be no thematic pattern to the highlighted reference points and no clue as to why the names of places that surface more than once in the text are only occasionally reproduced in bold font, all highlighted geographical markers fall within the limits of the Dominican Republic, with the exception of Spain (which is not included on the map). The spatial pattern of the bolded place names verifies that Prestol Castillo fixates on the eastern side of the Dominican-Haitian border. The Dajabón province constitutes new, unfamiliar territory for the newly arrived author, but it is Haiti in particular that represents the unknown for Prestol Castillo. His blatant unfamiliarity with Haiti as well as with *rayanos* and ethnic Haitians living in the Dominican Republic is one of the reasons why the author struggles throughout *El Masacre* to deviate from the established national discourse that plotted Haitians as the antithesis to Dominicans. Prestol Castillo's attempt to highlight place names along the border region, such as Dajabón and Monte Cristi, aligns with Ian Duncan's definition of the provincial novel. Duncan defines the provincial novel—as opposed to the regional novel—by its difference from a novel about the capital, comparing and contrasting these provincial spaces with the epicenter(s) of the nation. In *El Masacre,* Santo Domingo, Prestol Castillo's earliest geographical place cited in the novel, represents the nation's social, economic, and political epicenter. As Franco Moretti asserts in *Graphs, Maps, Trees: Abstract Models for a Literary History,* maps in literature can offer "a model of the narrative universe which rearranges its components in a non-trivial way, and may bring some hidden patterns to the surface" (53–54). At first glance, a focus on the bolded geographical markers as a unit of study in *El Masacre* substantiates Prestol Castillo's distancing from Haiti. When one takes a closer look at the narrative passages in which the bolded place names occur, however, a different pattern emerges, one that instead draws the two national communities together rather than positioning them as antitheses.

The fact that all bolded locations, with the exception of Spain, are in the Dominican Republic does not mean that Haitian cities are never mentioned in the text. Ouanaminthe, or Juana Méndez, the Dominican pronunciation of and nickname for the border town and the Haitian counterpart to Dajabón, is mentioned numerous times, as is Jacmel, the capital of Haiti's Southeastern Department. Likewise, Dominican Republic is bolded on page 65, whereas the country name Haiti never appears stressed (italicized or bolded). At first glance it appears that

Prestol Castillo sought to call attention to the importance of Dominican land over Haitian land. However, while Haitians and Dominicans of Haitian descent are among the primary subjects of the novel, the author's emphasis is on community members who inhabited these spaces, the same resilient individuals who were forced to flee or who lost their lives during the massacre. In this sense, the bolding of Dominican place names accentuates the Haitians' place within those places and provides an answer to the author-narrator's rhetorical question toward the end of the novel, on page 71: "¿De quién es esta tierra?" (Whose land is this?). One can interpret "esta tierra" (this land) as all the points on the map in figure 2, all products of Haitian hands, inhabited by Haitian bodies. Furthermore, the passages in which these bolded place names appear highlight the presence of the Haitian subject within those places. Santiago de la Cruz, a town in the province of Dajabón, for example, is cast as a town where Haitians live and work.[34] The first mention of Santiago de la Cruz in the book reads: "'Dominiquén pas vaut' . . . Lo ha pensando siempre mientras vive como dominicano en una tierra que no es la suya. 'Dominiquén pas vaut' . . . mientras servía como esclavo para el patrón mulato de **Santiago de la Cruz,** trabajando en el alambique o en el cañaveral; o arreando ganados hasta Puerto Plata, desde Dajabón" (59–60). This passage highlights, as do various others in which a bolded place name appears, the integral role Haitians play in Dominican communities. Here, an anonymous Kreyòl speaker tauntingly reminds himself of who works the eastern lands of the island, concluding that it is he and his Haitian brothers who work tirelessly at the hands of unjust Dominicans. He repeats in Kreyòl, perhaps to embolden himself, "Dominiquén pas vaut," which in English means "Dominicans are worthless."

Another example of the bolding of a place name in a passage that stresses the place and role of Haitian subjects is a description of Angela Vargas, a devoted Dominican teacher in an impoverished border town working in a school with Haitian pupils as well as pupils of mixed Haitian and Dominican descent: "Angela Vargas . . . es la única persona que sabe eso de que hay una **República Dominicana.** ¿Qué es eso? . . . dirían los asombrados habitantes del paraje" (65). Here, it is apparent that the inhabitants of the border town have no concept of nation-state. Bewildered and innocent, they ask their teacher, "What is this . . . the Dominican Republic?" The bolding of certain geographical markers at specific moments in the novel, then, can be understood as purposeful on the author's part, beyond signaling his newfound familiarity with the border region, if the context of each quotation is taken into account and the passages are read as narrative representations of Dominican spaces shared by both Dominicans and Haitians.

Similarly, geography is at the core of Prestol Castillo's 1943 publication *Paisajes y meditaciones;* even the title draws the reader's attention to the importance of place. As with *El Masacre,* although the title alone foregrounds geography as essential to the text, the ways that the work underscores third space go beyond this titular reference. In *Paisajes,* the words *ruta, camino,* and *paisaje(s)* appear numerous times and with varying connotations. This repetition draws attention to the limitless, flexible definition of routes in reference to the Dominican-Haitian border and the fact that these passageways are ephemeral and often dictated by political agendas. Frequently, *ruta* is a reminder of a historical route, such as "la vieja ruta" (34) or the route that "ya la había trazado un antiguo bucanero" (58). The notion of a route serves as a historical marker, highlighting paths of the past and signaling their change over time. Additionally, the words *paisaje* and *ruta* denote a physical map of the island. On page 55 Prestol Castillo uses the phrase containing *paisaje* as a transitional phrase after addressing the spiritual, historical, and cultural differences between Dominicans and Haitians: "Ahora volvamos al paisaje, que tiene la loma de siempre y el eterno negro." The word *ruta* is also used in a metaphorical, historical sense to refer to the history of the Dominican Republic: "Y es que nuestra Historia jamás ha tenido semejante ruta" (44). When distancing the history of the eastern side of Hispaniola from that of the western side, Prestol Castillo's use of the word *ruta* signals the importance of geography and place within this history.

Moreover, the text itself follows the author-narrator's route, atop a mule, along *la línea*. Although *Paisajes* was published in 1943, Prestol Castillo confirms that his *ruta* took place in 1938: "Mi ruta fué [*sic*] en 1938" (14). The confirmation of the date of the author's "border study" is key because it suggests that the trip took place just months after the 1937 Massacre. Since the massacre occurred near the end of 1937, Prestol Castillo likely began his border "route" just months after his initial appointment in Dajabón. The author's ownership of the route—"*mi ruta*"—implies that the notion of a path or passageway is subjective; thus any *camino* is unique to each *caminero*. When Prestol Castillo refers to the *castizos* (individuals of mixed descent) roaming the border region, he writes: "Los hombres han vagado sin rutas nacionalistas" (41). This statement suggests the idea of a route as existent but indefinable. Prior to this statement on page 41, the author claims that these border inhabitants are individuals with a "nebulosa noción de nacionalidad" (nebulous notion of nationality). Aside from the tongue twister's attempt to define the *castizos,* the phrase can also be read as marking Prestol Castillo himself as an intellectual who is unable to come to terms with his own self-identification. He, too, has a "nebulous notion of nationality" in that he sympathizes with or at least understands the situation of the Haitians and Haitians of Dominican descent. However, he proves unable to perceive a trace of himself in these hybrid subjects.

Much like Marrero Aristy's *Over, El Masacre* can be linked to Trujillo propaganda for the ways it exemplifies primitivistic, anti-Haitian discourse. Trujillo was irreversibly transparent about pointing his accusatory finger at the Haitian population for the deterioration of the border region despite the 1936 Trujillo-Vincent Treaty.[35] In a speech in Dajabón only days before the massacre decrying the growing number of Haitians in the area and their strengthening influence on *la frontera*—a warning not enough Haitians and Haitians of Dominican descent took seriously— Trujillo explicitly stated that action would be taken: "¡Los haitianos! Su presencia en nuestro territorio no puede más que deteriorar las condiciones de vida de nuestros nacionales. Esa ocupación de los haitianos de las tierras fronterizas no debía continuar. Está ordenado que todos los haitianos que hubiera en el país fuesen exterminados" (qtd. in Cambeira 183–84). Just as Trujillo refused to stand by while the western territory of the Dominican nation became increasingly populated by Haitians, Prestol Castillo proved unable to accept or uncomfortable with the simple role of observer, a muted *testigo* to the horrific events of the massacre. Prestol Castillo unifies the soldiers, cattle ranchers, and Haitians by a common preoccupation: survival. The narrator presents the different national and ethnic groups portrayed in *El Masacre* as products of their environment, engaged in a daily battle to acquire the resources needed to subsist in what can be considered a "cultura de carencia" (Rondón 37). Recognizing the consequences of an environment dominated by a lack of basic needs, the narrator explicitly portrays thievery as unavoidable. It thus becomes difficult for the author-narrator to point an accusatory finger at Haitians involved in petty thievery when they were taking back the fruit of their own labor. The author-narrator indicates numerous times the root of the thievery: "robar para comer" (99). The characters in *El Masacre* compose a cast of minute "villains": the *hateros* exploit the Haitian workers, the Haitians steal Dominican cattle, and the makeshift soldiers kill innocent Haitians and Dominicans of mixed descent.

Blatant assertions such as "otra causa de extinción del ganado era el robo de los haitianos" (29) support the *ladrón* classification and allegations that Haitians are cattle thieves. Prestol Castillo, however, is hesitant to equate the Haitians with criminals, describing the return of the cattle at nightfall and recognizing the Haitians as the cultivators of Dominican land left unattended after the massacre: "Vemos estos inmensos prados de la frontera y asalta una pregunta: ¿De quién es esta tierra? . . . Enantes, abandonada. Luego cultivada por Haití, que la pobló de estancias y frutales—cafetos, aguacates, mangos, sombríos—y ahora desolada, bajo crimen. ¿Para qué? . . . ¿Quién vendrá a esquilmar estos cafetales abandonados, estas praderas vacías?" (71). Furthermore, the author perceives the cattle after the genocide as "vacas tristes" (23), suggesting that even the once "stolen" animals grieve the Haitians' absence. While Prestol Castillo is not convinced that the Haitians are the enemy—and in the above quote portrays them as the cultivators and fruit-bearing hands of Dominican land—neither are the soldiers. As Sommer clarifies, "Many *reservistas* understand that they, like the Haitians, are victims of Trujillo, the sole beneficiary of the massacre" (*One Master* 166). Capitan Ventarrón and his men turn to alcohol to forget the atrocities their hands commit and to assuage their guilt, but they are unable to wipe away the blood on their hands or running through their veins. Ventarrón, for example, "recordó en un momento que su abuelo era de Haití" (28). In Sommer's analysis of *El Masacre* as a populist romance she asserts that the soldiers are "portrayed almost uniformly as reluctant to kill the Haitians, or at least ambivalent because of the way traditional anti-Haitian sentiments conflicted with their first-hand experience with hard-working and modest Haitian neighbors" (*One Master* 169). Similar to the ambivalent *reservistas,* the Dominican cattle ranchers and civilians are unable to fully comprehend the scope of the massacre: "Los dos hateros blancos ven pasar el acontecimiento y no aciertan a explicárselo" (Prestol Castillo, *El Masacre* 90).

While the *hateros* exploit the Haitian workforce, they recognize their importance to the economy of the northwest border region, and the aftermath of the massacre is an eerie silence. The stillness and desolation in the wake of the massacre are referenced countless times in the novel, as if to confirm that the border community is not whole without the Haitian presence: "Es silencio, quietud en el paisaje y en el llano verde" (43); "Una paz que espanta" (47); "la aldea de Dajabón es callada y sin luz" (72). The response of silence to the massacre is, in a way, the environment, *la tierra dominicana, fronteriza*—a land cultivated by the hands of individuals of Haitian descent—paying tribute to lives lost. While at times one could fleetingly read the enemy as the Haitians, the drunk *reservistas,* or the unknowing *hateros,* the blame clearly falls on the "superior commander" (Prestol Castillo, *El Masacre* 46, my translation). Unlike Marrero Aristy in *Over,* Prestol Castillo does not turn toward a foreign oppressive power but instead blatantly portrays Trujillo as villain. While Sommer agrees that the true enemy in *El Masacre* is Trujillo, she confirms that the enemy is not deciphered with ease:

> The enemy is so confusing here. The government and Dominican nationalist tradition identifies the Haitian as Usurper, as when the imaginative federal judges explain away the massacre as "combates campales entre bandas de campesinos haitianos, usurpadores, y bandas de campesinos dominicanos" (117). But the combination of the words "campesinos" with "usurpadores" for the Haitians remains an unconvincing juxtaposition. The idea of hardworking and modest-living Haitian farmers cannot conjure up the image of an illegitimate and oppressive exploiter. Even the judges' fabrication makes one think of a balanced struggle in which neither side is inherently right or wrong. (*One Master* 186)

This juxtaposition of the characterization of the Haitian subject in *El Masacre*—the fact that non-Haitians are also described as thieves and as the exploiters—is of foremost importance. The representation of the Haitians as tireless workers and "good" men, referred to numerous times in the novel as *buenos hombres,* offers a stark contrast to the more negative portrayal in the fragments that adhere to the anti-Haitian ideology of the era. Prestol Castillo's work engages in a balancing act between a personal, semitestimonial denunciation of the 1937 Massacre and adherence to Trujillo anti-Haitian discourse. *El Masacre* transforms into a hybrid model that both critiques *and* aligns with the national ideology.

El Masacre confronts the primitivism inherent in the irreversibly linked ideologies of both Peña Batlle and Balaguer. Looking more closely at the ways in which Prestol Castillo imagines the Haitian subject (and its interstices with the Dominican subjects) as well as the specific instances when his language has been regarded by certain critics as "primitivist," I believe that the primitivism modeled by Peña Batlle and Balaguer is not entirely repeated or justified in Prestol Castillo's *El Masacre*. For both Peña Batlle and Balaguer, equating the Haitian community to a social group marked by barbarianism is central to the progress of the Dominican nation as it proclaims the absence of these animalistic traits in Dominican society. While Haiti "vive inficionado de vicios numerosos y capitales y necesariamente tarado por enfermedades y deficiencias fisiológicas endémicas" (Peña Batlle 67), *El Masacre* is set in the Dominican Republic, not Haiti, and also paints a vivid picture of Dominican *hateros* and *reservistas* before and after the massacre. The division for Prestol Castillo is much less clear than it was for Peña Batlle in *Historia* or Balaguer en *La isla al revés*.

The author does not cast Haitians against Dominicans and describe the differences between them. Instead, the border culture in *El Masacre* serves as a major source of hybridization and racial mixing. It is clear that as a new arrival to the border region mere days before the massacre began, Prestol Castillo did not fully understand the Dominican border communities. Was this lack of information about the region his impetus for the border journey narrated in *Paisajes*? Anzaldúa alludes to the "confusion" that can manifest within the space of the border: "The ambivalence from the clash of voices results in mental and emotional states of perplexity" (*Borderlands* 100). Anzaldúa's "clash of voices" along the Río Grande is similar to the merging between two "voices" that reverberates along the Río Massacre.

The nationalities Prestol Castillo attempts to re-create on paper are more complex than Haitian *or* Dominican; they are more often Haitian *and* Dominican. The second chapter opens with a focus on the Río Massacre—"un río pequeñito que divide dos países" (*El Masacre* 24)—where two women, one Dominican, the other Haitian, are washing clothes together at the water's edge. The sweat, song, tears, and laughter of these two women runs through the river that is both a water source and a natural border. In chapter 4, a young Haitian who had grown up in the Dominican Republic meditates on her options: "¿Salir? . . . ¿Huir, correr, hacia Haití? . . . Pero . . . ¿Cómo? . . . Es de Haití, pero allá no conoce a nadie" (32). The reader is introduced not only to numerous Haitians with no connection, linguistic or cultural, to the western side of the border but also to individuals of mixed nationality. One example is the family of the Dominican Manuelita, her Haitian husband, Yosefo, and their seven children of mixed descent. Albeit saved from the massacre, "los hijos de Yosefo van a la otra tierra, la de su padre" (49). For the children, Haiti is not only "otra tierra" but one that is nonnavigable for the young Haitian Dominicans who cry out in Spanish when they are forced to witness the massacre. The author-narrator alludes to the irony of the family's move with a hypothetical question concluding the family's story: "¿Quién los entenderá en Haití?" (49).[36] Because they do not cry out in Kreyòl, the children will not be understood; in Haiti they are voiceless.

Despite Prestol Castillo's inability to completely separate the Haitian from the Dominican in the border town of Dajabón, Victoriano-Martínez asserts that "Prestol Castillo no parece reconocerse en el haitiano o el rayano frente al cual siente y demuestra cierta simpatía en su texto" (114). Because of the author's inability to abandon his elitist assumptions and fully recognize the commonalities linking all residents of Hispaniola oppressed by Trujillo's reign, himself included, he sometimes repeats the official Trujillo discourse when describing the Haitian subject. The author-narrator *does* describe the Haitians in animalistic terms: "Alma seca, vagabunda, del paisaje, que se guía por los olores, husmea las piedras, devora las distancias. El perro fronterizo, el perro, haitiano" (99). There are plentiful examples in *El Masacre* of Prestol Castillo's regurgitation of the jargon born of the *dominicanización* of the border region to describe Haitians. Victoriano-Martínez further remarks that in Prestol Castillo's 1973 novel, "el ser haitiano es un ser animalizado, reducido a pura naturaleza, a nuda vida" (116). While there is no denying that Prestol Castillo at times equates the Haitian subjects to animalistic beings in *El Masacre,* it is important to clarify that the "seres haitianos" in *El Masacre* are not reduced to a *collective* barbarism; the author rejects presenting the Haitians as anonymous subjects.[37] On the contrary, readers of *El Masacre* are introduced to Tamí (26), Moraime Luis (32), Jean Pié (40), Yosefo (47), Mustalí Dois (59), El Patú and his young son, Tusent (75), Yusén (82), Mandín (96), and countless others. The Haitians in *El Masacre* are brought to life; these are not nameless, dehumanized individuals whose lives Sargento Tarragón (commanding the Dominican forces carrying out the genocide) and his men take.

A further sign of the lack of anonymity when referring to the Haitians and Haitian Dominicans, in *El Masacre* Prestol Castillo also includes the names of individuals with no anecdotal reference in the text. Tamí, for example, is mentioned in passing: "viejos, como Tamí, el limosnero" (26); Jean Pié's life is remembered only briefly: "Jean Pié, con 80 años, lo degollaron" (40).[38] Like Tamí and Jean Pié, many Haitians are mentioned in the text only fleetingly, hinting at the existence of unnumbered Haitians and Dominicans of Haitian descent affected by the massacre, greatly exceeding in number the Haitians formally addressed by the author-narrator. This avoidance, conscious or not, to group Haitians as a collective community characterized primarily by barbarism, does not deny the fact Prestol Castillo resorts to a primitive ideology at times. The use of anti-immigrant and anti-Haitian language, however, possibly signals an internal struggle for the author himself. Diógenes Céspedes affirms the author's muddling of elitism and his possible condemnation of the 1937 Massacre while also expressing his skepticism regarding Prestol Castillo's outcry: "El hecho de que relata la matanza de los haitianos, que describe una cierta oposisión al régimen de Trujillo, que el narrador se refocile añorando sueños aristocráticos en una estancia patriarcal, no nos produce ni frío ni calor" (150). The author's internal struggle may derive from his role as both judge (magistrate of Dajabón) *and* writer. The author's struggle, permeating the pages of *El Masacre,* intensifies in *Paisajes y meditaciones,* published during the *trujillato* and dedicated to *el Generalísimo* himself. In *Paisajes y meditaciones,* the same struggle does not permeate the writing, and the author's eulogizing of Trujillo is not met with uneasiness or uncertainty.

Prestol Castillo's anti-Haitianism is more straightforward in *Paisajes y meditaciones,* the author clearly influenced by elitist assumptions and the national discourse. Prestol Castillo defines the *castizo* in *Paisajes y meditaciones* as synonymous with the Haitian subject and marks the *castizo* as "un hombre que no tiene medidas civiles, sino medidas zoológicas" (23). The author later describes the spiritual being of Haitians as "retardado, chato, primitivo" (30), and he blatantly portrays Haitians as barbarians throughout the text.[39] Not only are the textual examples of this ideology multiple but the author also cites originators of the barbaric representation of Haitians within the Dominican conception of nationality, such as Peña Batlle. Peña Batlle is quoted numerous times and exalted as "el primer especialista dominicano en cuestiones de frontera" (35). In some instances, it is clear that Prestol Castillo replicates both Peña Batlle's and Balaguer's understanding of the epistemology (with roots in the spiritual ancestry) of Haitians as opposed to Dominicans. He notes in the chapter "¿Somos distintos a Haití?" that "Nuestro negro,—similar al haitiano en la morfología—ha diferido totalmente del vecino en su ruta de evolución espiritual. El nuestro fué, espiritualmente, un español" (43). Pages later, he clarifies: "El negro del Este es un auténtico español" (46). Compared with the transparent primitivism in *Paisajes y meditaciones,* the same ideology in *El Masacre* is decidedly less barefaced. Why did the author-narrator tone down this language in his novelistic re-creation of the 1937 Massacre, especially as he was engaged with this specific train of intellectual thought when he wrote *Paisajes y meditaciones* less than five years after the massacre took place? This disparity highlights the broader scope in which the 1973 novel represents the Haitian subject.

Tipping the scales of Prestol Castillo's internal struggle inherent in *El Masacre* regarding the reality of the horrific massacre is an event the author-narrator refers to as a "delirious fever" (139). In the aftermath of the massacre and his attempt to come to terms with the genocide, Prestol Castillo has a nightmare about Touissant Louverture in which the

Haitian general declares that he will kill the inhabitants of the neighboring Spanish colony, including the children and women. In the dream the author-narrator imagines himself in the role of the revolutionary leader: "Soy Santos Louverture Toussaint" (137). In the narrator's lengthy dream monologue Toussaint proclaims: "Esta tierra es mía. . . . He pisoteado los blancos franceses . . . I ahora, pisotearé a los blancos españoles de Santo Domingo. Los degollaré" (137). This passage, toward the novel's end, is a reminder of the devastation and destruction imparted by the Haitian army, led by Dessalines and Christophe, at the start of the nineteenth century and in the wake of the Haitian Revolution. Toussaint's appearance also hints at the abuses committed by Jean-Pierre Boyer during the unification of the island and the aggressive politics orchestrated by Faustin Soulouque in 1849 and 1855 in his attempts to reconquer the Dominican Republic.[40] When the narrator awakens from his nightmare, the first thing he "sees" is an ocean flowing red with blood, just as the Massacre River had. Clearly the narrator's vision and thought are impaired by the vivid dream, as he wakes with visions of the blood-red water and the screams of his dead neighbors in his ear.

The chapter ends with a summary of his nightmare that mirrors the official, dominant discourse of the time: "Me sorprendió meditando sobre la historia presente que veía con mis ojos, escrita en caracteres de sangre, y aquella historia de impiedad, despotismo y crímenes cometidos por los *haitianos,* aprendida en las clases de historia, en la infancia" (140, my emphasis). Still in a state of shock following the events of the massacre, in the end the author-narrator labels the Haitians as the criminals, influenced by the events haunting his dreams. The dream sequence attempts to counteract the injustices committed during the Trujillo-ordered massacre by recalling colonial-era battles that took place well before Dominican Republic's independence. Prestol Castillo's use of his "clases de historia, en la infancia" as a reference point for the historical context of his dream, however, nullifies the blame he places on the Haitians. As previously noted, the novel begins with a characterization of the author-narrator's childhood teacher: "El maestro hablaba rutinariamente. No conocía su país . . . El maestro era extranjerizado en sus preferencias" (15). If the narrator's teacher knew nothing of the history or geography of the border region—and it was possibly the same teacher or a teacher similarly educated, elitist, and *capitalista* who presented the history of the Dominican Republic and Haiti as one-sided—then Prestol Castillo's blatant finger-pointing at the Haitian community after his dream appears less significant. In the novel's phrase "crímenes cometidos por haitianos," *dominicanos* could easily replace *haitianos,* and Prestol-Castillo has a backhanded way of highlighting this.

Manuel Robert, an alcoholic Dominican who loses his wife and children during the massacre, is described in the wake of the tragic event as "Otro hombre," "un producto del Corte" (97). These words also fittingly capture the author-narrator after the massacre. While Prestol Castillo does not entirely abandon his elitist assumptions, as evidenced by his return to jargon mirroring the vocabulary of early twentieth-century Trujillo intellectuals, the experience of *el corte* also changes him and alters his understanding of Haitians and Dominicans of Haitian descent. He is no longer an "extranjerizado" like his childhood teacher, who viewed the Dominican-Haitian border as a black hole in Hispaniola's geography and history. In *El Masacre,* the author-narrator exemplifies, perhaps unconsciously, how traditional, nationalistic discourse has identified Haitians as violent, barbaric savages by his use of primitivistic discourse. In this way Prestol Castillo offers an answer to the question, if not an excuse for, why such discourses "affect the Dominicans' collective unconscious" (Fumagalli 142), including his own. The author-narrator pushes back against the authoritative discourse by recognizing Haitians affected by the massacre as individuals. He also defies the dominant Trujillo ideology by divulging his personal confrontation of the border region after the massacre.

Reading *El Masacre* as a repudiation of *el corte* becomes the obvious choice when readers look more closely at Prestol Castillo's 1943 *Paisajes y meditaciones,* a prime example of a text *El Masacre* could have mirrored more closely in terms of content had the author wanted to follow the strict guidelines of the controlled, dominant discourse. Victoriano-Martínez asserts that the author perceives the massacre "desde la posición de un funcionario trujillista que participa en el encubrimiento del genocidio y se limita a narralo" (117–18). Prestol Castillo, however, does not just narrate *el corte:* he experiences it, suffers through it, and painfully addresses the aftermath. Howard critiques the author-narrator for his inability to confront the realities of the massacre (143), but the fact that Prestol Castillo's chronicle of the horrendous event is the only eyewitness account, regardless of possible fabrications or additions, problematizes this critique. While *El Masacre* is a subjective account of the 1937 genocide, the author-narrator's decision to record the event in novel form constitutes the most obvious, transparent attempt to address the realities of the massacre. The "notas de la frontera" composing *El Masacre* can be read entirely as a confrontation of the 1937 genocide, and Prestol Castillo's insistence on telling the truth, applauded by Sommer, confirms the author's deep-seated desire to do justice not only to those who suffered at the hands of Sargento Tarragón and his men but also to his own conscience, a conscience troubled by his reluctance to denounce the events with only words as opposed to actions, as evidenced by his reverence for the border-town teacher and his quasi girlfriend, Angela Vargas.[41] The author-narrator self-identifies numerous times as a coward (142), and this anxiety about cowardice is likely a response to the contradictory, paradoxical nature of the text and to *El Masacre*'s "inability and unwillingness to either fully embrace or resolutely reject dominant discourses" (Fumagalli 141). On page 50 of *El Masacre* the author-narrator makes reference to a writer who was ordered to the border by Trujillo to cover up the realities of the genocide: "El periodista sabrá que miente, contra su conciencia." Might one consider Prestol Castillo's occasional lapses in an otherwise overwhelming denouncement of the massacre in the same light? He, too, as a product of an elitist society imprisoned by the authoritative, Trujillo-censored discourse, lies against his own will.

Both Marrero Aristy's *Over* and Prestol Castillo's *El Masacre se pasa a pie* are considered literary successes in the Dominican Republic, boasting more prints run and copies sold than the majority of twentieth-century texts on the island. While the novels' publication dates are separated by thirty-six years, they were written within the same two-year period, at the height of Trujillo's reign. Admittedly, Marrero Aristy and Prestol Castillo were not the only Dominican writers active during the general's thirty-one years in power. Other notable authors writing during this time include Juan Bosch, Ramón Lacay Polanco, and Aída Cartagena Portalatín.[42] These two texts, while offering a literary commentary on the *trujillato*, prove increasingly interesting for the ways that they alternatively portray the Dominican neighbor, Haiti. Veering, albeit not entirely, from the national discourse supported by the dominant Trujillo ideology and *los trujillistas teóricos*, both *Over* and *El Masacre* offer a representation of the Haitian subject that counters and challenges Trujillo-driven ideology.

Both novels, while offering a less antagonistic portrayal of the Haitian subject than the vast majority of literary texts written and published during the *trujillato*, do not deviate completely from the antinegro state-sponsored ideology of the period, as they also incorporate the official discourse. *Over* and *El Masacre* describe Haitians in primitivist language, at times characterizing their neighbors as barbaric, uneducated, and unhygienic. The authors' sympathetic representation of the Haitian subject, alongside this regurgitation of the dominant, state-sponsored ideology, reveals an alternate understanding of the treatment of Haitian laborers and Dominicans of Haitian descent in the Dominican Republic. In *Over,* the North American managerial forces appear as both villainous and oppressive within the *ingenio* environment. *El Masacre,* in a more overt attack, blames Trujillo and his henchmen for the massacre and the deterioration of the communities on the Dominican-Haitian border. The fact that Trujillo emerges as the villain in Prestol Castillo's bestseller is the reason that the novel was not published until well after the dictator's assassination. The notion of censorship and the unrivaled power of the state-sponsored band of Trujillo intellectuals for the majority of the twentieth century also explains why Marrero Aristy and Prestol Castillo, residing in the Dominican Republic during the *trujillato,* published texts such as *La República Dominicana* and *Paisajes y meditaciones,* overtly praising the dictator and his anti-Haitian policies.

The geographical anonymity traceable in both *Over* and *El Masacre se pasa a pie* results in a temporary erasure, albeit literary, of the Dominican-Haitian border, a metaphorical dissipation of the borderline that Marcio Veloz Maggiolo's novels, examined in the following chapter, further illustrate. Marrero Aristy sets his novel, criticizing Dominican society and those in power, on an anonymous plantation, while Prestol Castillo begins his text with a reference to a misunderstanding and misrepresentation of the Dominican Republic's border region. This geographical uncertainty is essential to the novels' alternate envisioning of Haitians and Haitians of Dominican descent in Dominican literature from the Trujillo Era. Beyond emphasizing the blurring of lines separating Haiti and the Dominican Republic, the cartographic ambiguity in Marrero Aristy's and Prestol Castillo's bestsellers also allows other messages to emerge. Within the context of the twentieth-century sugar plantation, for example, a representation of ambiguous space links to the *desnacionalización* of the Dominican Republic. The rising global demands of the sugar industry resulted in a significant uptick in the country's international workforce. These newcomers included not only Haitians and *cocolos* hired as contract laborers but also North American managers. The historian Lauren Derby writes that the sugar boom in the early twentieth-century Dominican Republic was "a foreign affair" (*Dictator's Seduction* 17). Marrero Aristy and Prestol Castillo craft ambiguous portrayals of plantation space and border space. The loss of a sense of belonging that these portrayals imply parallels the dismantling or disturbance of a national spirit that many Dominicans felt in the early to mid-twentieth century. Moscoso Puello, for example, in his novel *Cañas y bueyes* overtly blames the sugar industry for the erasure of a Dominican national identity. Marrero Aristy and Prestol Castillo render geographical ambiguity a tool to address the inherently confusing or disjunctive concept of border space or third space. At the same time, though, Marrero Aristy and Prestol Castillo write Haitians and Dominicans of Haitian descent *into*—as opposed to out of—their understanding of the Dominican nation. Bhabha's theorization of postmodern space(s) as split and fractured in *The Location of Culture* marks third space as undefined and vague; ideas of "nationness" are interstitial and overlapping, as opposed to stable, and they are characterized by their discordance, juxtaposition, and fragmentation (217). The on- and off-border spaces in *Over* and *El Masacre se pasa a pie,* through their ambiguous representations of geography, mimic Bhabha's desire to frame displaced, evolving, and increasingly transnational, transracial, and transethnic communities as a postmodern reality and a positive consequence of fluid borders.

2   A Disappearing Act
Marcio Veloz Maggiolo's *Línea*

> El discurso literario de Marcio Veloz Maggiolo es un grito adolorido, una denuncia estremecedora de una época sellada por el terror, el crimen rampante y la frustración. Un discurso que nos invita a no olvidar.
>
> —Carlos Esteban Deive, "Marcio Veloz Maggiolo
> o la pasión por el saber"

Marcio Veloz Maggiolo, the most prolific Dominican writer of the twentieth and twenty-first centuries, wears many hats.[1] Winner of the Dominican Republic's Premio Nacional de la Novela in 1962, 1981, and 1992, Veloz Maggiolo is not just a novelist but also a poet, playwright, essayist, archaeologist, anthropologist, and historian.[2] Making a mark in multiple fields is a significant feat for an accomplished scholar and writer. As Carlos Esteban Deive remarks in regard to Veloz Maggiolo's broad intellectual impact, "Lo que nos asombra de él no es esa variedad de intereses. Lo realmente significativo, lo que lo destaca y distingue, es que en cada una de esas facetas de su quehacer ha sabido regalarnos la impronta de su capacidad, su ingenio, de su inteligencia privilegiada y de su audacia de creador e investigador" (65–66). In large part, the author's wide-ranging interdisciplinary interests have allowed him to converse with Hispaniola's past in a unique and informed manner. Veloz Maggiolo was born in Santo Domingo in 1936, during Trujillo's reign. His literary corpus reflects his experience growing up and receiving his education in a country under the rule of an infamous *caudillo*. Veloz Maggiolo is a writer and, moreover, an intellectual who traverses borders. Not only does his work, both literary and otherwise, highlight the cross sections between different academic fields but Veloz Maggiolo's novels fixate on the physical border and the "cross sections" between two national communities. The two novels examined in this chapter, *El hombre del acordeón* (2003) and *La vida no tiene nombre* (1965), reveal the complexities of the Haitian-Dominican border region and the relationships between Dominicans, Haitians, and Dominicans of Haitian descent.[3]

Veloz Maggiolo's all-inclusive vision of Hispaniola and the border region is the primary focus of the present chapter. Both *El hombre del acordeón* and *La vida no tiene nombre* carve a space for Haitians and Dominicans of Haitian descent in the author's unique reenvisioning of Dominican history.[4] Veloz Maggiolo, perhaps more than any other contemporary Dominican writer, contextualizes and problematizes the (non) existence of the Dominican-Haitian border. *El hombre del acordeón* is literary proof that despite the existence of a geopolitical border, any attempt to "filter" culture is irrelevant; what is "Dominican" to one is "Haitian" to another. The novel embodies Bhabha's inherently hybrid third space and fictionalizes a seamless border community in which the limitations of preexisting social, cultural, and racial boundaries are blurred, purporting "innovative sites of collaboration" (Bhabha, *Location of Culture* 1–2). Similarly, *La vida no tiene nombre,* while reflecting on foreign invasions of the Dominican Republic much as Veloz Maggiolo does in *De abril en adelante* (1975; From April on), situates Dominicans of Haitian descent as integral, patriotic members of the early twentieth-century Dominican Republic. Veloz Maggiolo's literary approach to the Trujillo Era cannot be classified as testimonial literature, but both *El hombre del acordeón* and *La vida no tiene nombre* are realistic accounts of the Dominican Republic in the twentieth century. Similar to testimonial narrative in which subaltern peoples on the margins of society represent themselves in literary form despite possible linguistic, cultural, and/or political restraints, both texts "concentrate on the debasement suffered by citizens, rather than on the way that it was or could have been overcome" (López-Calvo 113).

As Fumagalli notes, Veloz Maggiolo "weaves a vivid and diversified tapestry with the complex human, political, and cultural fabric of the northern borderland" (152). The ambiguous and shifting border territory of the Dominican Republic and Haiti correlates directly to the violent, repressive Trujillo regime, and the presence of the *frontera* permeates Veloz Maggiolo's fiction. The scholars Neil Larsen and Ana Gallego Cuiñas have studied at length the repeated return to the Trujillo Era in contemporary Dominican narrative. Likewise, countless critics have pointed to what De Maeseneer refers to as the "brega con el pasado" (*Encuentro* 23) in which Dominican writers find themselves incessantly engaged, unable to break with the past. Latin American literary traditions are often rooted in national historical events, and these foundational historical moments repeatedly are represented by discovery and independence. The unique, constant anchor for Dominican novels, however, is the *trujillato*. As Horn suggests, "More than any other Dominican medium—whether music, theater, film, or visual art—post-dictatorship writing, both fictional and nonfictional, took on the task of critically accounting for the dictatorial past" (56). Gallego Cuiñas, in *Trujillo, el fantasma y sus escritores* (2006; Trujillo, the ghost and his writers), offers various terms to identify this subgenre of historical narrative: *novela del trujillato, narrativa de Trujillo, narrativa trujillista, narrativa trujilloniana* (16). In addition to there being an overabundance of terms, critics disagree on which novels should be categorized as Trujillo narrative.[5] Giovanni Di Pietro, for example, classifies novels written during the thirty-one-year reign of the dictator, 1930–61, as Trujillo narrative (205). Gallego Cuiñas casts the net more broadly by instead determining that any novel written post-*trujillato* reflecting upon the regime can be categorized as "trujillista" narrative (17).[6]

It is important to note that an interest in the figure of the dictator is not a Dominican phenomenon but can be traced to the decade following the Latin American literary Boom of the 1960s, with novels such as Gabriel García Márquez's *El otoño del patriarca* (1975; *The Autumn of the Patriarch*, 1976), Alejo Carpentier's *El recurso del método* (1974; *Reasons of State*, 1976), and Augusto Roa Bastos's *Yo el Supremo* (1974; *I, The Supreme*, 1986). Prior to the Latin American literary movement and the post-Boom period that followed, Miguel Ángel Asturias's canonical novel *El Señor Presidente* (1946; *The President*, 1963) focused on the figure of the dictator. The aforementioned novels of the Latin American Boom mark a pointed interest in the aesthetics of the text, and they frequently enlist the dictator as protagonist, imagining and revealing the tyrant's private thoughts and desires.[7]

Trujillo narrative is one of the dominant literary discourses in the Dominican Republic, and Veloz Maggiolo entered the literary scene during the years just prior to the end of the Trujillo dictatorship. Thus, any study of *narrativa de dictador/dictadura*, or in the case of the Dominican Republic, Trujillo narrative, would be remiss if it did not include the literary production of Veloz Maggiolo. His longstanding presence as a Dominican writer whose literary corpus directly reflects and critiques the Trujillo regime shifts the question critic Neil Larsen poses in his study of *narrativa trujillista* from "¿Cómo narrar el trujillato?" to "¿Quién narra el trujillato?" An irrefutable answer to the latter question is Marcio Veloz Maggiolo. Veloz Maggiolo's narrative production substantiates Larsen's statement that the image of Trujillo and his regime in Dominican literature "refuses to disappear" (123, my translation). While Trujillo narrative is not the focus of this chapter, this persuasive "Trujillo phenomenon" (Gallego Cuiñas 12) constitutes an ideal starting point prior to examining both *El hombre del acordeón* and *La vida no tiene nombre*. Even Veloz Maggiolo's first novel, *Judas* (1962), is a commentary, albeit understated, on the Trujillo dictatorship.[8] The novel centers on the life of the biblical Judas and considers what led him to betray Jesus Christ.[9] Trujillo narrative often parallels historical fiction, and Horn claims that Dominican dictatorship literature is "most often placed by critics under the rubric of 'historical fiction'" (59). Relatedly, the critic Tessa Morris-Suzuki asserts that the historical novel "has become one of the chief vehicles through which the peoples of modern times were encouraged to imagine the past in national terms" (49). Veloz Maggiolo, however, addresses the Dominican Republic not just in national terms but in *trans*national terms, taking into account the complex relationship and interweaving of cultures between the Dominican Republic and Haiti.

The narrative of Veloz Maggiolo focuses not just on the figure of Trujillo but also on those oppressed during the thirty-one-year regime. Veloz Maggiolo's fiction gives voice to those who did not fit neatly into the political and state-crafted vision of a white, Catholic, Spanish nation during the *trujillato*, in particular Haitian and Haitian Dominican subjects. Deive confirms Veloz Maggiolo's focus on those victimized by the Trujillo regime: "Su narrativa reproduce, recreándola, la historia de la República, especialmente la más inmediata y dramática. No es una narrativa de héroes, sino de víctimas, de personajes generalmente marginados y sufrientes, perseguidos por la tiranía o atormentados por un destino incierto y evasivo, derrotados y amargos" (67). While Dominicans of all classes, races, ranks, and professions suffered at the hands of the Dominican tyrant, Veloz Maggiolo consciously includes the Haitian subject in his literary reflection on the Trujillo regime and its aftermath. As Rafael Rodríguez-Henríquez suggests in respect to Veloz Maggiolo's interest in fictional characters beyond the Dominican subject: "Su indagación acerca de la identidad dominicana es presentada en sus novelas desde una visión abarcadora de todos los grupos humanos que han contribuido a la misma" (iii). Without question, Haitians have contributed greatly to the agricultural and economic landscape of the Dominican Republic and have altered the construction of identity on the eastern side of the island.

In *El hombre del acordeón, línea* with a lowercase *l* refers to an overarching understanding of "border"; *Línea*, on the other hand, pertains to the northern border region of the Dominican Republic.[10] The novel is set, more specifically, in a town called La Salada, a community within the limits of La Línea. Both la línea and La Línea double as spaces that defy categorization: they are ambiguous, fleeting, transcultural, and transnational zones that are difficult to define. To reference Anzaldúa's Náhuatl term, *nepantla,* the Dominican-Haitian borderlands for Veloz Maggiolo are "tierra entre medio" ("(Un)natural Bridges" 243).[11] Or rather, the spaces occupied by border inhabitants alongside the Massacre River, separating the two countries of Hispaniola, can be understood as "in-between" spaces. I propose that while the border region in *El hombre del acordeón,* La Línea, may be the most precise example of a Dominican liminal threshold that is neither "here" nor "there," the same applies for more interior regions of the Dominican Republic. *La vida no tiene nombre,* for example, is set inland, in El Seibo. The easternmost province of the Dominican Republic, El Seibo is not physically located on the Dominican-Haitian frontier. Veloz Maggiolo, by writing Haitians into this space, asserts that Haitians and Dominicans of Haitian descent also inhabit this physical space. In this way, Veloz Maggiolo's work portrays an alternate representation of Haitians that extends beyond the border where *rayano* culture flourishes and the mixing of religion, food, and music from both Haiti and the Dominican Republic is more prominent. Returning to Anzaldúa's notion of *nepantla* to better understand Veloz Maggiolo's representation of both the physical border region and the ideological borders that exist to distinguish Dominicans and Haitians in areas beyond the border, AnaLouise Keating's approach to the idea proves helpful: "During nepantla, individual and collective self-conceptions and worldviews are *shattered* as apparently fixed categories—whether based on gender, ethnicity/'race,' sexuality, religion, or some combination of these categories and often others as well—are destabilized and slowly stripped away" ("Risking the Vision" 143). These two less-studied Veloz Maggiolo novels, *El hombre del acordeón* and *La vida no tiene nombre,* are prime examples of both on- and off-border narratives that, despite a clear difference in geographical setting, offer similar portrayals of the Haitian-Dominican dynamic. La Línea and El Seibo both serve to raze the "fixed categories" that traditionally define either side of the border, instead motioning toward alternate ways to approach hybridized spaces.

Moreover, this chapter postulates that Veloz Maggiolo's literary representation of the Haitian subject likewise serves to "shatter," "strip away," and "destabilize" the dominant discourse related to Haitians and Dominicans of Haitian descent in the Dominican Republic. His novels, in particular *El hombre del acordeón* and *La vida no tiene nombre,* break with the historical, patriarchal Dominican tradition that defines Haitians as the barbaric racial and ethnic Other. As noted previously, Veloz Maggiolo is an intellectual who wears many hats. His numerous anthropological articles—many with a central focus on the history and culture of Hispaniola—often contain passages that relate directly to his fiction. His 1984 article "Apuntes sobre autoctonía y etnicidad," for example, hints at a basic definition of cultural identity: "Por debajo de la identidad cultura, en los sustratos de la identificación hombre-paisaje, hombre-tierra, está la organización ideológica" (55). It is precisely the Dominican ideological organization as related to cultural identity that Veloz Maggiolo's novels problematize. Both *El hombre del acordeón* and *La vida no tiene nombre* relay a literary depiction of the Dominican Republic in which national identity is not uniformly opposite, nor does it reject, Haitian culture. The author's interest in reformulating a complex history of Dominicans and Haitians—resisting "the prevailing conception today of a Dominican nation and Dominicanness as being in radical and transhistorical opposition to Haiti and Haitianness" (Turits, "World Destroyed" 593)—is well documented in his 1972 essay "Tipología del tema haitiano en la literatura dominicana." This essay not only signals the importance of Haitians in Dominican letters but also recognizes the diverse, complicated and convoluted representation of the Haitian subject within the literature of the Dominican Republic. While the goal of this chapter relates directly to this important essay—which Veloz Maggiolo refers to as "el primer intento" to examine the varying representations of Haitianness in Dominican literature (12)—it also aims to problematize any desire to "typify" the representation of a single ethnic group within literature. The following close readings of *El hombre del acordeón* and *La vida no tiene nombre* question Veloz Maggiolo's five "positions," or representations of the Haitian subject in Dominican literature (prior to 1972, when the "Tipología" essay was published), and reject the typification—a simplification that strips past collaboration between the two countries of its multiple layers—of a complex and long-standing relationship.

The (Un)delineated Line in *El hombre del acordeón*

> La única línea clara para reconstruir hechos donde lo mágico puede superar a la realidad fue la influencia política que predominó entre los habitantes de la frontera y los rayanos que supervivieron en la misma decidiendo ser, desde aquellos momentos, dominicanos.
> —Marcio Veloz Maggiolo, *El hombre del acordeón*

El hombre del acordeón is a literal title in the sense that the story recalls the life—and more importantly the death—of Honorio Lora, one of the favorite *merengueros* of the novel's dictatorial figure. Honorio Lora, inhabitant of the border region and individual of legendary musical talent, *is* "the man of the accordion." To revisit the moments leading up to the mysterious death of the famed musician is to enter into *rayano* territory and confront the traditions that define the rural border town of La Salada. While the novel's setting on the Dominican-Haitian border is essential to the storyline, Veloz Maggiolo's representation of a traditionally marginalized region of the Dominican Republic offers an entryway into the merged cultures of the Haitians and Dominicans straddling the frontier. The transcultural and transnational elements abound; religion, music, and food commingle on the ambiguous *frontera*, highlighting the hybrid nature of the border region. Contradictory accounts of the death of Honorio Lora frame the novel in a unique way, and each testimony calls into question a previous "truth." The parsing of the novel into twenty-one short chapters and the myriad attestations to the life and death of Honorio Lora lead critic De Maeseneer to label the work as closely mirroring a "detective narrative," with the massacre as the historical backdrop (*Seis ensayos* 35).[12] The (nameless) principal narrator is a journalist by profession who takes upon himself the task of organizing the multiple testimonies that complicate the mysterious homicide of Honorio. The journalist is also a composer who adeptly interprets Honorio's lyrics—read as both precursors and critiques of the 1937 Haitian Massacre and challenges to General Brigadier—and he is the (temporary) owner of Honorio's magical accordion. The novel refers to Trujillo as "Brigadier," a name change forced upon the narrator, who confirms: "Inventé nombres y heredades cuando me encargaron, por órdenes del Brigadier, ya Presidente, recuperar la historia de los pueblos fronterizos" (14).[13] Confronted with the task of chronicling the border region and addressing its history, the narrator is from the beginning forced to lie, to "invent."

I begin this on-border analysis of *El hombre del acordeón* with a closer look at the novel's setting on the banks of the Massacre River. Following a discussion of the geographically engrained vision of the border, I examine the chaotic, choppy organization of the text and, lastly, I provide a tripartite analysis of the representation of the Haitian subject in the novel. This three-pronged analysis highlights (1) the (un)writing of the border (a line described on page 14 of *El hombre del acordeón* as "no tan delineada"); (2) the notion of rebellion in the text; and (3) the nonexistence or impossibility of "una historia simple." I consider the same three factors in my analysis of *La vida no tiene nombre*, connecting the two novels—written nearly a half century apart—and theorizing a common trajectory of Veloz

Maggolio's treatment of the Haitian subject. Both novels succeed in unifying the Haitian-Dominican communities—*El hombre del acordeón* from an on-border setting and *La vida no tiene nombre* from off border—and proving, much as the ancient vodou belief does, that two (different) things can be the same. As Joan Dayan notes, "The history told by these [vodou] traditions defies our notions of *identity* and *contradiction*. A person or thing can be two or more things simultaneously . . . we begin to see that what becomes more and more vague also becomes more distinct: it may mean *this*, but *that* too" (33). The Dominican-Haitian frontier, much like the vodou belief described by Dayan, is also *this* and *that*, both *here* and *there*; its ability to shift beyond physical, political confines makes it the ideal point of departure and return for Veloz Maggiolo's narratives.

Anzaldúa's understanding of *nepantla* is key to a conceptualization of *El hombre del acordeón*'s setting, a space in which two towns straddling the border fuse into one. La Línea is an inscrutable space, a physical territory that can be mapped but not defined, and its bewildering existence aligns with Anzaldúa's *nepantla:* "Nepantla is tierra desconocida, and living in the liminal zone means being in a constant state of displacement—an uncomfortable, even alarming feeling. Most of us dwell in nepantla so much of the time it's becoming a sort of home" ("(Un)natural Bridges" 243). In this sense, the Haitian and Dominican inhabitants of La Línea, the *rayanos,* are also *nepantler@s*. These subjects straddle a border that "was not clearly marked"[14] and in doing so lose a sense of space. At the same time, these "border beings" also create and demarcate their own sense of home, which extends beyond the geographical or political. Being unsure of one's belonging to a geographical space can indeed produce, as Anzaldúa asserts, an "alarming feeling," but it is most alarming for those who are foreigners or outsiders to this "in-between" terrain. It was this very sense of "alarm" or uncertainty that produced fear in the minds of Trujillo (or Brigadier in the novel) and other "white" elites; what Anzaldúa marks as an "alarming feeling" speaks directly to the force behind the 1937 Massacre and its goal to consecrate the frontier. *El hombre del acordeón* is set shortly after the massacre, but numerous unabashed recollections of Honorio Lora's life and death bring the horrific event to the novel's forefront. The event of the massacre, then, reclaims and repurposes the sense of alarm within the border region that for the first part of the twentieth century found a home in the negrophobic, anti-Haitian and antiblack nationalists. After October 1937, however, Haitian presence on Dominican territory was no longer a matter of everyday practice, a natural and relatively uncontested "come"-and-"go" atmosphere, but instead cause for "anxiety and fear" (Fumagalli 158). In *El hombre del acordeón*, Veloz Maggiolo normalizes the Haitian-Dominican border experience by giving voice to inhabitants of both sides, allowing for a collaborative detailing of La Línea that is inclusive of both Dominican and Haitian perspectives, confirming that "anxiety and fear" do not control or define the hybrid space for those who live within its limits.

Geographically speaking, a discussion of La Línea—or the fictional town of La Salada—is curious because the town on the Haitian side of La Salada is referred to in the novel as Ouanaminthe (22). Ouanaminthe, however, is *not* a fictional point; it is the Haitian counterpart of the Dominican border town known as Dajabón. If the town name La Salada functions as a mask, much as the name Brigadier does, why is the town name Ouanaminthe unaltered? While the community of La Salada is yet another of the narrator's "inventions," the inclusion of an actual geographical location such as Ouanaminthe, as well as other direct textual references to Montecristi and Manzanillo, serves to foil the narrator's attempt to eclipse the exact location of La Salada. Veloz Maggiolo remodels fictional space in *El hombre del acordeón* by renaming what readers familiar with Dominican geography assume to be Dajabón, positioning the invented town of La Salada as the Dominican counterpart of Ouanaminthe. Anne-Kathrin Reuschel and Lorenz Hurni address tactics to uncover the fictionalization of geography in literature, and they recognize that familiarity with a given space is necessary if one is to differentiate invented space from references to actual places: "Good general knowledge of the region is essential to separate places that no longer exist from those that have been invented or modified by the author" (297). I believe that Veloz Maggiolo purposely modifies the name of Dajabón in an effort to position the border town as a synecdochic representation of other Haitian-Dominican towns. In this way, his description of La Salada following the massacre—offering a vivid depiction of the dynamism and interconnectivity of border communities—speaks for La Línea at large and allows for a broader understanding of the transnational northern border region. The author's reference to the invented La Salada (as opposed to Dajabón) also functions as a reminder of a historical pattern of misnaming on the island. As Dixa Ramírez writes: "Persistent misnaming of either or both sides of the island in various fields of scholarship and over two centuries has compounded archival erasure or miscategorization. That is, non-Dominican and non-Haitian scholars writing about the island referred to either side accurately or mistakenly as San Domingue/San Domingo/Saint Domingue/Santo Domingo/Hayti/Haiti/Hispaniola/Española" (9).

Veloz Maggiolo, then, deliberately misnames Dajabón and in doing so successfully yields a limitless and boundaryless border region in his novel.

The setting on the Dominican-Haitian border allows a representation of the Haitian subject to form part of the novel's core, and so do the choppy, fragmented organization of the text and Veloz Maggiolo's utilization of various literary devices. The chaotic ordering and constant shift in narrative voice produce a literary disarray that mimics the border region itself. The first paragraph of *El hombre del acordeón* references this disordered aspect, which defines the work: "No se pretende que todo quede tan en orden como debiera ser. Es como hacer una colcha con retazos de diferentes tipos de tela y de colores como las que hacían las abuelas durante los años nebulosos de la infancia" (11). The patchwork metaphor here represents not only the overlapping testimonies recalling Honorio Lora's death but also the border itself. Much as Veloz Maggiolo attempts to create a typology of the Haitian subject in Dominican literature in "Tipología del tema haitiano," in *El hombre del acordeón* he points to the (im)possibility of defining—or "typifying"—the Dominican-Haitian border. To typify is to attempt to represent or define what is normal, but the border is *not* normal; the border region defies rules, politics, and geography, and this defiance makes the space a model heterotopia. The *frontera,* then, imposes limits (or has limits imposed upon it) but obeys none. This rebellious nature of the border allows Veloz Maggiolo space to create, space to weave the *tela,* or patchwork, that represents La Línea—a magical element that adds to its uniqueness. The novel defines the magic permeating the border zone as something similar to magical realism: "Cuando las cosas simples tienen la posibilidad de expresarse por sí mismas, se expresan, porque 'todo tiene su propia alma y personalidad'" (12). The use of flashbacks in the novel accentuates the apparent magical elements of *la raya.* Fernando Cabrera comments on the use of flashbacks in Veloz Maggiolo's novels as follows: "El uso del flash back como recurso de reconstrucción de los hechos, en más de una ocasión, se toman coordenadas temporales distintas para narrar, asimismo es aprehensible el cambio de sujeto narrativo" ("Marcio Veloz Maggiolo" 54).[15] The journalist and primary narrator who selectively presents the testimonies orders them in a way that convolutes the passing of time, shifting from past to present just as easily as the border inhabitants cross from one country to the other.

While the use of certain literary devices, such as flashbacks, creates a unique time frame in *El hombre del acordeón,* these devices also serve to unwrite the physical border by weaving together disparate historical moments, in this way revealing the border's temporary, fleeting nature. The border region, and more specifically Veloz Maggiolo's fictional town La Salada, succeeds in representing a hybrid zone where Haitian and Dominican cultures blend into one. Hybridity implies the formation of something new by combining two (or more) elements, an understanding that gives way to the creation of third space. Bhabha links the two concepts intricately. His third space is "based not on the exoticism of multiculturalism or the *diversity* of cultures, but on the inscription and articulation of culture's *hybridity*. To that end we should remember that it is the 'inter'— the cutting edge of translation and negotiation, the *in between* space— that carries the burden of the meaning of culture" (Bhabha 38). Thus, hybridity engenders third space and gives way to the in-between site (third space) that by definition resists binarisms, externally imposed labels, and unitary identities. Without hybridity and hybrid zones of contact like the fictionalized La Salada, third spaces do not exist. Veloz Maggiolo's novels succeed in conceiving of Hispaniola's border region as a merging of two separate entities into one unique and innovative site, a third space that traverses differences and encourages innovation.

In *El hombre del acordeón,* La Línea, understood as the general "border region" in the novel, expands beyond a hybridized status traditionally described as two parts forming one. Instead, it is a unified, singular, anomalous zone that stands on its own, a model third space in the fictionalized community's ability to navigate across and within conflictive ideologies to form a space of negotiation and collaboration. La Línea lends itself to a complete erasure of the border. La Línea is a community that exists *on* the border but also *on top of,* or *encima de,* the border. The presence and culture of the town overcomes the physical presence of the border. Veloz Maggiolo's fiction emphasizes the connection between two cultures, a linkage key to an alternate representation of the Haitian subject. Foucault highlights a similar hegemonic dualism in his understanding of heterotopic spaces. Conceiving of heterotopic spaces as a way to conceptualize borderlands relates directly to the third principle of Foucault's definition, which can be read in relation to a border dichotomy: "The heterotopia is capable of juxtaposing in a single real place several spaces" (25). A heterotopic space represents both the smallest parcel of the world and also the totality of the world. Veloz Maggiolo's La Línea, a fictional border town, is, likewise, seemingly insignificant. La Salada, an apparently ambiguous, unimportant border town, is a small parcel of La Línea, just a speck on Hispaniola's map; yet it is also a point where cultures converge, perhaps the location, albeit a fictional one, that best represents the totality of the island. Representative of spaces where two cultures meet, La Salada and La Línea both function as their own whole(s) in *El hombre del acordeón*.

Veloz Maggiolo, then, "erases" the border, both la línea and La Línea, by enforcing its totality.[16] The prime vehicle for this erasure in *El hombre del acordeón* is music. Obeying no borders, music plays an important role in the novel: "El merengue, la música más importante de la zona, había penetrado igualmente en las galleras haitianas llamándose *meringue*" (17). Make no mistake, *merengue* and *meringue*—linguistic roots aside—mean one and the same, a music that penetrates both sides of la L/linea. While Fumagalli notes that merengue is "widely recognized as a quintessential expression of Dominican identity" in her study of *El hombre del acordeón*, she also problematizes the origins of the musical genre, noting that one theory claims the genre originated in the Dominican Republic. An alternate theory, however, is that Dominican merengue developed from Haitian *meringue,* or *mereng* (153). Regardless of merengue's origins, in la L/línea everyone appreciates the music masterfully composed by Honorio Lora. The "Papá Dios del merengue" (19) and the "merenguero favorito" (12) of Brigadier, Honorio Lora transforms the merengue into a music that knows no borders. He crafts "un ritmo afrohispano" (20) that pays tribute to two different cultures and exemplifies the "unitarian current" that runs through both countries.[17] Moreover, when Honorio Lora plays with his musical trio, the instruments they play are described as powerful tools that "definen los límites del tiempo" (19). While the accordion, the guitar (or güira/güiro), and the drum define the limits of time, they also blur notions of time as the novel's chaotic organization—ordered around Honorio Lora's music and the interpretation of his verse—convolutes the past with the present. The same beats and rhythms are heard both east and west of the border, speaking to the universality of Honorio's art.[18]

Religion, much like music, also defies the border in *El hombre del acordeón*. The narrator states openly that the inhabitants of the border, *los rayanos*,[19] "creen en ambas religiones: la de los curas católicos y la que se desarrolla del otro lado de la frontera en donde los dioses tienen otras alternativas y modos de actuar, nombres y poderes diferentes" (84). This particular sentence is significant, as neither religion is given a name. While this anonymity facilitates an approximation to both religions, the description of the second religion—"la que se desarrolla del otro lado de la frontera"—recasts both religions as antagonistic. The narrator associates himself with the first religion by distancing himself from the second despite evading connecting either religion with one side of the border over the other. By alluding to the second religion, understood by the reader as vodou, the narrator uses phrases such as *otras alternativas y modos de actuar* and *poderes diferentes* to mark the stereotypical Haitian-based religion as the outlier, the foreign, the "Other." Regardless of the narrator's supposed affinity for the Catholic religion, Afro-Caribbean culture and vodou play important roles in Veloz Maggiolo's novel, and it is through a vodou ritual known as a *desunén* that Honorio Lora makes his return as a *lwa*.

The *desunén* solidifies Honorio's presence, both physical and spiritual, on the border after his death. The Haitian *bruja* from Ouanaminthe, Polysona Françoise, is charged with performing the *desunén* with the help of her *ti sorcier*, or aide, Remigia (a former lover of Honorio's). The *desunén*, as described by Remigia, joins the three elements of the deceased—*Go bon angé, Ti bon angé,* and *Metet*—resulting in the return of the spirit in *loa* or *lwa* form, able to impact the living and seek revenge for one's death (85). The *desunén* succeeds in bestowing Honorio with "permanencia como figura del panteón rayano" (81). Notably, the *desunén* takes place on Haitian soil, confirming the attachment of *rayanos* and Haitians in Ouanaminthe to Honorio and his song: "El toque de *desunén* es fácilmente captable por los fronterizos, y atrae a los rayanos como si fuera miel llamando a las abejas" (87). In fact, the very first mention of Haiti in the novel coincides with the first mention of the *desunén*, emphasizing the location where "el hombre del acordeón"'s cadaver was brought back to the living world in "la tierra haitiana" (13). The presence of Haitian "magic" (practiced by the *bruja volandera* Polysona) and vodou is an allusion by Veloz Maggiolo to the negation of Haitian influence in the Dominican Republic; at the same time it serves as validation of the stronghold of Haitian religion in Dominican culture. He stated in an interview: "La influencia haitiana [in the RD], aunque ha sido negada, ha sido muy importante desde el punto de vista de la religiosidad popular, hasta el punto de que ... existe ya un vudú dominicano muy establecido" (Veloz Maggiolo, "Entrevista con Marcio Veloz Maggiolo"). Veloz Maggiolo overtly references an established form of Dominican vodou, also referred to as "The 21 Divisions" or "Los Misterios."[20] The *lwas* central to Dominican vodou, however, differ from those of Haitian vodou, and the Dominican tradition is a syncretic blending of various religious practices, including Catholicism, Yoruba religions, and Haitian vodou.

Related to religion is the overarching, existential question concerning the possibility of life after death. This question relates not only to the subsistence of a soul or spirit but also the physical location of the body: Where do we bury our dead? What significance might this final resting place hold? In *El hombre del acordeón* the common tomb, or *tumba común*, known by the name El Vetusto, is a magical cemetery where the blood of Haitians and Indians mixes beneath the soil. The magic inherent in this cemetery, located in La Salada, is a testament to its ability to withstand drought. According to the narrator, the *tumba común* "se alimentaba de muerte" (40). Perhaps another quality attributed to the space's ability to persevere and withstand nature's attempt to derail it is the element of racial and ethnic mixture that defines it. While the unique cemetery "había sido primero un lugar de habitación de indios precolombinos y luego un camposanto cristiano de finales del siglo XIX y comienzos del XX" (40), the character in *El hombre del acordeón* named fray Antón, La Salada's Catholic friar, adds that the bones buried in El Vetusto include those of "franceses que dieron origen a la esclavitud de donde surgieron los haitianos" (41). And not surprisingly, in the wake of the 1937 Massacre, Haitians also were put to rest in the *tumba común*. The narrator confirms the presence of Haitian remains: "Ignacia Marsán sabía que los haitianos y los indios se mezclarían en el fondo de las fosas dando como resultado tormentas y momentos duros para el pueblo" (43). Ignacia Marsán, Honorio Lora's most prominent, long-term lover, in part blames the shared tomb for the town's constant battles and conflicts. Furthermore, El Vetusto serves to root the town of La Salada in a cross-cultural, multinational history. The mass gravesite deconstructs the royal trinity with which Trujillo sought to define his countrymen; neither white nor Catholic nor Spanish reigns supreme in la L/línea. The space of la L/línea, then, is representative of the Nuyorican Tato Lavieria's "Ni de aquí ni de allá," a negation of a homogenous, singular identity. The existence of El Vetusto, while rejecting Trujillo's homogenous vision of the Dominican Republic, also questions the existence of *brujas volanderas,* who, once on the verge of extinction, also inhabit the cemetery of La Salada.[21] Rodríguez-Henríquez alludes to the anonymity of El Vetusto: "El nombre del cementerio, no registrado en los sistemas de búsqueda, apunta a la vieja existencia del lugar, con lo que se alude a la mezcla racial, y al origen híbrido que tienen las brujas en la República Dominicana, y en otras culturas" (151). El Vetusto, however, succeeds in emphasizing not only the "origen híbrido" of the Haitian and Dominican *brujas* but La Línea it its entirety.

As shown in the previous paragraphs, the representation of religion and music in the novel, as well as the organization of the novel itself, addresses the border by mimicking its hybrid character. The nature of the border as "no tan delineada" (14), however, confounds *El hombre del acordeón*'s constant allusions to the border. The more the novel describes or classifies la L/línea, the more it appears to resist or defy categorization.

Thus, by writing the border, Veloz Maggiolo *un*writes the border, speaking to the absence of a fixed division between two countries and instead highlighting the coexistence and interdependency of two cultures. Each border inhabitant is in a sense akin to *El hombre del acordeón*'s secondary character Julio Flor—"con mujer e hijos en Ouanaminthe y mujer e hijos en La Salada" (22)—as the *rayano*'s ability to belong to both spaces challenges and emphasizes the understanding of the border as a space traditionally conflictive and oppressive. De Maeseneer describes the *zona liniera* portrayed in *El hombre del acordeón* as "un ambiente de mezcla, de magia, de hibridez, de resistencia al régimen" (*Seis ensayos* 118). This description of the border zone of La Salada does not reflect a relation defined by conflict that plays out at the *frontera*, but instead one where an organic harmony arises. The borderlands assume a life of their own, exemplifying a hegemonic dualism defined by Eugenio Matibag as a borderland in which cultures do not erase borders but instead multiply them, reduplicating themselves "both on the margins of the national territory but also in the heart of each society" (ix). Scott Michaelsen and David E. Johnson, in their introduction to *Border Theory: The Limits of Cultural Politics*, discuss how borders serve to multiply cultures, commenting on the "identity relationality that makes it seem as if cultures are still to be 'crossed'" (9), as opposed to an approach to the border that considers the interplay and interdependence between both sides. It is this model, one that uplifts the connections between two communities and centers on the whole that is the merging of two cultures and societies, that *El hombre del acordeón* offers the reader.

Beyond Lyrics: Rebellion in *El hombre del acordeón*

Examining the notion of rebellion in *El hombre del acordeón* allows us to analyze the role of the Haitian subject within the novel, as the entire work can be read as a denouncement of the 1937 Massacre. All accounts of the death of Honorio Lora seem to agree that especially in his final weeks the *merenguero*'s verses "iban contra la autoridad establecida" (60). Overtly challenging the atrocious events of the massacre, in which approximately fifteen thousand Haitians and Haitians of Dominican descent were killed, Honorio's rebellion recontextualizes the historically muted genocide and gives voice to the border inhabitants. His confrontation in verse also challenges and critiques the official history and culture concerning the border communities. As Rafael Rodríguez-Henríquez writes, "La novela propone la reconciliación etnográfica en un plano cultural híbrido, donde imperan las voces marginales/marginadas, lográndose así una pluralidad de voces que a veces se presentan de un modo conflictivo" (75). The plurality of voices at play in *El hombre del acordeón* represent the novel's challenge to authority at the most basic level. Veloz Maggiolo writes the Dominican Republic without writing *out* the Haitian presence and thus foregrounds the rebellion in the novel against the 1937 Massacre and the "lesser-than" treatment of Haitians in the Dominican Republic. González-Cruz alludes more specifically to rebellion as a constant in Veloz Maggiolo's literary corpus.[22] He notes: "Sus primeras novelas . . . revelan ya el carácter de saludable irreverencia que predominará en todos o casi todos sus cuentos y en las novelas que siguen" (107). In the paragraphs to follow, I frame the rebellion in *El hombre del acordeón* by considering Honorio Lora's lyrics as the most transparent critique of the massacre and the Trujillo regime.

Honorio Lora's lyrics of "protesta" and "amargura" (35) in part render Ignacia Marsán's fateful warning to Honorio that "hay músicas que matan" (37) reality.

> A los negros lo mataron
> del río Masacre a la vera,
> y a la pobre Ma Misién,
> a la pobre, quién la viera.
> Los dientes de cara ai soi,
> sonrisa de mueite entera.
> La comadre Ma Misién
> se murió de matadera. (35)

As Ignacia relays to the narrator, Honorio's lyrics only strengthened in protest as he continued to address the massacre with his music, painting the horrific reality of the event that claimed the lives of thousands of *rayanos* and Haitians whom the *merenguero* considered his friends. Another verse shares that during the massacre even the weapon of choice—the machete—protested the killings: "que no lo maten poi Dio, son también dominicano" (42). This personified verse is particularly revealing in confirming that Honorio Lora, *dominicano,* claims the *rayanos* as his compatriots. Honorio's link to the *rayano* and Haitian population is not only expressed in these lyrics but also confirmed by his affinity for *clerén* (a distilled spirit made from low-cost cane sugar in Haiti) and his friendships with those killed in 1937: "[Honorio] había perdido grandes amigos, si se incluye al rayano Tocay, autor de alguna de las letras de sus canciones, y a su mujer Ma Misién" (53). The Ma Misién mentioned here is the same *rayana* Honorio remembers in his song lyrics that reference "la pobre" and "la comadre" Ma Misién (35). The narrator also mentions other Dominicans who loved "los seres fronterizos y rayanos," those who found themselves "dolidos por los *hermanos* muertos" (62, my emphasis), thus offering a vision of a bonded borderlands community. At the same time, it is worth noting that Honorio Lora is not the only accordionist who calls La Línea home. A female accordionist, La Postalita, unlike Honorio, supports Brigadier. The figure of La Postalita—loyal to the regime—strengthens Honorio's rebellion against the *trujillato* and solidifies his refusal to join the pro-Trujillo chorus. Instead, the *santo merenguero* uses his voice and lyricism to transform his merengue into rebellion, a move that subversively counteracts Trujillo's state-sponsored promotion of merengue. "Trujillo used merengue as direct propaganda," writes George Lipsitz (136), and beyond commissioning musicians to sing his praises, he used the musical genre as a means to exacerbate "racial and class divisions within the country" (137).[23] The hastened growth of the merengue tradition during the *trujillato* occurred largely because Trujillo censored musical production during his regime and attempted to limit options to his preferred musical taste, positioning merengue (as opposed to the popular Dominican *bachata*) as his choice for the "national music" of the Dominican Republic.[24] In *El hombre del acordeón*, music becomes a vehicle for resistance. Trujillo's claim to a nationalist, bourgeois Dominican merengue notwithstanding, both in the novel and in Dominican history anti-Trujillo voices surface through this musical genre. Moreover, Honorio Lora's cross-border merengue succeeds in emphasizing, rather than negating, the African influence of the genre.[25]

It is clear in the novel that denouncing the massacre is one and the same with denouncing the Brigadier (Trujillo) regime, and Honorio's death also points to the conflation between these two reprobations in the novel. One could not challenge the general's actions without challenging the man himself. It is in large part this acknowledgment that validates the "sospecha de que Honorio había muerto por órdenes del General" (119). Honorio Lora's disapproval of the massacre, evidenced by the change in his merengue verses in the wake of the event, expands beyond lyrical protest. The magical power of his instrument—metaphorically alluded to numerous times in the novel as a weapon or *fúsil*[26]—and the *desunén* speak more broadly to Honorio's expostulation of the regime. As the accordion was a gift from Brigadier to his preferred *merenguero*, the instrument's synonymy with weaponry is ironic. The "weapon" gifted to him by Brigadier transforms into the musician's own death wish. The accordion opposes the regime even when the aftermath of the 1937 Massacre dismantles previous spaces of resistance. As Fumagalli asserts: "The massacre here seems to have therefore succeeded in sealing the frontier, forcing people to embrace fixed nationalities and to discard their affiliation to the complex and variegated world of the *raya*. The novel, however, also shows that there was still space for resistance, as the 'illegal' presence of those *rayanos* who were forced to identify themselves with, and move to, Haiti testifies; yet, as one of them puts it, their presence on Dominican territory was no longer a matter for everyday practice but cause for 'anxiety and fear'" (158). Honorio Lora and his accordion, then, establish a new space for resistance vis-à-vis a musical genre that reverberates on both sides of the border. While the vision of La Línea offered by the narrator before 1937 is one in which goods and resources come and go freely from the Dominican Republic to Haiti and vice versa, the fear instilled in the border inhabitants—namely, the *rayano* and Haitian populations—after the massacre temporarily halts this flow of resources. This cannot, however, put an end to Honorio's lyrical resistance to the regime, which intensifies after the massacre. This musical contestation permits Honorio's *desunén* on the Haitian side of La Línea in Ouanaminthe; the fact that he died for criticizing *el corte* allows him to be treated as a follower of vodou, practiced by the Haitian Polysona Françoise and others (85). His music, then, gained the *merenguero* an acceptance, or welcome, that crossed borders. His critique of the ethnic genocide of Haitians and Dominicans of Haitian descent, which coalesced in his popular merengues, drifted across the border and positioned Honorio as a voice for those affected by the massacre on either side of the *raya*.

Aside from containing specific examples of Honorio's lyrics acting in protest of the 1937 Massacre and General Brigadier's ethnic cleansing, *El hombre del acordeón* can be read as a general rebellion against the identification of Haitians as the Other in the Dominican Republic. While the work does not fit the categorization of a historical novel and the characters and the town of La Salada are fictional, Veloz Maggiolo's recreation of La Línea reveals the hybridity of the borderlands. Novelizing the protest of Honorio Lora and his will to stand "contra la autoridad establecida" (61) results in an alternate, fictional version of historical events. *El hombre del acordeón* represents a type of narrative that Trouillot describes as going "back and forth over the line between fiction and history" (*Silencing the Past* 8). Veloz Maggiolo's novel exemplifies the susceptibility of history to invention, and the entire text toys with the notions of credibility and veracity. Vetemit Alzaga, the father of the narrator and one of his many informants, identifies as a "cuentero de pura fibra" (13).

Vetemit refers to Honorio Lora's death and rebirth(s) as "parte de las historias verdaderas que ahora se quieren negar" (12). The novel's insistence on a negation of the truth, or "history" as understood by some, connects to Trouillot's recognition of "the need to impose a test of credibility on certain events and narratives because it matters *to them* whether these events are true or false, whether these stories are fact or fiction" (11). If one approaches Trouillot's warning in regard to the credibility of a given narrative (including his notion of a "collective past") within the context of *El hombre del acordeón,* a new understanding of La Salada or La Línea as a hybrid space emerges. Approaching Veloz Maggiolo's fictional border community as third space blurs the differences between *fronterizos* and *rayanos;* Dominicans, Haitians, and Dominicans of Haitian descent coexist in a space defined by negotiation and contact, where Honorio's music echoes without limits.

(The Impossibility of) "una Historia Simple"

Related to the underlying theme of credibility and the possibility of a "truthful" or "accurate" record of past events in *El hombre del acordeón* is the (in)existence of "una historia simple" (83). The narrator utilizes this exact phrasing when attempting to describe the questionable burial of Honorio Lora: "Honorio Lora fue traído, velado en la iglesia de fray Antón y enterrado con su instrumento. *Una historia simple*" (my emphasis). Directly following the narrator's use of this phrase to describe Honorio's afterlife as "simple" and uncomplicated is an allusion to the contradictory versions, or "versiones contradictorias" (83), of the *merenguero*'s burial. Thus, this preemptive allusion to "una historia simple" appears immediately undercut. The narrator's self-identification as an untrustworthy inventor adds to the multiple layers of "truth" in the narration of Honorio's (after)life. Moreover, the discussion surrounding identity that permeates the entire novel, exemplified by the Hispanicizing of Haitian last names, foils any understanding of the fictional La Línea's history as "simple."

Not only does the narrator categorize others, such as his father, Vetemit Alzaga, as inventors and falsifiers of truth but he recognizes his own affinity for invention. Although he praises his good memory even into his old age, he admits that it wavers, "parpadeando a veces" (14). His confession of an imperfect memory is followed by his self-classification as "un cuentero." This identification is particularly significant, while also ambiguous, as *cuentero* in Spanish refers to both a storyteller and a gossiper or even liar. Although he classifies himself as *cuentero,* the narrator seems to chart a distinction between himself as "storyteller" (if one chooses to interpret *cuentero* in this way) and Vetemit Alzaga, who, as mentioned previously, "era cuentero de *pura fibra*" (my emphasis). The description of Vetemit as *cuentero* is repeated numerous times in the novel, almost always with a negative, uneasy connotation, making the reader wary of Vetemit's border accounts.[27] As the narrator reiterates his father's description of Honorio in his youth he adds words of warning: "No vayan a creerlo todo de un cuentero" (24). The narrator himself, on the other hand, leads the reader to believe that he only invents when necessary, for example, when ordered by Brigadier to "recuperar la historia de los pueblos fronterizos" (14). Regardless of the reason behind the narrator's "inventions," the *cuentero* classification can also be read as a strategy to mitigate Brigadier's (Trujillo's) vengeance, similar to Freddy Prestol Castillo's decision to label *El Masacre se pasa a pie* as fiction and not a testimony based on true events. Another noteworthy emphasis on the relation between memory and the passage of time is the narrator's employment of the term *cuentero:* "De modo que, cuentero o no, oficio en decadencia, mi parecer es que lo que aquí narro *alcance* veracidad, porque, si tengo culpas, debo señalar que 'culpas son del tiempo y no de quien narra'" (25, my emphasis). Confirming the irony of a "truth within reach" and the narrator's self-doubt concerning his storytelling tendencies—"cuentero o no"—in this sentence the first-person narrator apologizes preemptively for any liberties taken, placing the blame on the lapse of memory associated with age and temporal distance. Regardless of the verdict regarding the narrator's identification as *cuentero,* of interest here is the fact that only Dominicans are scrutinized for their tendency to lie or bend the truth. The narrator clearly portrays Vetemit as untrustworthy both as father figure and as community member. In a sense, from an ethnic and racial standpoint the tables are turned. At no point in the novel are Haitians or *rayanos* cast as *cuenteros,* or liars, a stereotype of Haitians in the Dominican Republic.[28] *El hombre del acordeón* presents Haitians and *rayanos,* populations gravely affected by the 1937 Massacre, as innocent victims forced to flee the Dominican Republic for Haiti, a country many had never considered home. A closer look at the characterization of Dominicans as opposed to Haitians and *rayanos* in the novel allows for a consideration of the ways *El hombre del acordeón* addresses identity.

"La gente había encontrado eso que ahora llaman 'la identidad,' una cosa que se puede inventar y dar personalidad a quien no la tiene" (92). This line from the novel frames the representation of identity, marking it as flexible and influenced by those in dominant societal positions. In *El hombre del acordeón* Brigadier controls Dominican identity and erases—forcing the narrator in his role as "historiador official" to also erase—*negro* or *negra* as a possible racial classification for Dominicans. Following Brigadier's orders, the narrator asserts: "En el documento de identidad personal y los carnés del Partido aparecía 'indio' en vez de negro, o bien 'indio oscuro,' o 'indio lavado,' usándose el término 'trigueño,' o sea del color del trigo, para mulatos claros y el de 'moreno' para los negros de verdad" (93). Kimberly Eison Simmons, in *Reconstructing Racial Identity and the African Past in the Dominican Republic,* also references these state-sanctioned identities when she confirms that the term *indio* was institutionalized by Trujillo as a "non-black, mixed, race/color category" (29) intended to differentiate Dominicans from Haitians, who were identified on the census, or *cédula,* as "black." The novel itself is proof that such imposed identities—negating the black elements in Dominican society—do not have a stronghold in la L/línea. Honorio himself, at the center of the novel, is the champion of hybrid identity. His third and final burial converts him into a being that is half Christian and half vodou. Although these descriptors refer to religion, as opposed to race or ethnicity, the notion of blending is key. More specifically, the commingling of Haitians and Dominicans is best exemplified in *El hombre del acordeón* by the last names, or *apellidos,* of residents of La Salada and surrounding border towns. To no surprise, Vetemit is charged by his son, the narrator, with playing a leading role in the name shifting that served to falsify the origins of La Salada residents. Encouraged by Brigadier, Vetemit changed Haitian last names of La Línea residents to Spanish ones. The narrator shares that Brigadier lauded a certain merengue in large part because Vetemit had changed the last name of a family of fishermen from Manzanillo, a border town in the Monte Cristi province, referenced in a national legend (and later in the merengue lyrics), to the Spanish *apellido* Mártires (72). Outwardly a supporter of Brigadier and his regime, chronicling the border region to his liking by writing out the black presence, Vetemit also makes reference to the black *Dominicans* who died during the massacre. Vetemit shares that these victims shouted out to those yielding machetes, "We, too, are Dominican" (42, my translation). The name changing—or confounding of the national roots of a given last name—extends to Brigadier himself, as he attempted to persuade others that "el apellido ancestral de su abuela era español, puesto que Chevalier en francés significa 'caballero' en lengua de Castilla" (57). Honorio, as protestor of the regime, criticizes the purposeful name changes in song: "Juanita la loca / cambio de apellido, / pero nunca pudo / cambiar de vestido" (73).

To return to the subtle mockery in the novel of Honorio's (life and) death—or the history of la l/Línea at large—as "simple," Jean Price-Mars's use of the term *double attitude* to describe the relationship between Dominicans and Haitians is relevant. The term addresses how Dominicans contradicted and convoluted the simplistic binary (Dominicans as *non-Haitian*) and created a complex situation in which Dominicans opposed other Dominicans and Haitians opposed other Haitians. In this way, a "parallelism of this double attitude" resulted, as "those of one country who held a stake in dealings between the two nations articulated and acted upon beliefs and convictions that ran counter to those of others of the same country" (Matibag 11). The relationship between Dominicans, Haitians, and the "in-betweens" (or *rayanos*) in the border region further complicates the existence of a "double attitude." While any multilayered relationship is difficult to conceptualize, in La Salada, for example, the crossings (of which Honorio's friend Tocay, with families on both sides of the border, is a good example), cover-ups, and name changes only further confound the relationship.

Veloz Maggiolo affirms that for the purpose of his essay "Tipología del tema haitiano" he is primarily interested in analyzing narratives that posit "como tema *central* el hombre de Haití" (13). In *El hombre del acordeón*, however, at the center of the narrative is not only the Haitian subject but a Dominican man and *fronterizo* whose life is tied directly to Haiti and the borderlands, or La Línea. Veloz Maggiolo's requirements for what constitutes "Haitian narrative" aside, the 2003 novel can indeed be categorized by the parameters identified by the author himself in his "Tipología del tema haitiano." The Haitian subject in *El hombre del acordeón*, then, can be read as both the *haitiano compadecido* and *el haitiano integrado*. As the essay was written decades after the novel was published, no classification of the work is included.[29]

In reference to *El hombre del acordeón*, the "Tipología del tema haitiano" can be read as a precursor to the novel's denouncement of the 1937 Massacre and the author's will to address the genocide in the essay. Veloz Maggiolo points to a historical pattern of neglecting the event: "La matanza de haitianos del 1937 no fue difundida ni por la prensa dominicana ni por medios de comunicación relacionados con el país" (27). *El hombre del acordeón* represents the author's attempt to avenge the silencing of this genocide, and the novel both searches for and convolutes "distintas verdades" (De Maeseneer, *Encuentro* 113) in relation not only to Honorio's mysterious death but also to a one-sided Dominican history. While the novel exposes "la mentira de la historia" (114), it also speaks to the border crossing of more than human bodies. Honorio Lora's music is a significant social motivator that crosses over the border, consecrating a mystical significance of the *santo merenguero*'s instrument: "El acordeón es una herramienta narrativa que servirá para abordar el asunto histórico relacionado con Trujillo, por lo inclusivo se narra la historia del instrumento en el país, también se relatan, insistentemente, las circunstancias que atañen el robo y rescate del mismo, hasta el final de la obra, donde el instrumento, al adquirir una dimensión mágica, se depura de su valor práctico para sí alcanzar una significación más simbólica" (Rodríguez-Henríquez 126). This symbolic significance relates to the hyperhybrid characteristic of la L/línea, envisioning Hispaniola and its *rayano* and *fronterizo* populations as part of a whole, avoiding the more traditional focus on two halves or "unequal" parts.

La vida no tiene nombre: A Novel about Two Occupations

La vida no tiene nombre, released in 1965, shortly after Trujillo's assassination, was Veloz Maggiolo's first publication linked to the Latin American literary boom of the sixties.[30] *La vida no tiene nombre,* however, is worthy of recognition not only for its inclusion of numerous hallmarks of Boom novels, such as a nonlinear organization and multiple narrative perspectives, but also as a novel with a marked interest in the Haitian subject.[31] A young Dominican Haitian man is *La vida no tiene nombre*'s first-person narrator and protagonist. Both the novel's classification as Veloz Maggiolo's first text identifiable as Boom narrative[32] and its notable focus on the Haitian subject come as no surprise given that portrayals of *lo haitiano* in the Dominican Republic are a constant in Veloz Maggiolo's literary corpus. Another constant in Veloz Maggiolo's literature is an interest, even obsession, with history. In the case of *La vida no tiene nombre,* the 1916 US Marine occupation in the Dominican Republic serves as the work's historical backdrop, and the novel's publication in 1965 came just a few short months before a second invasion by the US Marines. The work's subtitle, then, *Novela de la Ocupación,* has dual meaning, as it refers to not one but two occupations. This subtitle, as I show in the paragraphs to follow and as reflected in my own subhead, would make more sense as *Novela de ocupaciones*.

Veloz Maggiolo sets *La vida no tiene nombre* in 1916, during the beginning of the US Marine occupation that lasted until 1924.[33] With the official proclamation by the US military government that the Dominican Republic was "in a state of military occupation" by the forces under the command of Captain Henry S. Knapp, Dominican sovereignty collapsed (Moya Pons, *Dominican Republic* 320). Dominican hostility and resistance toward the occupation plagued the United States' eight-year presence in the country. Pressure from Dominican rebels, referred to in *La vida no tiene nombre* as "revoluciones montoneras" (88), required unplanned monetary investment in the invasion and forced La Guardia Nacional (the National Guard) to respond. The novel defines the National Guard as "una milicia que los americanos han inventado, con la cual persiguen a los dominicanos que andan alzados por los campos" (6). The *guerrilla* rebellion against the United States' armed intervention is the primary focus of Veloz Maggiolo's brief historical novel.[34] This historical positioning of the novel and the Haitian Dominican protagonist who identifies as a revolutionary rebelling against the US Marine presence root the novel in a complicated, transnational political history and align the novel with Seymour Menton's definition of *novela histórica*.

Menton defines the literary subgenre as follows: "Hay que reservar la categoría de novela histórica para aquellas novelas cuya acción se ubica total o por lo menos predominantemente en el pasado, es decir, un pasado no experimentado directamente por su autor" (32). *La vida no tiene nombre* portrays, from a fictional perspective, the plight of a Dominican Haitian rebel—a "Dominican" patriot who falls victim to racial discrimination and social injusticias—and in doing so also emphasizes the fundamental role memory plays in Veloz Maggiolo's narrative. Rodríguez-Henríquez, in *Fuentes de la imaginación histórica,* one of the first critical studies dedicated solely to the literary production of Veloz Maggiolo, refers to the intersections of fiction and history in Veloz Maggiolo's work as "memoria imaginativa." This "imagined memory" helps to fill historical voids—especially when the allusion to "imagined memory" appears related to experiences of marginalized subjects like the Haitian Dominican Ramón—and also answers, at least partially, to magical elements in *La vida no tiene nombre* classified as "beyond this world." While Veloz Maggiolo's later novels, including *El hombre del acordeón,* contain elements of what can be considered magical realism, *La vida no tiene nombre,* in its portrayal of the absurd in everyday life, shares characteristics with Carpentier's "marvelous realism." González-Cruz asserts that *La vida no tiene nombre* is "quizá la [novela] que mejor trata el tema socio-político dentro del marco del absurdo. Porque aquí Veloz Maggiolo no tiene que valerse de la fantasía para su ficción novelesca: el absurdo lo constituye la existencia de cada día en la República Dominicana. La trama ocurre alrededor de 1912: colonialismo americano, ausencia de libertad, intrigas políticas, etc." (113). The novel's title emphasizes this absurdity, speaking to the utter waywardness of life and suggesting that fiction does not need to be invented given the absurdity and uncanniness of life itself. The protagonist and narrator of *La vida no tiene nombre,* Ramón, is a perfect example of a fictional character trapped in an absurd reality. Ramón is unable to detach himself from a historical period of national chaos and confusion; he is a victim of his race and class. Son of a Haitian servant raped by her "white" Dominican employer, Ramón voluntarily enlists in the revolutionary troops under the command of the Dominican general Matías Remigio. Ramón's Dominican father and half brother, however, align themselves with the lucrative outside forces, supporting the invasion and, according to Ramón, betraying the Dominican nation. Sharing his thoughts from a jail cell as he awaits execution—a fact revealed in the first few pages of the novel: "estoy preso por los delitos" (7)—Ramón relays and details his attempted evasion of the National Guard and eventual capture. Ramón unknowingly succumbs to his brother's plot to murder their father, a plot that leaves the (Dominican) brother as sole inheritor of the father's fortune. While the narration describes Ramón, nicknamed "El Cuerno,"[35] and his life during the rebel fight and addresses his decision to join the revolutionary cause, it also reveals a distinctive historical, social, economic, and political background.

The moment of publication of *La vida no tiene nombre* reflects the second invasion of the US Marines. Nineteen sixty-five was the year when Juan Bosch's socialist politics, and his Partido Revolucionario Dominicano (PRD), failed to unite the country and oppress opposing external forces. Bosch's brief presidency, from February 27 to September 25, 1963, was made possible by Trujillo's assassination, and many viewed this shift in political tides as the harbinger of a hopeful future for the country. In light of several constitutional changes instated by Bosch, largely related to limits on landownership and improved workers' rights, he was forced out of office by former Trujillo military officers and fled to exile in Puerto Rico. In response to the political pandemonium that ensued following Bosch's forced exile, on April 28, 1965, US military troops landed again on Dominican soil, this time to offer support to the neo-Trujilloist (anti-Bosch) political forces. This second occupation, in which a physical US presence did not last through the end of the year, heavily influenced the negotiations between the two Dominican governments during the time, the *gobierno constitucionalista* and the *gobierno de reconstrucción nacional* (the two opposing forces in the short-lived civil war). After a mere four months the civil war ended, and in August of the same year the

Dominican Republic formed a new government. The US occupational troops remained on the island until free elections were held and a new constitutional government came to power. Unsurprisingly, given his support from the Trujilloist army officers, Joaquín Balaguer and his Partido Reformista prevailed, forcing Bosch back into exile, this time in Spain.[36] *La vida no tiene nombre,* published for the first time in February 1965, preceded the start of this second military intervention by only two months—a time offering a renewed sense of political freedom and societal optimism but also a time of increasingly conflictive politics.[37]

The novel's publication shortly before the second US invasion is noteworthy, but so is the aforementioned newly liberated literary climate in the sixties in the Dominican Republic, following Trujillo's assassination in 1961. The Dominican critic Soledad Álvarez, in her article "*La vida no tiene nombre,*" describes the changes in the intellectual sphere in the country after 1961: "El tornado político removió todos los cimientos de la vida y la sociedad dominicana. Y en la euforia no sólo fueron derribados los símbolos visibles de la era. Con la retórica y el arsenal ideológico que imponían los nuevos tiempos, los intelectuales y escritores jóvenes se plantearon, un tanto a ciegas, la tarea desmesurada para sus fuerzas de remover los cimientos de la cultura elitista, autoritaria y excluyente sobre la cual se había montado el sistema de significación trujillista" (96). Veloz Maggiolo's literary publications during the decade immediately following Trujillo's assassination include *Judas* and *El buen ladrón* (1960; Judas, The good thief);[38] *La vida no tiene nombre; Nosotros los suicidas* (1965; We the suicidals); and *Los ángeles de hueso* (1967; The angels of bone). The end of the Trujillo regime elicited a response from the intellectual community, and Veloz Maggiolo's novels condemn the Trujillo Era. Many of the young intellectuals who published alongside Veloz Maggiolo in this crucial historical moment belonged to the Generation of 48—or *los del 48*—and attended the *tertulia* La Bombonera (Álvarez, "*La vida no tiene nombre*" 95–96). The critic Fiallo Billini describes the passionate response and mobilization of the Dominican society after 1961 as follows: "decapitada la tiranía, tiene lugar en la República Dominicana una crisis de hegemonía . . . que causa inmediatamente la movilización de la sociedad civil."

It is arguable that all four of Veloz Maggiolo's novels published in the 1960s can be classified as "Trujillo narrative," and this historical thematic, including direct narrative links to Trujillo (in *La vida no tiene nombre,* for example, Trujillo appears as a trainee of the US Marines), is not unique for this time frame. The novel's inclusion of a Dominican Haitian narrator and protagonist, however, veers from the norm. Other

Dominican novels published around 1965 include, but are not limited to, the following: Rafael Meyreles Soler's *Así mataron a Trujillo* (1965; How they killed Trujillo), Arturo Espaillat's *Trujillo: Anatomía de un dictador* (1967; Trujillo: anatomy of a dictator), and Eduardo Matos Díaz's *Quiénes y por qué eliminaron a Trujillo* (1975; Who killed Trujillo and why). These novels' titles not only reflect an interest in a narrative depiction of or a contestation to the Trujillo regime; they also demonstrate an overall increase in publications in the immediate wake of the *trujillato*. Gallego Cuiñas recognizes both trends during this specific time frame: "El número de novelas se incrementa y adquiere un mayor protagonismo el trujillato" (135).[39] While *La vida no tiene nombre* merits classification as Trujillo narrative for its interest in the figure of Trujillo, albeit a characterization of the dictator prior to his 1930 rise to presidency, Trujillo is not the principal focus. More than a Trujillo narrative, Veloz Maggiolo's 1965 novel is perhaps a "(Dominican)-Haitian narrative," detailing the struggle of a Dominican of Haitian descent during the 1916–24 occupation. In the following pages I consider (1) the ways in which *La vida no tiene nombre* (un)writes the border by (dis)placing the Haitian subject from the border itself; (2) the theme of rebellion in the text; and (3) how the selection of Ramón as protagonist-narrator complicates Dominican identity.

On and Off the Border: El Seibo

In contrast to *El hombre del acordeón* and *El Masacre se pasa a pie*, analyzed in chapter 1, *La vida no tiene nombre* does not embed the Haitian subject within the physical space of the border. While *La vida no tiene nombre* is *not* set on La Línea, the cultural, racial, and ethnic signifiers that traditionally define *la frontera* and the border inhabitants follow the protagonist into the eastern region of the Dominican Republic. The Dominican Haitian Ramón Vieth's protagonism in *La vida no tiene nombre* recontextualizes and challenges where a *nepantler@* can reside within Hispaniola. Anzaldúa's *nepantler@s* live "in the liminal zone," and they are thrust into a "constant state of displacement, an uncomfortable, even alarming feeling" ("(Un)natural Bridges" 243). While the off-border spaces are not traditionally characterized as ideological "liminal zones," this uncomfortable or alarming feeling that Anzaldúa describes exists for Ramón too. The setting of *La vida no tiene nombre* is rural, and the first sentence of the novel grounds the text in the importance of land and the sugar industry: "Las tierras del este son pródigas en caña de azúcar y yerba para el ganado" (5). This rural setting exhibits prominent traits of the naturalist movement, and the comparative phrases abound; for example, the author describes Ramón's father's face as "arrugado y amarillo como panal de abejas," and about the clouds in the afternoon he writes, "Las nubes ruedan por el aire como pelotas de lodo" (13).[40]

Veloz Maggiolo's purposeful setting of the novel in the province of El Seibo, in the easternmost region of the Dominican Republic,[41] reflects not only his desire to frame the narrative around a typical Dominican landowner and his offspring but also his interest in expanding the space Haitians traditionally inhabit in Dominican literature. The second sentence of the novel refocuses the primary interest of the narrative, moving from the land itself to the hands that work the land: "Son tierras donde los hombres no tenemos ni siquiera precio; donde los hombres trabajamos como animales, de sol a sol, por unos cuantos centavos americanos" (5). This sentence speaks to the absurdity of life itself and to the inconsequential status of minorities and nonelites in Dominican society at the turn of the twentieth century. Further, this off-border setting allows a more pointed, nuanced depiction of the Haitian subject. This alternate space, as García Canclini suggests, warrants a "move from interpreting the confrontation between *identities* to examining the *cultural* processes that either connect or alienate" historically disparate groups (*Hybrid Cultures* xli, my emphasis). What, then, connects the people of Hispaniola? Does an off-border setting make possible a space where notions of citizenship or identity are more malleable? What does it mean to be culturally or socially marked as Haitian (or Haitian Dominican) in a rural and off-border site? Ramón, while recognizing his mother's Haitianness, identifies as a proud Dominican: "Yo llevaba en mi alma el deseo profundo de demostrarle a los Vieth (así se apellidaban mi padre a sus hijos) que era más dominicano que ellos, que sentía mucho más que ellos amor por esta tierra que tanta traición ha engendrado en los últimos años; por eso, un buen día me enrolé en las tropas alzadas del general Matías Remigio" (26). Not only does Ramón boast of his own Dominicanness but he takes it a step further by claiming to be *more* Dominican than his half siblings, children of a woman "más blanca que Simián," Ramón's Haitian mother (19). Written more than a half decade before TC/0168/13, the novel has many connections with the Dominican Tribunal Court ruling. In the wake of *la sentencia,* Dominicans of Haitian descent in the Dominican Republic are also making transparent their "amor por esta tierra [dominicana]" by fighting for their citizenship rights. As it is for Ramón, it is the country in which they were born, whose language they speak, and whose cultures and customs they know.

Ramón, unlike most *cuerno*, or bastard, children, was given the last name of his father: "Parece que un día papá, en una de esas borracheras indecentes, decidió, para mortificar a sus hijos blancos, darme su apellido, un apellido que debería llevar legalmente, pero que no utilizo más que en los casos necesarios" (19). While this last name, Vieth, provides Ramón flexibility in certain social situations—the protagonist using it in "casos necesarios"—it is a notably non-Dominican name. Ramón states his father's origin: "Sin embargo mi padre no era dominicano, era de un país muy lejano que se llama Holanda, pero tenía muchos años en Santo Domingo" (25–26). Like Ramón's mother, Simián, his father is *not* a native of the Dominican Republic, but he has lived and worked in the country for years. Simián, on the other hand, is a recent Haitian migrant to the Dominican Republic. Veloz Maggiolo's use of *Vieth* instead of a more established Dominican surname, Spanish in origin, speaks to the transnational, international scope of the El Seibo province and the Dominican Republic at large; in this way he creates a beyond-borders community not only reaching to Haiti but spanning international borders.[42] Given her geographical positioning in the eastern region of the Dominican Republic, Simián,[43] already cast as an outsider because she is "non-Dominican," becomes even more of an outcast. Ramón clarifies his mother's origins: "Mi mamá, que tal vez ya ha muerto, provenía de lejos, casi del extremo oeste de la isla, desde una lejana aldea situada en algún rincón de Haití" (19). Ramón's unfamiliarity with Haiti is apparent here. He does not know where his mother is from, only that her hometown is on the far western side of the island. This allusion to the "far western side" suggests that Simián traveled the island of Hispaniola from one extreme to the other, from the furthest western point to the eastern limit, "hasta llegar a los lados de El Seibo, débil y violada varias veces por los campesinos de la parte sur" (19).

La vida no tiene nombre also reflects anti-Haitian jargon as it portrays the racism Ramón faces living in the interior of the Dominican Republic. Ramón, despite his last name, is unable to escape the characterization as the "Otro-vecino." When his father calls him a "maldito haitiano," however, the harsh words do not affect him: "Decía que yo era haitiano como si eso fuera un insulto, a mí siempre que me lo dijo me daba por pensar que si él consideraba a mi mamá un animal por el hecho de ser haitiana, él, papá, debía ser un animal peor y hasta más insignificante que mamá puesto que se ayuntó con ella cuantas veces le dio la gana, y seguramente que al hacerlo no sintió ni el asco ni la conmiseración que a veces aparentaba para los negros" (22).

Not only does Ramón refuse to consider his Haitianness an embarrassment or accept the racial and ethnic tag as an insult but he turns the primitivist-based insult on his father. Ramón describes his father, Señor Vieth, as "un animal peor y hasta más insignificante que mamá" (22). The father, and not his Haitian son, is the backward, wild savage, unable to control his sexuality or his temper. The novel's portrayal of Señor Vieth as a *mujeriego,* incapable of controlling his sexual desires, contributes to the gendered discourse present in *La vida no tiene nombre,* a rhetoric palpable in other works of Veloz Maggiolo's.[44] The "gender matrix" (Horn 67) in this novel, however, challenges conservative, nationalist Dominican thought by applying this sexual profiling not to the Haitian protagonist but instead to his (naturalized) Dominican father. The novel also ridicules the *hacendado* "father figure" for his wavering treatment of Haitians; although Señor Vieth sexually harasses Simián, Ramón confirms that his father sometimes felt or demonstrated commiseration toward the predicament of Haitians (22). Ramón is willing to criticize his deceased Dominican father from the ironic safety of his jail cell, admitting that when his father died he no longer felt imprisoned by his unwavering power, instead professing, "Sentí una alegría" (77).

Padres-Villanos: Ramón's Two-Part Rebellion

Unsurprisingly, Trujillo narratives traditionally cast *el Generalísimo* himself as the novel's villain. While *La vida no tiene nombre* can be categorized as Trujillo narrative for its overarching interest in the figure and his prominent role as a promising, young, US-trained Dominican during the first occupation, the novel places Trujillo as a "background villain."[45] Or rather, the novel presents Trujillo as a piece or fragment of the foreign military force and, more specifically, the US-trained Guardia Nacional. Ramón introduces the United States and the US Marine forces in the first pages of the novel as the obvious enemy, describing the *gringo* troops as "de un país que se llama 'Los Estados Unidos.' Un país que a pesar de su nombre no quiere unirse a nosotros y ayudarnos, sino darnos mal trato y mala vida" (7). Ramón's enlistment alongside the Dominican rebel forces solidifies his rebellion against the Guardia Nacional and the US Marine occupation. This rebellion—which also includes a representation of the national father figure and future "padre de la nación"—and Ramón's unwillingness to succumb to outside forces are coupled with his rebellion against his own father. The narrator becomes filled with hate upon simply thinking of his father (17),[46] in large part because he is unable to forget the countless times his father hit and sexually abused his mother, Simián.

La vida no tiene nombre casts Trujillo as the less obvious father figure (compared with Señor Vieth); the novel chronicles his role in the nation prior to his rise to the presidency. Ramón comes into direct contact with the young Trujillo as a *gavillero* awaiting execution. Notably, not only is Ramón proud of his inclusion as a member of the rebel forces but he recognizes the significance of his patriotic contribution—as a Haitian—to the country's fight: "El hijo de la haitiana luchó por la causa de los patriotas dominicanos" (27). The young Trujillo, then, is the individual who delivers Ramón to the Americans for his execution, leading him to a room full of "oficiales gringos" (81). While Trujillo's physical presence in the novel is fleeting, his violent disposition is highlighted; Ramón remembers that "me levantaron con violencia" (81), emphasizing a disposition that later defined the dictator. Gallego Cuiñas comments on the presentation of the *trujillista* military in Veloz Maggiolo's work, noting its inclusion in the author's later work, *De abril en adelante* as "sumo exponente de la crueldad y la bestialidad" of the US invasion (156). This same cruelty permeates the depiction of the US Marine–trained Guardia Nacional in *La vida no tiene nombre*. Ramón goes as far as to describe the troops as "los gringos del infierno" and classifies Trujillo and others who joined forces with the outsiders as "dominicanos que han vendido su alma" (83). In this way, *La vida no tiene nombre* construes as polar opposites the Dominicans who "sell their souls" to the US Marines and "sell out" their native country and the rebel forces, including Haitian Dominicans such as Ramón, who fight for national interests and dethrone official (exterior) political institutions.

While Ramón makes clear that he is proud of his role in the *revoluciones montoneras,* he also expresses his disenchantment with the rebellion, in this way speaking to the failure of the *proyecto nacional,* or national project, a theme common to both Dominican and Latin American narratives that also serves as evidence of Veloz Maggiolo's skepticism of the social and cultural optimism that followed Trujillo's death. Ramón outlines the plight of the rebels and questions the value of fighting for Dominican compatriots who "le negamos el agua para la sed y el candil para lo oscuro." At the end of a nearly page-long rant delivered to his fellow black *gavillero,* Juan, Ramón concludes: "¿Cómo crees que podemos pelear así? Hacerlo es seguir forzándolos revólver en mano y eso no es liberarlos, a nadie se libera por la brava, quien no tenga conciencia de que tiene que ser libre que se hunda, que se lo lleve el diablo" (53–54).[47]

Ramón's disenchantment with the rebel forces is largely based on the fact that violence, as opposed to goals such as justice and liberation for the Dominican people, becomes the heart of the rebellion. Ramon's critique of the rebellion can be compared to the ending of Mariano Azuela's seminal novel about the Mexican Revolution, *Los de abajo* (1915), which highlights the irrationality and senselessness of war when it lacks an ideological thrust. Ramón's disillusionment with the *gavilleros* further problematizes his construction of the two *padres-villanos,* but it also points back to the absurdity of life, referencing the novel's title. The narrator-protagonist is a metaphorical and literal "prisoner" of the asininity and irrationality that defines life on all levels and for all individuals, Haitian or Dominican.

The absurdity of life reflected in the title *La vida no tiene nombre* also speaks to the complexity and nonconformity of the narrative itself, typical of literature pertaining to or in the wake of the Latin American Boom. The novel's portrayal of two villains—the eventual *padre de la nación,* Trujillo, and Ramón's own father—accompanied by a portrayal of the disillusioned rebels fighting against the Guardia Nacional signals the various narrative levels of *La vida no tiene nombre.* Much like *El hombre del acordeón,* Veloz Maggiolo's occupation-centered novel transgresses any classification of "una historia simple." The placement of the testimony in the hands of the Haitian Dominican protagonist, Ramón, makes room for an alternate representation of the Haitian subject in Dominican literature that distorts the vision of the country as white, Spanish, and Catholic and places race in the context of an important historical moment in the Dominican Republic. The novel's keen interest in and development of the role of the Haitian or Haitian Dominican *off* the border serves to dissipate both the metaphorical and the literal, tangible *raya*. This emphasis also expands the space(s) inhabited by Haitians in the Dominican Republic and allows Ramón's voice to emerge as a clear testament to the discrimination against Haitians in the Dominican interior.

La vida no tiene nombre at times compares the racism Haitians face in the eastern region of the Dominican Republic to the racism encountered by poor, black Dominicans in the country. Ramón writes of those on the *hacienda* who were treated better than his mother, Simián, for no reason other than the color of their skin: "En la hacienda había otras negras que eran mejor tratadas que Simián. Esas no venían de Haití, eran dominicanas y mi padre no las odiaba tanto" (25). This statement highlights a historically rooted and culturally ingrained animosity that Dominicans harbor toward their Haitian neighbors, understood as a consequence of earlier French and

Spanish colonial policies and the Haitian Occupation. It is clear, too, that Ramón is cognizant of this history, at times conflicted, between the two countries of Hispaniola, as he references the Haitian Occupation (1822–44) as a possible motive for Dominicans' disapproval of Haitians when talking about Simián, "descendiente de unos que cierta vez invadieron a Santo Domingo: los haitianos" (25). While Ramón divulges that Haitians are treated more poorly than black Dominicans or even black immigrants from other neighboring Caribbean nations, frequently referred to as *cocolos,* Ramón demonstrates that his *haitianidad*—a source of pride for the narrator-protagonist—does not suppress his *dominicanidad*. Ramón endeavors to show that he is "más dominicano" (26) than his Dominican half siblings by joining ranks with the rebel forces. Ramón's reference to the first and longest Haitian occupation of the Dominican Republic, stating that his mother is a descendant of those who invaded Santo Domingo (thus recognizing that he also is a descendant of Haitians), perhaps links his idealism and pride in his dual status as Haitian *and* Dominican to the twenty-two-year Haitian domination and its leader. Did Ramón's outlook, then, grow from an idolization of Jean-Pierre Boyer and his nineteenth-century ideals? It is possible that Boyer, who desired to merge Haiti and Santo Domingo as one united front, represents for the young *gavillero* a role model, a powerful Haitian leader who sought to eliminate slavery and re-vision agricultural space and use in Santo Domingo.[48] His vision of camaraderie and brotherhood between the Republic of Haiti and Santo Domingo in the early nineteenth century is one Ramón likely respected; Boyer proclaimed in January 1922: "Pues según ofrece viene como padre, amigo y hermano a abrazaros todos bajo la egida tutelar de una sola constitución" (qtd. in Moya Pons, *La dominación* 31).

While the narrator self-identifies as a proud Dominican patriot, he also affirms his Haitian lineage. Likewise, Ramón's father's family and the community do not allow him to forget or downplay his Haitian heritage, nor do they accept him as a Dominican. As son of a Haitian, servant mother, El Cuerno is marked as *un haitiano* in El Seibo. Ramón demonstrates his understanding of his predicament by telling Juan that "los dominicanos nacimos para que nos pisen" (53). Nonetheless, the revolutionary theme in *La vida no tiene nombre,* guided by Ramón's testimony as he awaits his execution, is impactful—more so as Ramón is not just another rebel fighter but a *Haitian Dominican* rebel fighter. De Maeseneer agrees: "La aproximación por parte de este revolucionario sencillo, hijo natural de un padre dominicano traidor y de una haitiana, es muy impactante" (*Encuentro* 44).

To further comment on Veloz Maggiolo's telling of the story of the 1916–24 occupation through the eyes of a Haitian Dominican revolutionary, the fact that the novel perennially positions Ramón as a victim of Dominican society, and not a victimizer, is key. Even upon revealing the violence of the *gavilleros,* Ramón refuses to agree to senseless killings; rather, he voices his disagreement with the rebels' growing affinity for theft and violence. The reader sides with the narrator as his puppet-like role in his "nameless life"—with no real control over his life and no ability to seek new opportunities—positions him as a disposable member of Dominican society. El Cuerno hypothetically asks, further alluding to his inability to change life's course: "¿Qué culpa teníamos Simián y yo en todo esto?" (26). Ramón's life "se ha reducido a la guerra" (52). This pessimistic viewpoint also surfaces in the protagonist-narrator's description of the vodou rituals practiced by Haitians living in the *bateyes:* "Los haitianos de los demás bateyes vinieron a la hacienda, encendieron una hoguera en un pelado del monte, y empezaron a cantar y a saltar alrededor de la misma con tres aullidos de desesperación" (29). While these "aullidos de desesperación" represent the plight of Haitians both on and off the border, Ramón's voice as a Haitian Dominican *gavillero* expands the stereotypical role of the Haitian subject in Dominican literature and bestows new meaning to the aforementioned shrieks of desperation: they are also shouts of and for inclusion, rebellion, and solidarity.

"Pocas Obras [Dominicanas]" on the Haitian Subject

Veloz Maggiolo asserts in his aforementioned "Tipología del tema haitiano" that "pocas obras y pocas veces el tema del haitiano había sido tocado por autores nacionales" (94). The relevancy of this statement well into the twenty-first century is debatable. While the theme of Dominican-Haitian relations does not eclipse the ever-present representation of Trujillo and the *trujillato* period in Dominican national literature, for example, literary representations of the Haitian subject have increased in number since the late seventies, especially when one considers the literary corpus of Dominican American authors examined in the following chapters. As Veloz Maggiolo's "Tipología" confirms, Dominican works prior to 1977, including Manuel Mora Serrano's *Juego de dominó* (1973; Game of domino) and Juan Bosch's story "Luis Pié" (written in 1942), represented Haitians in literature. Other noteworthy works underscoring the relations between Haitians and Dominicans published after Veloz Maggiolo's essay include Diego D'Acalá's *La frontera* (1994; The border), Mélida García's historical novel *Oro, sulfuro y muerte* (1999; Gold, sulfur, and death), Favio Ramón Montes de Oca's *Trujillo y los secretos de su hija rayana* (2011; Trujillo and the secrets of his *rayana* daughter), Alanna Lockward's *Marassá y la nada* (2013; *Marassa and the Nothingness*, 2016), and Rita Indiana Rodríguez's *La mucama de Omicunlé* (2015; Omicunlé's servant), among others.[49] I chose to focus solely on two novels written by Marcio Veloz Maggiolo in this chapter because of his return in his literature to the Trujillo regime and his repeated examination of the role of Haitians before, during, and after the *trujillato*.[50] Veloz Maggiolo's incessant asking in his narrative who forms part of the Dominican society is crucial to examining the role(s) he assigns to the Haitian subject:

> La concepción de Veloz Maggiolo sobre la identidad dominicana insta a reflexionar sobre quiénes son los dominicanos, generalmente en relación con el resto de Latinoamérica y el mundo. Es preciso aclarar que el cuestionamiento de la identidad en sus narraciones tiende a inclinarse por la protagonización del "otro," pero se presenta, sin lugar a dudas, desde una óptica histórica totalizadora que enfoca todos los grupos humanos de nuestra historia cultural. (Rodríguez-Henríquez 65)

Veloz Maggiolo's decision to position the Other as protagonists—the Haitian Dominican Ramón and the border subject Honorio Lora—is a prime example of the author's purposeful placement of non-Dominican minorities to narrate the Dominican nation.

Literature reexamines history and provides a new way of interpreting the past that conflicts with the patriarchal, dominant understanding of important historical moments. Valerio-Holguín notes: "In the long run the texts that have succeeded in denouncing at an international level the human rights violations committed by Trujillo's regime are not testimonial accounts but rather historical novels" ("La reinterpretación" 207). I would argue, however, that the work of Veloz Maggiolo goes beyond the realm of testimony or traditional historical narrative and succeeds not only in denouncing the Trujillo regime but also in rewriting the role of nonelites in events of great consequence to the history of Hispaniola, such as the first US Marine occupation and the 1937 Haitian Massacre.

3 "Here We Are the Haitians"
Seeing Haiti from the Diaspora

Latina Memoir from an "Insider/Outsider Perspective"

A popular Haitian proverb, included in Edwidge Danticat's novel *Claire of the Sea Light* (2013), speaks to the importance of knowing and caring for others: "Fòk nou voye je youn sou lòt" (164). The proverb, translated into English as "We must keep an eye on one another" or "We must look after one another," can also be understood as a call for humanity to "see" and to know others. Much as the saying in English "I see you" has a connotation beyond the sensory act of seeing and instead is synonymous with understanding someone or recognizing their point of view, the Haitian proverb emphasizes the multiple connotations of vision, underscoring the desire and the will to see both the unfamiliar and the familiar. The two memoirs analyzed in this chapter, the first of two chapters centered primarily on Dominican American literature, "see" Haiti and Haitians from both on- and off-border—or on- and off-island—spaces. By sharing their experiences in the form of self-writing the authors succeed in outwardly envisioning Haiti as an integral component of the Dominican and Dominican American reality. The memoirs, Raquel Cepeda's *Bird of Paradise* (2013) and Julia Alvarez's *A Wedding in Haiti* (2012), are autobiographical texts with a collective pulse, interweaving the histories and lived realities of Haitians and Dominicans both in the US diaspora and on the island of Hispaniola.

While these Dominican American memoirs "see" Haiti and Hispaniola from different perspectives, the fact that they are written from the diaspora grounds the texts in what Gina Athena Ulysse refers to as an "insider/outsider perspective." Ulysse divulges, in her introduction to *Why Haiti Needs New Narratives: A Post-Quake Chronicle* (2015), the onset of her decision to compile her writings on and related to Haiti in book form. Regarding the uniqueness of her perspective and the gap her narratives fill, she writes: "I offered a multifaceted insider/outsider perspective on this developing moment in Haitian history, a post-quake chronicle. (I think of it as a memoir of sorts)" (xxvii). In a different way,

Cepeda and Alvarez also offer an "insider/outsider perspective," as both memoirs express feelings of belonging and exclusion in varying geographical settings. *Bird of Paradise* and *A Wedding in Haiti* not only comment on the authors' perspectives as insiders *and* outsiders, a common trope of the diasporic experience, but also explore the same sentiments Haitians experience both in the Dominican Republic and the United States. Cepeda and Alvarez build on the shared perception of identifying as both insiders and outsiders to reassess the Haitian-Dominican relationship. In addition to addressing the two memoirs, this chapter looks at recent multimodal autobiographical and testimonial expressions, including documentary film, alongside Cepeda's and Alvarez's texts to explore the multitudinous ways writers, performers, and directors "see" Haiti.

The historian and performer Edward Paulino's one-man autobiographical play, *Eddie's Perejil*, directed by Samantha Galarza, shows one Dominican American's understanding of Haiti and the complex relationship between the two nations of Hispaniola. The play ends with an invitation to the audience to spread flower petals on the Dominican and Haitian flags displayed in front of the stage.[1] This final, ritualistic call to action, involving the audience in the act of performance, functions not unlike a makeshift altar to the lives lost during the 1937 Massacre, the historical event on which the play centers. Paulino shares that the first blow to his "love affair" with the Dominican Republic, his refuge from his life in public housing in New York City, began with his discovery of the 1937 Perejil Massacre. His personal relationship with his beloved Dominican Republic continued to spiral downward when he met Sonia Pierre (1963–2011), a human-rights advocate in the Dominican Republic, and learned how Dominicans of Haitian descent like Pierre are continually denied citizenship in what is in many cases the only country they have ever called home. The final straw, however, ending his decades-long obsession with all things Dominican, was his discovery of his own racial privilege in the Dominican Republic. It was a visit to Vesuvio, the famous, upscale restaurant in Santo Domingo, that sparked Paulino's most jarring realization in regard to the Dominican Republic and race. After acting out his exquisite meal in the capital in *Eddie's Perejil*, Paulino narrates his epiphany: "Holy shit. I was now the *blanquito*. The joy that I had felt in the D.R. all those years was based on privileges because of how I looked."

All three of Paulino's epiphanies referenced above relate directly to the notion of racial privilege as a have or have-not. More specifically, his final coming to terms with his *madre patria* reflects how a given individual's racial privilege shifts from on-island to off-island or diasporic spaces.

Paulino's self-discovery regarding the social and cultural repercussions of being "light-skinned" in the Dominican Republic read as the inverse to the Dominican Chiqui Vicioso's oft-cited words describing her first experience in the United States: "Until I came to New York, I didn't know I was black" (Shorris 146). While Vicioso embraced her blackness in the United States, identifying herself as a black woman and an Afro-Latina, it was on Dominican soil that Paulino became uncomfortable with the entitlement associated with being light-skinned.[2] As Paulino expresses in *Eddie's Perejil,* he had a privilege he did not deserve and therefore, in his words, "could not have." Related to the racial negotiations at the heart of both *Bird of Paradise* and *A Wedding in Haiti,* dictated by space and reflective of differences between racial identifications on the island and in the US diaspora, Paulino describes a situational whiteness that he maneuvers differently according to his geographical location. Because he is on the "other side" of what can be considered a US racial schema that traditionally functions as a binary and differentiates only between whiteness and blackness, Paulino's personal racial tribulation aligns with that of other Latinos/as in the US diaspora as they grapple with external understandings of race and their multiple schemas. Wendy Roth, in *Race Migrations: Latinos and the Cultural Transformation of Race,* identifies a variant of the US binary racial schema that subsumes a third racial category: Hispanic/Latino. In this "Hispanicized US schema," individuals can be classified racially as Hispanic or Latino/a as opposed to solely black or white. In this two-part US racial schema, only non-Latinos/as are typically referred to using the binary classification system (28–29). Key to navigating the myriad racial schemas and their variants in the United States is the insistence on the hybridization of such racial categorizations. As Roth writes, "The fusing of concepts is a form of cultural change, and the blending of new and old ideas about race points to how cultural change is spurred by migration" (30).

How this "blending," the joining and disjoining of various racial schemas, manifests in Latina memoir is the focus of this chapter. More specifically, this chapter considers the representation of Haitians and Haiti in Dominican American memoir in order to explore how these portrayals are assessed by authors navigating US racial, social, and cultural realities. If movement is analogous with migration, how does this shifting of space or nation-state—a significant change in a given individual's physical grounding—mark Latina literary expressions? Moreover, do racial perceptions or classifications in literature set in the United States differ from those in literature set in the country of origin, in this case the Dominican

Republic and by extension Hispaniola? Torres-Saillant addresses blackness and the Dominican state as follows: "A large part of the problem of racial identity among Dominicans stems from the fact that from its inception their country had to negotiate the racial paradigms of their North American and European overseers" ("Tribulations" 127). Such negotiations become increasingly complicated when an understanding of blackness created within the Dominican nation—however cognizant of Western powers and the tendency of US journalists and statesmen to conceive of the Dominican race as nonblack—is reappropriated in the space of the United States. Relatedly, since Dominican culture traditionally suppresses African influences, the state instead championing the Hispanic heritage of Dominicans, it is vital to consider how both blackness and Haitianness can at times appear celebrated or understood differently by Dominican Americans.

Historically, the United States has played an influential role in emphasizing and concretizing a racial ideology in the Dominican Republic that denies blackness and conceives of Haitians as the Other. The country also emerges as a space that confronts and challenges these very racial misconceptions for Dominicans living in the US diaspora. The diaspora proves key to a reexamination of the self as migrants are forced to reconfigure notions of home and community. In cross-cultural metropoles like New York, this challenge to an individual's identity commonly forges a connection with African roots and the African American community—a merging of two cultures and communities that forms the basis of the popular refrain for Dominicans in New York: "Nosotros somos los haitianos de aquí" (Victoriano-Martínez 222).[3] This saying asserts that in the United States, Dominicans become foreigners, an outsider perspective that allows them to understand firsthand the societal position Haitians occupy in the Dominican Republic. Juan Gonzalez confirms the "mix-up" that occurs between Dominicans and Haitians: "New Yorkers tend to mistake them [Dominicans] for blacks who happen to speak Spanish" (117). The fact that Dominicans in the United States begin to associate themselves with the Haitian Other instead of defining themselves *against* it—making visible links between the Dominican "us" and the Haitian "them"—elucidates the search for identity in Dominican American literature.

Collaboration between differing racial and ethnic communities, notably African American and Hispanic/Latino communities, dates from the civil rights era. A prime example from the late 1960s is the partnership of the Puerto Rican Young Lords Party with the Black Panther Party, the emerging Puerto Rican organization leaning on the established Black Panthers as a model for racial empowerment and social justice. Young Lord Pablo Yoruba Guzmán describes the origins of the Young Lords Party and the interracial and interethnic values at its core: "In New York, Puerto Ricans were growing up alongside African Americans in the same barrios, and only the fools among us ... could not see that we had a heck of a lot in common" (241). While Guzmán does not negate or attempt to dispute the high degree of racism toward each other on the part of Puerto Ricans and the African American community, and on the part of light-skinned and dark-skinned Puerto Ricans, he explains: "We had to deal with this racism because it blocked any kind of growth for our people.... Puerto Ricans like myself, who are darker skinned, who look like Afro-Americans, couldn't do that [escape], 'cause to do that would be to escape into a kind of fantasy. Because before people called me a spic, they called me a nigger" (236). The experience Guzmán relates mirrors the experience of Dominican immigrants in the United States; Puerto Ricans, Dominicans, Cubans, and other Latin Americans arriving in the US diaspora also were mistaken by New Yorkers "for Blacks who happen to speak Spanish" (Gonzalez 117).

The newcomer status of Dominicans in the US diaspora, who arrived later than other Hispanic Caribbean groups, such as Cubans and Puerto Ricans, makes firm conclusions about binational identities difficult. Puerto Ricans migrated largely to New York as legal residents of the United States, the majority as a result of Operation Bootstrap, which fostered a change in the Puerto Rican economy in the 1940s and 1950s. On the other hand, the Cuban migrant population, centered in Miami, saw its largest increase in number after the 1959 revolution of Fidel Castro. Often, the varying migratory waves to the United States are unique in their social and political composition, as exemplified by the multiple waves of Dominicans arriving in the United States. During the Trujillo regime, Dominicans fled the country as political exiles. After Trujillo's assassination in 1961, Dominican immigration remained largely political in nature as immigrants sought to escape the political uprisings and unstable governments, namely, the popular uprising in 1965 seeking to restore political power to Juan Bosch. According to Juan Gonzalez, "Between 1961 and 1986 more than 400,000 people legally immigrated to the United States from the Dominican Republic ... making Dominican migration one of the largest to this country of the past forty years" (117). Considering that the migration of Dominicans to the United States is a more recent trend (compared with the migration of Puerto Ricans and Cubans), it is not yet possible, less than a half century later, to fully understand how the binational identities created as a result of this migration reconfigure in a global context. It is possible, however, to reflect on the ways in which such a distancing from the island changes perspectives on Hispaniola and, in particular, the Dominican-Haitian dynamic.

Beyond the racial perception of dark-skinned Dominicans as "black" in the US diaspora, the geographical intimacy between Dominican and Haitian populations, notably in the state of New York, is revealing. Figure 3 displays data from the 2015 US census. Each pie chart represents the number of Haitians (dark gray) and Dominicans (light gray) residing in each county. The 2015 census records, under a "population characteristics" category, whether or not a given individual identifies as "foreign born." According to the US Census Bureau, "The foreign-born population includes anyone who was not a U.S. citizen or a U.S. national at birth" ("Quick Facts"). Within this category, individuals can select a country of origin, and the data in figure 3 represent the percentages of those who listed either the Dominican Republic or Haiti. Notably, there are inaccuracies in this visualization of Dominican and Haitian populations by county since many who identify as Haitian American or Dominican American were born in the United States and thus should not be included in the foreign-born category. The category, and census data in general, often neglects to include unauthorized immigrants residing in the United States, even though the census does count individuals regardless of immigration status in an attempt to document the growth of immigrant communities and accurately report US population statistics. While there are obvious inaccuracies in the populations of Dominicans and Haitians represented in figure 3, it does confirm that the two Caribbean immigrant groups share the same geographical space and are members of the same immigrant communities. While Dominicans represent the majority in the Bronx and New York (Manhattan) counties, neighboring Suffolk, Kings, and Nassau counties are approximately split between the two populations. This visualization of diasporic space shared by the two Hispaniola-rooted communities helps us understand why Dominican American writers might elect to link the two populations in literature. Figure 3 confirms the geographical crossover of Dominican and Haitians in New York. Raised and educated primarily in New York, Raquel Cepeda and Julia Alvarez highlight in their memoirs the relations between Dominicans and Haitians both in the US diaspora and on Hispaniola. Their narratives also portray a search for their own identities, inclusive of African roots. Both women, albeit in different ways, confront Hispaniola's past and create, through

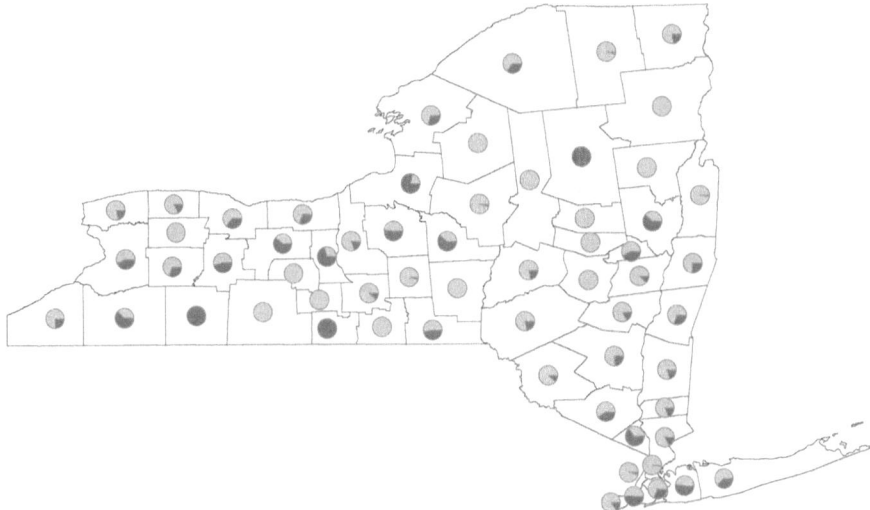

Figure 3. Dominicans and Haitians in New York State

their autobiographical frameworks, a contrapuntal, shared space where Dominicans and Haitians coexist.

Approaching one of these memoirs as off island and the other as on island, set in Haiti, is parallel to a consideration of the hyphenated identity of Latinos/as in the United States. While this discussion is applicable to the many different Latin American nationalities falling under the umbrella term *Latino/a/x* in the United States,[4] it is essential to at least briefly mention the term *domincanyork,* a sobriquet for Dominicans living off the island as members of a unique, bipartite entity. The term *domincanyork* is cast in a negative light by Manuel Núñez in *Ocaso de la nación dominicana* (1990; Decline of the Dominican nation). Núñez states that "la infravaloración de sí mismos," with respect to the "dominicanyorks," "lleva a los dominicanos a reproducir un sentimiento de incapacidad en sus propias fuerzas" (459). Josefina Báez, in her performance text *Dominicanish* (2005), inverts the negative connotation surrounding the term, much as the Puerto Rican American Tato Llaviera and others, such as Pedro Pietri and Miguel Algarín, did for the terms *Nuyorícan* and *AmeRícan*. In this way, Báez celebrates the dual identity and positions herself as writer and performer "en la lucha política por la identidad" (Victoriano-Martínez 179). Like Báez, Pérez Firmat recognizes the advantages of a binational or hyphenated identity, despite the difficulties surrounding its negotiation. He states in *Life on the Hyphen* (1994) that for Cubans at least, the "hyphenated" status should not be indicated by a minus sign, but instead by a plus sign: "Perhaps we shall call ourselves Cubans + Americans" (16).

In the first of the two close readings central to this chapter, I consider Cepeda's memoir *Bird of Paradise: How I Became Latina* for the ways in which the author rewrites the off-island, diasporic relations between Dominicans and Haitians. I consider how the US diaspora emerges as a new model of third space in which the fraternal relations between Haitians and Dominicans represent one of many cultural collisions and collaborations. Cepeda envisions a dynamic, transcultural diaspora that is a site of resistance but also of transformation. While *Bird of Paradise* is about the author's experience in New York City and the Dominican Republic, the story ends and begins in the United States. By contrast, Alvarez's memoir, *A Wedding in Haiti,* is set entirely on the island of Hispaniola, primarily in Haiti. A question that resurfaces in the close readings of both memoirs is how the specific space of the United States influences the writer when she revisits the history of her country of origin. Of primary interest is how these two memoirs rewrite Haiti by shining new light on the history between Haiti and the Dominican Republic and by rooting their narratives in a past and future of camaraderie and collaboration between the two countries. Moreover, a critical approach to memoirs written by two Dominican American women, Cepeda and Alvarez, proffers a female-oriented understanding of how Dominican Americans write both the United States' and Hispaniola's past and future. Here I build on Maja Horn's and Neici Zeller's work on gender discourses in the Dominican Republic and the Dominican diaspora. These close readings, with a Dominican American feminist lens, reframe the experience of the diaspora by focusing on female voices that fill the voids of Dominican discursive praxis and challenge the intellectual gap that Sylvia Wynter alludes to as "the silenced ground of women" (363).

"Enemies" on the Island, "Relatives" in Nueva York: Raquel Cepeda's *Bird of Paradise*

Raquel Cepeda's *Bird of Paradise: How I Became Latina*, deemed by the author "the first memoir to be written by a Dominican American author of [her] generation and released in the popular market" ("From the author"), has two parts. Part 1 details Cepeda's childhood in New York City with her father during the hip-hop generation and in Paraíso, Dominican Republic, with her grandparents. Part 2 discloses the author's

DNA test results and attempts to uncover her ancestry prior to the emergence of the umbrella identifier *Latino/a*. Cepeda contradictorily accepts and contests the results with a glance into her personal history, confronting her hyphenated identity. The memoir seeks to explain Cepeda's ancestry and in the process challenges the understanding of Dominican identity in a global society. While the narrative is autobiographical, the text is markedly collective, encompassing the diasporic experience not only of Dominican Americans but of a diverse community of immigrants to the United States that spans generations, with a desire to trace their origins and forge a connection with their past.

Marianela Medrano's poem "El corte" ironically labels Hispaniola as utopia, a Caribbean paradise. The poem begins by beckoning readers to visit the island: "Come on down Come on down see the / fantasy island / Where history hums like a tamed / dragon" (67). While Medrano's poem thematically centers on the 1937 Massacre, it also relates to the tendency of Dominican and Dominican American authors to return to the past, an inherent inability to untie history from narrative. The poem's nickname for the Dominican Republic—"fantasy island"—mirrors Cepeda's reference to the island as a "paradise." For both Medrano and Cepeda, these monikers mark a conscious return to the *madre patria*, looking in from the diaspora. As Cepeda tells the story of her mother, Rocío, Paraíso first surfaces as the town in which Rocío grew up. When Rocío marries the author's abusive, *mujeriego* father without her parents' blessing, it becomes clear that "Paraíso had turned into everything but paradise for the family" (10). Cepeda's mother immigrates to Nueva York with her new husband and becomes blinded by wedded bliss, resolving to create her own *paraíso* by cleaning homes of rich Americans and picking up extra factory shifts. For Rocío, "Paradise is a state of being, more than just the name of a suburb or a home" (8). Paradise, then, becomes a mirage, unattainable. Medrano, beckoning readers to "Come on down see the / fantasy island," precludes the likening of the island to any "fantasy" by recalling its troubled past. In a similar way, Cepeda challenges her mother's conception of any fantasy or paradise in New York, implying that paradise is not synonymous with a low-paying job and an abusive husband. Paradise, or the island of fantasy, whether Manhattan or Hispaniola, whether attainable or out of reach, is all-inclusive. On both "islands" Haitians exist in and are an important, integrated component of "paradise." This ironic usage of the term in Cepeda's memoir is also a reminder of the popular cruise line, Royal Caribbean, taking passengers to a beach in Haiti near the town Labadee without telling them they were porting in Haiti. Until recently, the cruise company dubbed the stop "a vacationer's *paradise*." Today the port is clearly labeled as a private beach in Labadee, Haiti, called Paradise Cove.[5] The descriptors *fantasy* and *paradise* in relation to Hispaniola also evoke the problematic motif of island isolation, a representation that stands to "relegate islanders to a remote and primitive past, denying them entrance into the modernity of their colonial 'motherlands'" (DeLoughrey 15).

Furthering the concept of *nosotros,* in reference to the collective pulse of Cepeda's memoir, is the merging of Dominicans and Haitians throughout part 1 of the text. As mentioned previously, *Bird of Paradise* has two parts. The first relates Cepeda's coming to terms with her own identity: "a Dominican who was been mistaken for everything but Dominican" (xiv). Part 2 details the results of her ancestral DNA test. Both parts look to the past to better understand the present and plan for the future. While Cepeda is Dominican American and in the title of her memoir refers to herself as "Latina," both parts of the memoir concern her effort to understand her ancestral origins "*before* we became Latino" (xiv). The results of Cepeda's DNA test are intriguing, largely because they include a direct link to the Dominican Republic's indigenous Taíno population, but I focus primarily on the part 1. My close reading highlights three specific aspects of the memoir: Cepeda's criticism of Dominicans who negate their blackness, the conception of a fluid or hyphenated identity, and specific examples of Haitians and Haitian Americans forming part of a Dominican American *nosotros*.

Bird of Paradise is Cepeda's first publication outside journalism; the author's previous journalistic publications include an edited volume titled *And It Don't Stop: The Best American Hip-Hop Journalism of the Last 25 Years* (2004). Cepeda confronts what it means to be Latino/a today not only in her 2013 memoir but also as cohost of the recently canceled Panoply podcast *Our National Conversation about Conversations about Race*.[6] Tackling issues of race, class, and identity, the podcast is sarcastic, blunt, and powerful, much like *Bird of Paradise*. Cepeda, in fact, received an award in 2014 at the United Nations for her memoir and "for the courage reflected in her literature, her commitment to denouncing violence against women, and for her work in helping young women's empowerment."[7]

In *Bird of Paradise,* Cepeda frequently references the antiblack, anti-Haitian ideology, with roots long enough to reach to the diaspora from Hispaniola and beyond. Her own father, Eduardo, part-Haitian, inspires the most blatant examples of negrophobia in the text. When she was a child, the *antihaitianismo* rubbed off on Cepeda. She remembers her father's brother, Jean, as "a darker-skinned version of Papito and way more sinister. I started thinking that what Dominicans said about *haitianos* was true: Their darker skin did make them more evil" (33). Cepeda's father mocks her, disapproving of her interests when as a young girl she shares her dream to be a break-dancer and rapper when she grows up. He equates her affinity for rap and hip-hop with all things black, noting, "She *wan's* to be so Black" (60). In a similar sense, Eduardo himself seeks to be anything but black, rejecting all things Afro. His response to the discrimination that the Latino/a population faces in New York City—although Cepeda concludes that "they" were not sure exactly what they were discriminating against, "white, Black, Native American" (138)—is to find a group against which *he* can discriminate. "Dad began to jump on the anti-Arabic bandwagon though he could easily be mistaken for a Middle Easterner" (139). Toward the end of part 1 of the memoir, no longer susceptible to the racial underpinnings of a family that discouraged her from celebrating or expressing her *dominicanidad,* she reflects on her adult life (xv). Cepeda expresses the desire to see her father suffer from an identity crisis as she had: "I wanted him to feel the pain and confusion I did all these years for simply reminding him of what he was, *un dominicano*" (140). Her categorization of her father as *un dominicano* reflects her decision to (subconsciously) erase the Haitian from her father's identity. The irony in *Bird of Paradise,* then, is that the author identifies as black but was brought up to deny her Afro roots. Cepeda's confrontation of an antiblack mentality not only questions the roots of such an ideology but offers a counternarrative. Through self-writing, Cepeda challenges a one-sided dominant discourse that paints Dominicans as racist and antiblack. *Bird of Paradise* stands to prove that an accompaniment to such racism and antagonism is acceptance and integration for blacks, including Haitians, in a diasporic community that has stereotypically negated its blackness.

Further evidence of Cepeda's father's whitewashing tendencies is his second marriage, to Ercilia, a woman described by Cepeda as "a gringa or *something close to one*" (41, my emphasis). The almost-but-not-quite attitude toward Ercilia's whiteness points to the fluid, social conception of race in the Dominican community. This sentiment is confirmed by Cepeda's confession: "Ercilia's whiteness is a figment of Papi's imagination" (66). The examples of shifting (racial) identities in *Bird of Paradise* extend well beyond Eduardo and his remarriage. The reality of hyphenated, multiple identities for Latinos/as in the diaspora is highlighted in the epigraphs of various chapters of the memoir, including chapter 7, which begins with a quote from Anzaldúa's *Borderlands:* "Simultaneously, I saw my face from different angles / And my face, like reality, had multiple characters" (87). The idea of the multiple self is best expressed by Anzaldúa's *mestiza* consciousness. Anzaldúa asserts that "*la mestiza* is a product of the transfer of cultural and spiritual values of one group to another. Being tricultural, monolingual, bilingual, or multilingual, speaking a patois, and in a state of perpetual transition, the *mestiza* faces the dilemma of the mixed breed" (*Borderlands* 100). In the Dominican Republic, the interplay between the terms *mestizo* and *mulato* is fraught with confusion. While the twentieth-century Dominican census traditionally recorded the majority of the population as "mestizo," often *mestizo* was used to refer to race, and *mulato* to color.[8] The contemporary understanding of the two terms has shifted. According to Simmons, in the Dominican Republic "*mulataje* is one of the two emerging racial projects challenging *mestizaje*. It articulates a new racial view and reflects a *negro-blanco* (black-white) mixture with assertions of being *mulato*" (117). In *Bird of Paradise,* Cepeda—just like Anzaldúa's *mestiza*—"undergoes a struggle of flesh, a struggle of borders, an inner war" (100). The memoir is a testament to this transitory but enduring phase of the life of a Dominican American woman caught in the "in-betweens."

Cepeda shares her journey to uncover her ancestral origins and her personal, familial history as a hyphenated individual. The balancing of a multiethnic, multiracial, and multicultural identity foregrounds the memoir. Cepeda notes, after moving permanently to New York City, that instead of Raquel, "maybe the name Rachel, as unremarkable as it sounds to me, suits me better now" (51). Likewise, the author points repeatedly to her dual identity. At first she does so with hesitation, wondering about the flight attendants on a plane to the United States "if any of them are Dominican, like me. Or *Americana,* like me" (42). Later, in college, Cepeda affirms her bipartite identity with confidence and prowess: "I'm dominiyorkian" (120). Cepeda's proud self-identification recalls the overarching premise of Josefina Báez's *Dominicanish,* which she begins by stating, "Yo soy una Dominican York" (7). While Cepeda, like Báez, seems to accept the hyphenated identity as "not a minus sign but a plus" (Pérez Firmat 16), she confirms in a podcast recorded by C-SPAN in early 2015 that she is "very comfortable being American and being Latino. For me, that hyphen is not something that separates me, but brings me to both" ("'White People'"). For Cepeda, labeling herself as solely one or the other—focusing on only one side of the hyphen—is wrong. Singling out *Dominican* or *American* fails to recognize fully that the two national, ethnic markers do not constitute two separate identities, but their fusion into one.[9]

A discussion surrounding the notion of fluid identity, or the "gray spaces" of race, in *Bird of Paradise* should also include the emphasized difference(s) between Latinos/as born in New York City and Dominicans who recently landed on US soil, the latter also designated *plátanos* or *campesinos*.[10] The newer arrivals consider the "true" dominicanyorks, the category in which Cepeda places herself, to be less "authentic" Dominicans:

> To many of the tens of thousands flooding the city, we're gringos, fake-ass Dominicans, though they are just a few years away from becoming as American as they perceive us being. In the time in between, the rift between "us" and "them" has become more volatile than standing on a fault line during an earthquake. Many of us born in New York City who feel like we have nothing in common with the *campesinos,* and assume they've come straight out of the farms and shantytowns of rural D.R., began choosing sides. (107)

Just as the *campesinos* feel animosity, and perhaps jealousy, toward the seemingly more assimilated Dominican Americans in the diaspora, Cepeda claims to speak for her own community of hyphenated subjects when she states that they "don't give a fuck about the *plátanos*" (107). This trivial rivalry, or misunderstanding, draws a new line between "us" and "them" for Dominicans of the diaspora. This stratification serves to polarize two parties that should instead lean on each other for support, especially as the "Americans" are "growing increasingly hostile to [a Dominican] presence. People across the nation are freaking the fuck out" (138).[11] Thus, both established Dominican Americans, those already embracing their Latino/a ID, and *plátanos* face discrimination in the diaspora, a discrimination that Haitians face too. This seemingly unavoidable discrimination results in a kind of "leveling" for Haitians and Dominicans. The sociologist Jorge Duany's conclusion that Dominicans in Puerto Rico find themselves on the lowest rung of the economic ladder owing to their "racialization" as blacks relates to the economic and social situation of Dominicans in the United States as well. Just as "American-born Latinos exist in a kind of liminal state" (Cepeda, *Bird of Paradise* 138), Haitians do too.

Dominicans' finding themselves in the same societal position as Haitians in the United States leads to a diasporic reconceptualization of the Dominican-Haitian relationship. Thus, instead of highlighting how the Haitian community differs from the Dominican community—often the reality on the island—the diaspora stresses what the two groups have in common. Hispaniola is a point of contact and similarity for Dominicans and Haitians in the United States, figuratively erasing the border that divides political and social realities on the island. Not only does Cepeda befriend Haitian

Americans but she openly admits to her Haitian ancestry. Her father's side is part Haitian, an ancestral connection that Cepeda confirms by incorporating brief Kreyòl dialogues into the text, for example: "Pou ki-sa, frem?" Papito asks. "Why, brother?" (39). Furthermore, Cepeda's best friends are Haitian, and these friendships sometimes result in the author being marked as "less" Dominican. A Haitian comments to her, "I thought you were Puerto Rican and something, or, like, Black and white," to which she retorts: "What about me isn't Dominican?" The response to Cepeda's question is a loaded one: "You're hanging out with Haitians, for one" (85). Although her association with Haitians suggests that she is "less Dominican," Cepeda questions her freedom to choose Claudine Jean-Baptiste, whose mother was born in Port-au-Prince (60), as a best friend: "I wonder if we would have been friends had we been living in the D.R. or Haiti. I imagined thousands of friendships disintegrating into the arid Caribbean air—POOF—before they could even begin. Teenagers, separated by an imaginary line, who will never laugh together or share fresh clothes" (84). Although the comment appears lighthearted, alluding to a teenage innocence of sorts, Cepeda's reference to an "imaginary line" is revealing. Her statement not only demonstrates how the diaspora is able to redraw and "soften" borders that appear more impermeable on the island but playfully criticizes an island-based political border that prevents friendships, forcing them to disintegrate "into the arid Caribbean air." Cepeda suggests that the US diaspora enables a disintegration of this line; Haitians are included in the "us" that permeates the memoir. In this sense, Cepeda—identifying as Dominican American and Latina—distinguishes between metaphorical borders in the diaspora and geographical borders in the Dominican Republic, suggesting that the diaspora permits and encourages the creation of third spaces that stand for diversity and inclusion, whereas the Dominican Republic does not.

Although *Bird of Paradise* reenvisions Haitian-Dominican relations in the space of the diaspora, the memoir also attempts to locate the origins of antiblackness in the Dominican Republic, contending that the diaspora is an extension of racial and ethnic prejudice. In an overt reference to anti-Haitian ideology in the Dominican Republic, when referencing the "bullshit" Dominicans speak about Haitians as a source of embarrassment, Cepeda claims: "It's part of the baggage *our* parents and grandparents lug over from the *madre patria*" (84, my emphasis). *Our* here refers not just to Dominicans but to Haitians as well; each group has its own "baggage" from the Caribbean island split into two nations. The diasporic, possibly generational shift discernible in *Bird of Paradise* not only stresses a fierce disagreement and moral discomfort with the anti-Haitianism that at times defines the Dominican community but works to dissolve the ideological border between the two. Just as Anzaldúa's invisible borders are written all over her, surging through her veins, such challenges serve to break down borders and disband dominant ideologies. "Dominant paradigms, predefined concepts that exist as unquestionable, unchallengeable, are transmitted to us through the culture" (38), are reclaimed by Anzaldúa as she owns her unique personal space and structures her path to *una cultura mestiza*. In a similar way, Cepeda's memoir opens the possibility for a Dominican Haitian culture within the US diaspora, challenging the supposedly "unchallengeable."

"We Just Came to See": Julia Alvarez's *A Wedding in Haiti*

Like Cepeda's memoir, Alvarez's *A Wedding in Haiti* is an autobiographical text that speaks to and for a collective audience. While Alvarez also comments on the past and present relations between Haiti and the Dominican Republic, she does so from an on-island and on-border setting. She locates her memoir entirely on the island of Hispaniola, along the border and in Haiti. Alvarez's memoir and Junot Díaz's "Monstro"—a science-fiction (sf) short story analyzed in the following chapter—are connected by their setting on Hispaniola. *A Wedding in Haiti* and "Monstro" also share an underlying, subtle theme of revealing Haiti, introducing the country to an audience seemingly unfamiliar with America's first black republic. This audience comprises not only Dominicans and Dominican Americans but an increasingly global and possibly less knowledgeable population. Alvarez in particular weaves into her memoir snippets from the annals of Haitian history, allowing an international readership to possibly "see" Haiti and Hispaniola for the first time, or perhaps from a new perspective. Díaz stresses this idea of "seeing" and the importance of not looking away: "After all, apocalypses like the Haitian earthquake are not only catastrophes; they are also opportunities: chances for us to see ourselves, to take responsibility for what we see, to change. One day somewhere in the world something terrible will happen, and for once we won't look away" ("Apocalypse").

In *A Wedding in Haiti* Alvarez goes from admitting that "we just came to see" (266) to exploring the internal weight of "seeing" and the responsibility of bearing witness: "The one thing we cannot do is turn away. . . . When we have seen a thing, we have an obligation to see and to allow ourselves to be transformed by what we have seen" (280).[12]

If Alvarez stresses the importance of "seeing" in her memoir, then what does *A Wedding in Haiti* show—what do readers "see"? On a visual level, there are photographs throughout the text. The uncaptioned photographs accompany Alvarez's own understanding of Haiti and perhaps attempt to capture what words cannot. She states in the first sentence of the author's note that "I am not claiming to be an authority on Haitian matters." As Susan Sontag suggests in *On Photography*, photography is inherently synonymous with authority and aggression: "In deciding how a picture should look, in preferring one exposure to another, photographers are always imposing standards on their subjects. . . . Those occasions when the taking of photographs is relatively undiscriminating, promiscuous, or self-effacing do not lessen the didacticism of the whole enterprise" (6–7). The majority of the photographs in *A Wedding in Haiti*, were taken by the author, and many others by her husband, who accompanied her on her travels. The aggression inherent in the act of taking a photo increases when images are published and dispersed to a wider audience, as the author decides not only which images are worth capturing but also which images are worth publishing: "In deciding how a picture should look, in preferring one exposure to another, photographers are always imposing standards on their subjects" (Sontag 6). While the photographs accompanying the text of *A Wedding in Haiti* reinforce the author's intent to share her experience visually with her readers, they also stress the impossibility of mirroring reality, a realization and preoccupation Alvarez shares with readers: "At the end of the day, you add it up, and you still feel ashamed—at least I do. You haven't improved a damn thing" (127).

While words and photographs attempt to render Haiti tangible to the reader, despite the implicit subjective lens of photography, the idea or assumption that a photo is "not enough" or that one must travel to a place to truly understand it also emerges in Alvarez's memoir. An interest in travel—and more specifically an interest in the routes that dictate travel—guides the autobiographical narrative. In an article published the year after *A Wedding in Haiti* in the travel section of the *New York Times*, Alvarez divulges her "lifelong wish of traveling the length of the border." She recommends places to stay and transnational cuisine for those traveling along the "seam of Hispaniola." In both the 2013 article and the 2012 memoir, Alvarez follows, in part, the same route that Prestol Castillo pursued atop a mule decades earlier, the inspiration for his *Paisajes y meditaciones*. The two authors, one Dominican and the other Dominican American, had similar motivations for taking the route; both *A Wedding in Haiti* and *Paisajes y meditaciones* are reflections on the shifting Dominican border policies and the Dominicanization of the Dominican-Haitian border. While Prestol Castillo traveled the route just months after the 1937 Massacre and endeavored to justify Trujillo's handling of border politics, Alvarez—eighty years later—openly reflects on and condemns Trujillo's plan to whiten and Hispanicize the Dominican-Haitian border. Many of the allusions to Haitian-Dominican history appear subdued in the memoir, leaving it to the reader to unpack their significance. Alvarez's comment on the massacre in *A Wedding in Haiti,* accompanied by a brief history of Haiti from French colony to the revolution to brutal twentieth-century dictatorships, is easy to miss. A Dominican vendor outside Dajabón weighs the *dulce de yagua* Alvarez purchases and comments, "Le falta conciencia para ser una y media" (122). Alvarez then adds, "I find myself wondering how such a fine moral sensibility would have responded to the 1937 Massacre" (123).

One of Alvarez's most recent works, *A Wedding in Haiti* has received little critical attention.[13] It is also Alvarez's only work set primarily in Haiti. In particular, the text marks a unique merging of genres as it moves beyond the one-sided generic definition of memoir and instead constitutes, as Alvarez herself labels the work, an *us-moir* ("A Promise Kept" 171). This genre-bending term describes an alternative to the often self-centered, introspective reading of a typical memoir, or *me-moir,* an alternative that focuses on the "we," or the Spanish *nosotros,* present in the text. The "us" in us-moir in *A Wedding in Haiti* lends itself to a multitude of interpretations. One might read the plural *we* in the text as Alvarez and her husband, Bill Eichner, or Alvarez and her Haitian friend and godchild, Piti. The plural here, however, is not limited to people; it can also stand for two geographical spaces: the Dominican Republic and Haiti. The us-moir speaks to the atrocities of the past and the poverty, destitution, and resilience of the present, while also anticipating future Dominican governmental actions dealing with Dominican-Haitian relations. Alvarez writes movingly about entering Haiti from the Dominican Republic: "The soldier nods, the gates part, and just like that, we're in Haiti, and free to proceed. No red tape, no need to wheedle our way in. Haiti will take us without blinking an eye or checking our documents" (31).[14] By contrast, but perhaps not surprising, the border crossing from Haiti back into the Dominican Republic, with three Haitians in tow, is not as simple. Alvarez makes references to the popular Dominican saying *El que tiene boca llega a Roma* (If you have a mouth you can get into Rome) in concluding, "If you are Haitian, getting into the DR is another story" (114). Although *A*

Wedding in Haiti was published the year before TC/0168/13, immigration law and policy pervade the "travel memoir." The reflections on the two border crossings—the first to attend Piti's wedding and the second to visit Port-au-Prince after the earthquake—each concern issues of immigration policy and acquiring the appropriate documentation.

Returning to Alvarez's uncomplicated entrance into Haiti and the book's interest in "seeing" Haiti, it is helpful to explore how the author "sees" Haiti in memoir form. With the Dominican border far from view, a different Haiti—one not depicted in the media—unfolds in front of Alvarez. She meditates on her second trip to Haiti following the 2010 earthquake: "I wanted to be close to Haiti in an intimate way, not the Haiti blaring all over the news, the Haiti of horrifics, the failed state, the death count rising. . . . I wanted to hold Ludy [Piti's infant daughter] and sing her to sleep with my old Dominican lullabies" (147). Alvarez expresses her longing to know the real Haiti through a desire to sing the Dominican lullabies of her childhood, in Spanish, to Piti's Haitian daughter. This sentiment roots her longing to "be close to Haiti" in a fondness for her own *patria,* the Dominican Republic, hinting at the centuries of not only disagreements and bloodshed but also solidarity and camaraderie between the two countries. Although Haiti bears scars from the past, both parts of the memoir show a country filled with hope, resilience, and determination. The relationship between the Dominican Republic and Haiti is a contrapuntal one, leading Alvarez to a subtle rewrite of José Martí's line referring to Cuba and Puerto Rico as "two wings of a bird that can't fly unless they work together." Alvarez substitutes the countries mentioned by Martí with two others, remarking: "Haiti and the Dominican Republic are the two wings of a bird that can't fly unless they work together" (177). Alvarez problematizes this metaphor by reflecting on the countries' past, remembering Haiti's "race-driven history, and not just during colonial times, and not just whites against blacks, but internally down the generations" (107) and the 1937 Massacre (123). Despite the often heavyhearted and somber tone of the memoir, Alvarez renders the suffering on the Haitian side of the border as palpable and tractable. It becomes clear that Haiti, time and time again, for historical, political, racial, and even natural reasons, has a target on its back. Alvarez was urged to see and write Haiti by her own impulse to "be by Haiti's side" (148), a side she remains near in a spatial sense, as a Dominican American, but also in a personal and spiritual sense, unable and unwilling to brush aside Haiti's will to be "seen."

Alvarez positions herself on Haiti's side not only in *A Wedding in Haiti* but also in earlier works, such as in her breakthrough novel, *How the*

García Girls Lost Their Accents. The Haitian character in *García Girls*, Chucha, is one example of the linkages between Haitians and Dominicans in the US diaspora. The protagonist of *García Girls* is Yolanda, nicknamed "Yo." For Alvarez, Yo (which in English means "I") is a purposeful nickname, emphasizing the character's biographical ties to the author herself.[15] Yolanda's family subtly resist the dictatorship and refuse to turn their eyes or hearts from the slaughter of Haitian nationals, taking in a Haitian fleeing the massacre. This Haitian is Chucha, the family's maid, whose inclusion as a character allows the novel to transform into, in Alvarez's words, a "revolution of truth-telling and self-invention" (*Something to Declare* 109).[16]

Chucha serves the family for thirty-two years, and it is in the chapter "The Blood of the Conquistadores" that her character, barely escaping death, comes to life. Yolanda's sister, Fifi, shares the story of her "neighbor":

> There was this old lady, Chucha, who had worked in Mami's family forever and who had this face like someone had wrung it out after washing it to try and get some of the black out. I mean, Chucha was super wrinkled and Haitian blue-black, not Dominican *café-con-leche* black. She was real Haitian too and that's why she couldn't say certain words like the word for parsley or anyone's name that had a *j* in it. . . . She was always in a bad mood—but you couldn't get her to crack a smile or cry or anything. It was like all her emotions were spent, on account of everything she went through in her young years. Way back before Mami was even born, Chucha had just appeared at my grandfather's doorstep one night, begging to be taken in. Turns out it was the night of the massacre when Trujillo had decreed that all blacks Haitians on our side of the island would be executed by dawn. There's a river the bodies were finally thrown into that supposedly still runs red to this day, fifty years later. Chucha had escaped from some canepicker's camp and was asking for asylum. Papito took her in, poor skinny little thing. (218)

Chucha's story warrants the construction of a crossroads between traumas as "the fate of Chucha and that of the Garcías tell of *national tragedies*" (Bess 97, my emphasis). These, however, are national tragedies that become transnational ones, endured by those on both sides of the island. These tragedies portrayed in *García Girls* can be read as political, with an overarching Caribbean character, because "the displacement of Caribbean people from their islands to the United States for political or economic reasons has produced a tension between the culture of the country of origin and that of the adopted homeland" (Luis, *Dance* 266). The danger the García family encounters and their escape toward the end of Trujillo's reign by fleeing to New York City emphasize the multilayered history of the Dominican Republic, Hispaniola, and the Caribbean at large, in this way addressing Glissant's understanding of the collective or shared reality unique to those whose histories have been erased by colonialism. In the opening chapter of *Poetics of Relation,* Glissant revisits the experience of deportation to the Americas and remarks, "Although you are alone in this suffering, you share in the unknown with others whom you have yet to know" (6). Alvarez, writing a new Dominican (American) history and thus filling historical voids, also presents a history that forms part of the greater Caribbean history—an all-encompassing, shared history that accommodates the diaspora and its subjects.

One can unravel a historical Caribbean parallel that spans generations upon considering the García family and their loyal maid, Chucha. In a sense, the Garcías' history and Chucha's history are one and the same. A decade or so after the slaughter of approximately fifteen thousand Haitians and Haitians of Dominican descent by Trujillo's henchmen, Yolanda's grandfather is incarcerated for taking part in an underground movement against the dictator. As a direct result, the SIM, Trujillo's "secret service," keep a nightly watch on her father (Alvarez's own father was also involved in plots against the dictator), monitoring his activities (6). Alvarez's character Chucha serves as a window into the shared history of the two countries of Hispaniola and represents a universal Quisqueyan subject. Just like the Haitian Kreyòl speakers who stutter as they pronounce the *j* in *perejil,* Yolanda experiences a similar difficulty. As she begins to recite poetry on stage, "her tongue feels as if it has been stuffed into her mouth to keep her quiet" (19–20). Although the author's alter ego in *García Girls* might appear tongue-tied, Alvarez does not hesitate when her pen hits the paper, and in this way she gives voice to the forgotten and/or suffocated stories like Chucha's. Thanks to Alvarez, Chucha and her story of survival persist, and critics like Bess, who concludes that Chucha "will be the one left to suffer true powerlessness while the wealthy and lighter-skinned Garcías escape to safety" (97), are proven wrong. Instead, both female characters—Yolanda *and* Chucha—transgress time, history, and geography. Alvarez and Piti in *A Wedding in Haiti* also prove transgressive; their experience in Haiti and the Dominican Republic, both shared and personal, speaks to Hispaniola's past and present. The memoir reflects on the horrific 2010 earthquake in Haiti and describes the country's resilience moving forward. Moreover, the testimonial text is precursory to TC/0168/13, as it underscores the difficulty of obtaining proper documentation for Haitians who choose to reside in the Dominican Republic.

Diverse Visions of Dominican and Haitian Transnational Testimony

In ways similar to those in which *Bird of Paradise* and *A Wedding in Haiti* challenge the Dominican diaspora's silenced histories by offering personal accounts in memoir form, the self-reflection inherent in the abovementioned *Eddie's Perejil* assesses and reassesses Hispaniola's past. The metanarrative implicit in the autobiographical play, for example, materializes when Paulino narrates his historical field research in which he interviews both survivors and those who carried out Trujillo's orders during the 1937 Massacre.[17] In this moving segment of the play, Paulino sits in a chair behind a camera set atop a tripod and reenacts his most memorable ethnographic interviews. While Paulino, behind the camera (which at the start of the play appeared hidden under the Dominican flag), assumes the role of the machete-wielders who carried out Trujillo's orders during the massacre, the multiperspective approach complicates the history of the 1937 Massacre. Paulino shares that the *perejil* story—about the "test" given to differentiate dark-skinned Dominicans from ethnic Haitians by asking the individual to pronounce the word *perejil*—was not entirely accurate, as "speaking Spanish wasn't going to save you." Moreover, the underlying narrative of the two Dominicans whom Paulino portrays hints at an offer of forgiveness for the perpetrators since they had been acting on an order they could not refuse if they wanted to live. Although the stakes and time period are different, the 2013 Tribunal Court ruling and the US diasporic reaction to the race-based ruling relates to or "replays" the same decisions Paulino references in *Eddie's Perejil*. As Reconoci.do's Ana María Belique, a Dominican of Haitian descent and one of the organization's most vocal leaders, has stated on various occasions since the 2013 ruling, "In 1937 they killed us with machetes, and now they are killing us with laws."[18] *Eddie's Perejil* is just one example of the alignment of Dominican Americans with the plight of Haitians in the Dominican Republic in regards to immigration law and of Dominican and Haitian communities in the US diaspora.

Because of the substantial response from the US diaspora to the Dominican Tribunal Court's 2013 ruling, formally identified as TC/0168/13 but referred to informally in the Dominican Republic and the Dominican diaspora as *la sentencia,* I end this chapter with a focus on two nonliterary works that exemplify digital and documentary-based activism: a Twitter-based response to TC/0168/13 from the US-based organization We Are All Dominican and the 2017 documentary *Hasta la Raíz.* These two platforms' implied linkages between Hispaniola and its US-based diaspora show that "what happens on the islands, and to U.S.-based Caribbean communities, is not contained by national boundaries but travels across the waters" (Reyes-Santos 110).

Similar to the Border of Lights virtual vigil, which seeks to connect and draw parallels between off- and on-island communities, We Are All Dominican uses the microblogging social-media platform Twitter to reach a wider audience. We Are All Dominican, "a collective of students, educators, scholars, and community members of Dominican and Haitian descent residing in New York City," campaigns for an inclusive national Dominican identity ("Vision and Mission Statement").[19] Like Border of Lights, the group claims to work in solidarity with movements led by Dominicans of Haitian descent advocating for citizenship rights in the Dominican Republic and, furthermore, "seeks to educate and activate the Dominican diaspora in order to challenge anti-Haitian and anti-Black discourses." This weighted phrase, taken directly from the mission statement, links global communities that disagree with the denial of Dominican citizenship to Dominicans of Haitian descent as dictated by the Dominican Constitutional Tribunal. The importance of the identification or classification of We Are All Dominican as "Dominican Americans and allies" speaks to a focused effort in the US diaspora to overcome and challenge racial prejudice and antiblack or anti-Haitian sentiment. While the group's Twitter platform has become a space where Dominican Americans can comment on Dominican American culture—from food to hair and beyond—the initial tweets responded directly to issues of statelessness in the Dominican Republic, often retweeting content from Reconoci.do and continuing to fight against, and raise awareness about, the October 2013 ruling. A tweet from September 23, 2016, shows a photo of protesters with Dominican flags and a cut-out poster of Sonia Pierre. The accompanying text reads: "3 years ago, DR gov created largest stateless population in Western Hemisphere. We Are All Dominican at DR consulate NYC saying basta!"[20] Cepeda and Alvarez, although not formally linked to the We Are All Dominican platform, have a a similar desire to "educate and activate" the Dominican diaspora. The pulse of social justice within the literary works of these authors is an example of the ways in which recent

Latino/a literature imagines creative ways to rethink the relationship(s) between a politics of social justice and market popularity. Raphael Dalleo and Elena Machado Sáez write that the relationship between these two factors represents "a combination that the critical reception denies by either rejecting one of these elements or articulating them as binary opposites" (3).

Literature such as the memoirs of Alvarez and Cepeda engenders "creative ways" to rethink relationships, not only between social justice and market popularity, but also between and among communities. Similarly, documentary film provides an avenue for exploring existing relationships in new, often less visible ways. *Hasta la Raíz,* directed and produced by the Venezuelan Juan Carlos González Díaz, depicts the struggle of Dominican descendants of Haitian migrant workers in the Dominican Republic. Following the path of three women to secure documentation in their birth country (the Dominican Republic), the documentary not only portrays the effects of TC/0168/13 on individuals but also follows the social movements that respond to the Dominican government's policies regarding the statelessness of thousands of Dominicans of Haitian descent, namely, the nonprofit Reconoci.do, which champions the rights of Dominicans of Haitian descent. Building on the testimonial pulse of the documentary, in December 2017 Reconoci.do published a collection of testimonies entitled *Nos cambió la vida.* The collection shares the consequences of the denationalization of Dominicans of Haitian descent brought about by the Tribunal Court's 2013 ruling. The various authors—from different geographical areas, such as El Seibo, San Pedro de Macorís, Barahona, and Santo Domingo—not only reveal their personal experiences with race-based discrimination both before and after TC/0168/13 but also divulge histories of gender violence and bullying.[21]

The testimony-based *Hasta la Raíz* and *Nos cambió la vida* do more than show how Dominican institutional policies stigmatize and disenfranchise Dominicans of Haitian descent; they also call for a global, digital public to advance an increasingly inclusive society. The screenings locations of *Hasta la Raíz* since the film's US premiere at the Dominican Film Festival in New York in July 2017 include multiple US university campuses, although according to the director, the film's target audience is, first, Dominicans of Haitian descent and, second, the Dominican public.[22] While the documentary's screenings in the United States signal a diasporic viewer base, the documentary itself withholds commentary on a global or US-centric response to TC/0168/13, focusing primarily on Dominican social movements. The metaphorical organization of *Hasta la Raíz* moves from "Las hojas," with a brief introduction to Dominican and Haitian history and the 2013 Tribunal Court decision, to "El tallo," focusing on social movements and protests in direct response to *la sentencia*. The title *Hasta la Raíz*, then, not only alludes to the similarities and differences between the Haitian ancestry of the three female protagonists but also problematizes the foregrounding and sustainment of anti-Haitian ideology in the Dominican Republic. The Dominican American and international responses to TC/0168/13 constitute a unique (and still growing and maturing) structure. Or rather, the Dominican diaspora could be classified as another "tallo," or root, in the documentary, given, for example, the impact of Dominicans living off island in Dominican politics or the historical role of the United States in the formation of Dominican racial identities. Although the root conceit that organizes *Hasta la Raíz* suggests a metaphorical plant indigenous to Hispaniola, its seeds have spread widely. US-founded groups like We Are All Dominican are just one example of a refutation of anti-Haitian ideology and a diasporic, digital response to TC/0168/13. The Dominican Americans Alvarez and Cepeda, by writing to and for an international audience and publishing memoirs with a collective pulse, in ways similar to *Hasta la Raíz* and *Nos cambió la vida* contribute to and foreground a testimonial perspective on Dominican-Haitian relations.

Dominican American "Us-moir"

Cepeda's *Bird of Paradise* and Alvarez's *A Wedding in Haiti* both speak to a diverse public. Their words reenvisioning Dominican and Haitian relations both on the island of Manhattan and on the island of Hispaniola appear destined not solely for Dominican Americans in the US diaspora but also for those residing in the Dominican Republic and Haiti. Moreover, the autobiographical works have extended meaning for an international readership that will benefit from "seeing" Haiti and Hispaniola, just as Alvarez professes her trip to Haiti allowed her to do.

I consider Cepeda's work an off-border or off-island memoir because it approaches Dominican and Haitian relations primarily from the space of New York City, marking a shift in relations as a consequence of geography. Alvarez's memoir, on the other hand, is an example of what I consider to be an on-border or on-island memoir, set on and around the Haitian-Dominican border. Like Cepeda, Vicioso marks the diasporic experience geographically. She labels her experience "the New York experience," and she describes it as "crucial" to her discovery of "Caribbean and racial identity" (264). There are regional differences in the diasporic experience of Latinos/as in the United States; figure 3 shows the intermixing of Dominican and Haitian populations in New York State. Given that the vast majority of foreign-born Dominicans in the United States live in the Northeast and more than half of all Dominican immigrants live in New York *and* that the state also is home to the second largest Haitian population (after Florida), the overlap in the Caribbean immigrant populations of Haiti and the Dominican Republic is not surprising (Grieco). While census data do not provide a "literary geography," confirming and visualizing the blended Haitian and Dominican communities in the US diaspora establishes a framework for understanding the turn of Dominican American writers toward Haiti. I consider Cepeda's memoir depicting the relationship between Haitians and Dominicans within the US diaspora here in order to better understand how and why Latino/a writers demonstrate this geographical split in literature. This fragmentation of sorts speaks to the porosity of borders and the writers' ability to imagine border spaces—physical and metaphorical, on- and off-island—as blank canvases.

The relation between Haitians and Dominicans that emerges in *Bird of Paradise* recognizes a unique definition of third space, one that does not just merge together two cultures but instead foments a racially and ethnically diverse community. Cepeda's memoir addresses the cultural collision(s) not just between the Dominican and Haitian communities but also those between Latino/a immigrants and the African American community in New York. An analysis of third space in the US diaspora, then, becomes more complex. In many ways these inherently off-island spaces by definition are also third spaces, disrupting previously established identities and forcing immigrants to renegotiate how they define themselves.

Alvarez, in *A Wedding in Haiti,* navigates Haitian-Dominican relations vis-à-vis her very own Haitian "road trip," following a route along the border and into the interior of Haiti that allows her to "see" Haiti in a new light. The author locates her 2012 memoir not only on border but entirely on island and introduces a hybrid third space that emerges as a means to articulate space that diminishes existing borders and makes possible a reconsideration of preconceptions of culture and identity, initiating "new sites of identity, and innovative sites of collaboration and contestation" (Bhabha, *Location of Culture* 1).

Although the setting of Alvarez's memoir reflects an on-border third space and Cepeda's addresses an off-border third space, it is important to remember that both Dominican American women write primarily from the United States. *Bird of Paradise* and *A Wedding in Haiti* seek to make connections, albeit connections stemming from the Dominican diaspora, that bridge relations between Dominicans and Haitians, much as *Hasta la Raíz* and the social-media platform of We Are All Dominican aim to do. The joining together of these two communities problematizes and reenvisions the past and future relationships between them. Representing the shared spaces and collaborative acts that in large part define Dominican-Haitian relations links the two memoirs as Dominican American "us-moirs."

4 Multiple Haitis

> The Haiti imagined in Cuba (or Jamaica, or Charleston, or New Orleans, or Bahia), this Caribbean or Black Atlantic, this Haiti of liberation figurative and literal—was this also Haiti's Haiti?
> —Ada Ferrer, *Freedom's Mirror*

Michel-Rolph Trouillot's article "The Odd and the Ordinary: Haiti, the Caribbean, and the World" begins by positioning Haiti on the "odd" side of the odd-ordinary binary as a means to challenge Haitian exceptionalism. Trouillot confirms Haiti's peculiarity at a superficial level, stating that "Haiti is unique. Haiti is different. Haiti is special" (3), but he protests the overemphasis on Haiti's singularity: "When we are being told over and over again that Haiti is unique, bizarre, unnatural, odd, queer, freakish, or grotesque, we are also being told, in varying degrees, that it is unnatural, erratic and therefore unexplainable" (6). Others have joined the Haitian anthropologist in his critique of a habitual classification of Haiti as out of the ordinary. The Haitian American Edwidge Danticat challenges this singular vision of Haiti in her collection of autobiographical essays, *Create Dangerously: The Immigrant Artist at Work* (2010). Danticat's essay "Another Country" describes how US journalism commonly presents Haiti as atypical. In this essay she questions why those living in the United States, for example, are unable to see the parallels between Haiti and the United States. Likewise, Gina Athena Ulysse's essay "Loving Haiti beyond the Mystique" suggests that Haiti's need for new narratives is a consequence of the country's "myriad contradictions" (95). Trouillot, Danticat, and Ulysse challenge a representation of Haiti as exceptional not by disparaging the unique facets of Haiti's history—its being, for example, the site of the first and only successful slave revolt in modern history—but by emphasizing that Haiti is multiple and exists in many spaces, including the diaspora.

Much like those by Trouillot, Danticat, and Ulysse, the portrayals of Haiti by the authors considered in this chapter go beyond narrow-minded, sometimes sensationalist conceptions of the country. The Dominican American Junot Díaz and the Puerto Rican American Daniel

José Older write Haiti from a Latino perspective; Díaz portrays Haiti as apocalyptic in his short story "Monstro" (2012), and Older considers Haiti vis-à-vis a US diasporic framework and space in his novel *Shadowshaper* (2015). My consideration of how two Latino authors (with different Hispanic Caribbean origins) portray Haiti in literature in part aims to draw ties between Haitians and their (Afro-)Latino/a neighbors within the space of the pan- and interethnic US diaspora. Scholars often exclude Haiti from modern-day understandings of Latin America even though it shares the island of Hispaniola and is geographically part of the Caribbean. Despite the linguistic and historical colonial divergences that often result in a positioning of Haiti as an aside in studies of the region, some academics have stressed the similarities between Haiti's culture and Latin American culture as well as Haiti's influence on the region, in particular with respect to Haiti's history as the first black republic in the Americas. In *Haitian Connections: Recognition after Revolution in the Atlantic World,* the historian Julia Gaffield critiques isolationist theories that claim the Atlantic World refused to interact with Haiti in the years following 1804. She instead argues that "the many and diverse connections between Haiti and the surrounding countries, colonies, and empires in the first years after the Haitian Declaration of Independence reveal that there was no straightforward or uniform response to the challenges and opportunities that Haiti afforded to foreign governments and individuals during the Age of Revolution" (182). The influence of Haitian independence, as Ada Ferrer and David Geggus further assert, reverberated widely in the neighboring countries and colonies of the new republic.

While the impacts of Haiti's independence in the Atlantic World speak to the historical connections between Haiti and Latin America, the affinities between Haiti and its neighbors also relate to the ways that some Haitian Americans self-identify today. The Haitian American scholar Ayanna Legros, for example, asserts her Afro-Latina identity as follows: "I identify as Afro-Latina because my family comes from an island in Latin America. I claim Afro-Latina identity to acknowledge the critical contributions Haiti has made throughout the region." Legros embraces her Afro-Latinidad, viewing Haiti's history as an essential part of black history in Latin America. In this she goes beyond the Harvard scholar Henry Louis Gates's inclusion of Haiti in his TV series *Black in Latin America*.[1] Gates focused one episode on Haiti and the Dominican Republic, but centered his analysis on the division between the two countries rather than their shared and interdependent history.

In *Shadowshaper,* parallels surface between diverse Caribbean communities in the US diaspora. The novel crafts a deep-rooted connection between two teenage protagonists—one Puerto Rican, the other Haitian—and also highlights the resurgence of Afro-Caribbean religions and spiritualties in the space of the United States. My analysis of this novel by a Puerto Rican American author breaks with the sustained analysis of Dominican, Dominican American, Haitian, and Haitian American texts. More than a consideration of the ways multicultural literature in the United States can model interethnic and interracial communities, an exploration of the space shared by Haitian and Puerto Rican communities in the United States in *Shadowshaper,* in addition to a continued interest in the shared space between Haitian and Dominican diasporic communities, highlights Glissant's rhizomatic understanding of community.[2] Glissant professes in *Traité du tout-monde* (1997; Treatise on the whole world) that places are by nature interrelated, suggesting that all the places in the world meet up with one another. Building on Glissant's belief that each neighborhood or community opens into or gives way to a more expansive, more inclusive environment, my analysis of *Shadowshaper* emphasizes the dynamic relations between space, place, and literature while also paving the way for a conversation about less visible US diasporic relationships. Moreover, Older's novel's interest in a literary cartography vis-à-vis the remapping of a Brooklyn community in the throes of gentrification both aligns with and expands the interest in the parallels between mapping and literature that guides chapters 1 through 3. While the present chapter, like the previous one, analyzes Latino/a texts, it also departs from a sole focus on Latino/a literature by examining two Haitian works: the Haitian Évelyne Trouillot's play *The Blue of the Island* (2012) and Haitian American Edwidge Danticat's *The Farming of Bones* (1998). Thus I will end this chapter by turning to Haiti and Dominican-Haitian relations as perceived by Haitians and Haitian Americans. Ferrer's words questioning the multiple, trans-Caribbean allusions to Haiti—"Was this also Haiti's Haiti?" (345)—are an important reminder that cross-island or cross-border currents run both ways.

For Díaz, the second Latino writer to win the Pulitzer Prize, Hispaniola's at times tragic, often corrupt colonial, revolutionary, and dictatorial history has transformed the island into the ideal setting for an apocalyptic plot in his short story "Monstro," first published in the *New Yorker.* He portrays Haiti as an apocalyptic dystopia, remarking in an interview: "So many apocalypses have already taken place on that island, including the one that gave rise to the modern world, I figured: what's one more?

If any place could take it, it would be that poor island. What sparked this story was: A couple years ago I got to thinking that our world has so many blind spots, so many places and people it intentionally doesn't want to see—if some menace began to coalesce in these spaces, our own unseeing would, in fact, blind us to the danger" (Leyshon 1–2).[3] Díaz's imagining Haiti and Hispaniola as dystopic space rivals the repeated categorization of Hispaniola as a utopia, with writers routinely honing in on the white sand beaches and the Caribbean breeze, portraying a tourist's paradise. The connection between utopia and dystopia is an unbreakable one; utopias cannot exist without their inverse. The opposition between the two coexisting and contrasting approaches to space enticed Foucault to label space as anxiety ridden: "In any case I believe that the anxiety of our era has to do fundamentally with space, no doubt a great deal more than with time" (23). While Díaz imagines Hispaniola and Haiti as dystopia in "Monstro," articulating an earlier vision of Hispaniola as utopia helps to later address the subversive elements in Díaz's representation of the island. The Dominican twentieth-century thinker Pedro Henríquez Ureña championed Hispaniola, and by extension the Americas, as utopic space.

Locating Haiti in America's Utopia

Pedro Henríquez Ureña, "America's teacher,"[4] is a pivotal figure not only in the intellectual history of the Dominican Republic but in the history of Latin America at large. Son of the Dominican politician and doctor Francisco Henríquez Carvajal and the Dominican educator and lyricist Salomé Ureña, Henríquez Ureña dedicated his intellectual life to rethinking Dominican national identity and, by extension, a Hispanic American consciousness. Henríquez Ureña's work is similar in scope to that of nineteenth-century intellectuals such as Andrés Bello, Domingo Faustino Sarmiento, and José Martí. His geographically diverse experiences—Henríquez Ureña lived in numerous Latin American countries, spending extended periods in both Mexico and Argentina—motivated his intellectual investment in the concept of Hispanic America as *magna patria,* or the Great Motherland, destined for unity and integration.[5] His vision of a *magna patria* guides his 1922 lecture "La utopía de América" (America's utopia). Henríquez Ureña first delivered the lecture in Buenos Aires at the University of La Plata alongside the Mexican thinker and politician José Vasconcelos during a visit to the Argentinian capital; his unified vision of America reflects an elitist cultural, social, and religious reality.

The Dominican intellectual's "America" aligns with the school of thought known as *americanismo*. The foundation of his utopic vision of the Americas is a cultural *mestizaje* firmly rooted in the European tradition that disenfranchises black, indigenous, and mixed-race individuals. In the chapter "La cultura y las letras coloniales" in *Obra dominicana* (Dominican work), for example, Henríquez Ureña says that Christopher Columbus's diary is the first, true expression of Dominican letters; negating indigenous populations, he heralds Columbus as the intellectual founder of the New World (204).

In Henríquez Ureña's quest to foment a critical Latin American consciousness, an "American Utopia" was one of his most passionate causes and a cultural project that guided his intellectual endeavors. In *Tracing Dominican Identity: The Writings of Pedro Henríquez Ureña*, Juan R. Valdez writes that while many studies centered on the intellectual life of Henríquez Ureña focus on his utopian project, scholars also herald Henríquez Ureña for his contributions to politics and culture as a Dominicanist, as opposed to an Americanist (17). Because of his dark skin, Henríquez Ureña's racial profile was questioned and critiqued. Valdez remarks: "Henríquez Ureña's racial profile was the object of attacks first in Mexico and later in Argentina. It must be noted that many Dominicans consider being called 'Haitian' one of the worst possible insults. Using the term 'Haitian,' his attackers questioned Henríquez Ureña's national origin and targeted his mulatto profile" (14). He was a proud Dominican who spent the majority of his adult life abroad. A long list of scholars herald Henríquez Ureña's investment in Dominican culture and nationalism,[6] but did his American utopia reflect his racially and culturally diverse homeland? As a mulatto, Henríquez Ureña endured being called "Haitian" pejoratively, but how Haitians—or any members of the African diaspora—fit into his Hispanist-rooted utopia is unclear. The 1922 lecture makes constant reference to a collective "we"—the phrases *our America* and *our utopia* pervade the lecture—but European values cloud a supposedly unified vision of America. Haiti, his beloved homeland's neighbor and a historically significant Caribbean nation, has no place within his linguistic, cultural, and racial paradigm.

Does Henríquez Ureña's Haiti, then, align or contrast with Díaz's fictional depiction of the country as an apocalyptic blind spot? For the Dominican intellectual, was Haiti a dystopic wasteland excluded from America's utopia? Regardless of the racial profiling Henríquez Ureña himself confronted abroad and the fact his father's politics briefly moved the family to Cap Haïtien, Haiti during Ulises Heureaux's presidency in the late 1880s, Haiti does appear as a blind spot in his twentieth-century utopia. Utopic projects like Henríquez Ureña's were often designed as transformative social motors, but any utopia is, by nature, unattainable. Henríquez Ureña clarified his futurist, idealist vision in his 1922 Buenos Aires lecture, stating: "Mira al pasado, y crea la historia; mira al futuro, y crea las utopías" ("La utopía"). This harmonious political project—a Dominican intellectual's visionary solution for Hispanic America in the early twentieth century—was a mirage, an ideal. A key distinction between Henríquez Ureña's American utopia and the multiple visions of Haiti examined in this chapter lies in the fact that utopia stands for imagined space. While Díaz, Older, Trouillot, and Danticat fictionally portray Haiti and its off-island intersections with other national communities, they do so by weaving the island's history into their works. In this sense, Foucault's heterotopia, or "other space," functions as a palpable, real alternative to a utopic framework, enabling a more complex and nuanced approach to third space. Describing identifiable geographical spaces—and, thus, approaching heterotopias and other flexible social space frameworks like atopias in contrast to utopias—aids in a conceptualization of space and an analysis of the fluidity of the Haitian-Dominican border in contemporary literature.

Haitian Contagion? Junot Díaz's Near-Future Epidemic

Although Díaz's two collection of short stories, *Drown* (1996) and *This Is How You Lose Her* (2012), meddle with notions of *haitianidad* as related to *dominicanidad* and toy with the classification of *Haitian* as a marker for both Haitians and Dominicans in the US diaspora, the majority of the stories take place on United States soil. For this reason, I will briefly comment on the representation of Haitians in *Drown, This Is How You Lose Her,* and Díaz's 2007 breakthrough novel, *The Brief Wondrous Life of Oscar Wao,* before turning to a more substantial analysis of the Dominican American author's science-fiction portrayal of the African diaspora vis-à-vis Haiti in "Monstro" (2012). While a transcultural mapping of sorts occurs in both collections of short stories—the narration moving from densely populated Dominican communities in New York such as Washington Heights to *la isla* for visits to relatives or vacation with a girlfriend—the narratives of both *Drown* and *This Is How You Lose Her* depict the experiences of a Dominican American male in the US diaspora. The narrator of the first story in *Drown,* "Ysrael," for example, comments on the ways his older brother mocked him: "He had about five hundred routines he liked to lay on me. Most of them had to do with my complexion, my hair, the size of my lips. It's the Haitian, he'd say to his buddies. Hey Señor Haitian, Mami found you on the border and only took you in because she felt sorry for *you*" (5). This same *tíguere* of an older brother who employs the "nickname" Haitian as an insult does not hesitate to engage in sexual relations with Haitian girls: "There was a girl he'd gone to see half-Haitian, but he ended up with her sister" (6). Both these quotes indicate the close links between Dominican and Haitian diasporic communities while also underlining the fluid racial categories shaping racial classifications specifically in the US diaspora. The appellation the narrator's brother, Rafa, uses—Señor Haitian—points to the fusion of the two sides of the border and also the collision of different conceptions of race in light of unique historical and cultural factors in both the Dominican Republic and United States. The description of the narrator's Haitian-like features illuminates, by placing an emphasis on physical qualities, the African ancestry of Dominicans. The fact that Rafa boasts to his brother about his sexual escapades with a "half-Haitian" is also significant, as it exemplifies the continued intermixing of two nationalities at times presented as antithetical even in the diaspora. Horn analyzes in detail the ramifications of Díaz's toying with the vestiges of Dominican masculinity, showing how he posits "Dominican" gender patterns as backward and "American" patterns as modern, disavowing "how both gender inequalities remain alive and well in the United States and how historically these formations have never been as separate as they now appear to U.S. mainstream critics and readers" (138).

This Is How You Lose Her also offers readers a vivid portrayal of the commonplace whitewashing by Afro-Dominicans in the diaspora. In the story "Invierno," Yunior—a repeat narrator from Díaz's earlier works—compares himself with his brother, focusing on his phenotypical traits. He references the fixed biological markers that often are the outward pillars of racism: "My hair still had enough of the African to condemn me to endless combings and out-of-this-world haircuts" (126). Robbing Yunior of the chance to own or show pride in his African roots, his father eventually forces him to shave his head. Yunior's bald head is representative of the contrast between *pelo bueno* and *pelo malo* typical in the Dominican Republic. This negation of blackness repeats throughout the collection, signaling the US diaspora as a heterotopic space where Otherness prevails, a space where immigrants are (dis)placed in situations in which they do not and cannot conform to the norms.

Díaz's *The Brief Wondrous Life of Oscar Wao* more explicitly expands the geographical center of its narrative to the Dominican Republic by directly confronting the interstices of the *trujillato* and its paternalistic, authoritative discourse, a discourse that traditionally associates blackness with Haitians. Díaz's reinterpretation of Hispaniola's history takes root in the Trujillo regime, and the novel responds to the *fukú* endured over three generations by the Cabral de León family, to which Oscar Wao belongs.[7] There is a palpable, albeit relatively fleeting mention of the 1937 Massacre in *Oscar Wao;* the reality of the horrifying event pervades the writing itself, constantly meriting mention in both footnotes and text. The massacre is mentioned in three footnotes (24, 25, and 26) and is frequently alluded to in the text. Such references are read by Díaz as "blank pages," or rather, as attempts to fill in historical gaps (119). Díaz expands on the notion of such historical black holes or voids in an interview: "If the novel was able to say the things that it does not, at the heart of the novel [*Oscar Wao*] the reader would immediately encounter the genocide of the twentieth century against the Haitians and Haitians of Dominican descent, but on the surface level the reader can also find in the novel the genocide of the Dominican Republic, the Caribbean, and of the New World. The book [*Oscar Wao*] approaches this theme indirectly, because the New World approaches it indirectly" (De Maeseneer, *Encuentro* 117, my translation). Another indirect refutation of and response to the Haitian Massacre in *Oscar Wao* is the recurring mention of a faceless figure. This "man without a face" haunts the novel, taking part in evil acts. When Oscar is dragged to the cane fields outside Santo Domingo by two Dominican men who want him dead, or at the least severely injured, he sees this mysterious figure: "They had guns! He [Oscar] stared into the night, hoping that maybe there would be some US Marines out for a stroll, but there was only a lone man sitting in his rocking chair out in front of his ruined house and for a moment Oscar could have sworn the dude had no face, but then the killers got back into the car and drove" (298). This allusion serves as a harrowing reminder of the anonymous victims of Trujillo. It can also be read as a subtle reference to the 1937 Massacre, as laborers, both Haitian and Haitian Dominican, were brutally killed with machetes. Many reports mentioned the disfigurement of victims' faces and bodies.[8]

The recurring inclusion of the faceless man in Diaz's work mirrors speculative fiction, in which a given text reveals supernatural or imagined elements. The "man without a face" is one of *Oscar Wao*'s many connections to sf.[9] However, *Oscar Wao* is not an sf novel; instead it is *about* sf. The critics T. S. Miller and María del Pilar Blanco suggest reading the sf genre in the novel as an extended metaphor, sf functioning as a lens through which to see the world and the manner in which Oscar Wao navigates the US diaspora, framing "his experience in the terms of genre fiction" (Miller 93). Even the historical framing of the novel as related to the Trujillo regime can be made relatable by sf pop-culture references, with Trujillo himself compared to the antagonist Sauron in *The Lord of the Rings*. Díaz, via myriad allusions to sf popular culture, manipulates the sf canon as a means to alternatively portray the Caribbean diaspora. Within this fantastical (diasporic) world vision, Hispaniola, notably the Dominican Republic, stands for ground zero, a space where fantastical elements can abound. The primary narrator of *Oscar Wao*, Yunior, situates the (cursed) story of the Cabral de León family within the aforementioned *fukú* and in doing so expresses the relation of Hispaniola to the sf genre. Yunior shares with readers Oscar's sf vision of the Dominican Republic: "What more sci-fi than Santo Domingo? What more fantasy than the Antilles?" (6). The sf nature of the island is reiterated in a footnote in which the narrator prods, "Who more sci-fi than us?" (21n6). The subjective designation of Hispaniola as the ideal site for the "perfect disaster" repeats in Díaz's "Monstro," published in the first issue of the *New Yorker* dedicated to science fiction, in 2012.[10] While "Monstro" instead plots *Haiti* as ground zero, both *Oscar Wao* and "Monstro" successfully insert sf into Antillean intellectual discourse and offer the speculative genre as a new, unique way to experience the Antillean (and African) diaspora.

If one considers a frontier or borderland metaphor ingrained in both *Oscar Wao* and "Monstro," Díaz's novel "about sf" centers on the border(s) between the United States and the Dominican Republic, whereas "Monstro," a genuine sf narrative, shifts toward a zombie-laden examination of the border(s) between Haiti and the Dominican Republic as well as between Haiti and the world.[11] Set in the near future, "Monstro" is about an epidemic in which the first sites of infection are Haiti's capital and surrounding areas. From the outset the story asserts the darkening effect of the disease, whose symptoms are described as "black pustules" of "black mold-fungus": "A disease that could make a Haitian blacker? It was the joke of the year." "Monstro," however, does not tell a linear tale of the Haitian-rooted zombie epidemic; instead the storyline skips from the narrator's knowledge of the rapidly mutating virus to his lustful obsession with a Dominican girl, Mysty, whom his dying mother refers to as "culo falso." The narrator, a Dominican American Brown University student who spends his summer in Santo Domingo, becomes increasingly absorbed in his friendship with Brown classmate and Dominican American heir to his father's fortune, Alex, and his almost-friend and want-to-be girlfriend, Mysty. As "Monstro" ends, the two storylines are on the cusp of colliding as the narrator, Alex, and Mysty head for the border to assess the disease called "La Negrura" (The Blackness). For Díaz, "Monstro" is a literary consequence of Haiti's pattern of adversity, showcasing how the country became the ideal setting for an apocalyptic plot. In the aforementioned interview Díaz labels Haiti and places like it as "blind spots," or sites that people intentionally look away from or block from view. Accepting Haiti and Hispaniola as a "blind spot" aligns the island with Foucault's notion of a heterotopic space, a space that is disturbing, transforming, contradictory, and easily forgotten. Building upon Foucault's structuralism paradigm, his article "Of Other Spaces" regards the present and future as "epoch[s] of space" or "epoch[s] of juxtaposition," in which the relation between time and history makes possible the delineation of different types of heterotopic spaces (22). Related to "Monstro"'s apocalyptic story plot, the first distinction of Foucault's heterotopology is a "crisis heterotopia." A crisis heterotopia is a site defined by a state of crisis, a space forbidden to those who have no relation to it, a "blind spot" or void for those whose lives are not rooted in the crises of that space.

Just as *Oscar Wao* merits classification as a novel *about* science fiction but is not itself a science fiction novel, the story "Monstro" is *about* Haiti but was not written from Haiti nor is it set in Haiti. The narrator instead approaches a plague-stricken Haiti from the perspective of a Dominican American young adult. From the beginning, the narrator makes clear that he self-identifies as one of the "pro-Haitian domos," unlike his *tíos,* who suggested at the onset of the disease that "someone needs to drop a bomb on these people." The reason behind the pointed, purposeful *mirada* toward Haiti that forms the core of "Monstro" can be partly assessed by considering Díaz's reflective essay written in the wake of the 2010 Haitian earthquake. Titled "Apocalypse," the essay offers the reader a lesson on what the 7.0-magnitude earthquake revealed about Haiti, and by extension about the modern world. Díaz's meditative response to the 2010 disaster explores poverty, poor political and structural infrastructure, and global inequality and capitalism. Díaz positions darkness as metaphor to attempt to grapple with social (as opposed to natural) disasters: "If, as Roethke writes, 'in a dark time, the eye begins to see,' apocalypse is a darkness that gives us light." He notes that this "peering into darkness" is not an easy task. A notion of darkness and the positioning of blackness or darkness as cultural and social metaphor—the narrator of "Monstro" originally labeling the Haitian plague "La Negrura"—guides Díaz's sf story.

At first mention in "Monstro," La Negrura appears to be termed a *disease*. In later textual references to the mysterious, new "disease," however, it is called an "infection," "a slow leprous spread," "zoonotics," and a "plague." The wide discrepancy between these terms perhaps relates to the disease's unique characteristics and its apparent ability to morph from a noninfectious disease into one that has infected nearly the entire Haitian population.[12] *Zoonotics,* for example, refers to noncontagious diseases spread between animals and people, such as dengue and zika, both common to the Caribbean region. Leprosy, on the other hand, is a bacterial and infectious disease that spreads by skin-to-skin contact. Further, *plague* in "Monstro" indicates yet another infectious disease, an epidemic disease spread by indirect contact or airborne transmission. Regardless of the terminology, with each subsequent textual reference in "Monstro," La Negrura becomes increasingly more contagious and aggressive. The sf literary critic Isiah Lavender posits contagion as metaphor. According to Lavender, racism, like infectious diseases, "morph[s] into a different structure with all the same signs, including social visibility and the fear of living with racial difference" (*Black and Brown* 119).[13] Not unlike contagious diseases, racist thinking can be transmissible when a white individual comes into (physical) contact with a nonwhite; it is an ideological contagion that confirms mythical fears about blackness. As Lavender writes, sf contagion narratives often themselves function as contagions, as literature can spread racist ideology. Díaz's desire when he crafted "Monstro," as Sarah Quesada notes, was for readers to see and perceive blackness in the same way as whiteness, "not as a complex or a condition" (297). "Monstro" forces the reader to confront racism, namely, the patriarchal Dominican national ideology that positions whiteness and Hispanicism in stark opposition to blackness and Haitianism. Díaz's story sarcastically toys with the ironic reality of blackness as a condition, since the disease at first appears to prey on the weakest links in a metaphorical and social sense—"It seemed to hit only the sickest of the sick"—but also on the "blackest" or "darkest" links: La Negrura as "disease," "zootonic," or "plague" racially tags its "viktims."

The term *viktims,* for those who have succumbed to the constantly evolving disease, references the Kreyòl translation of *victim.* Throughout the story, this term is continuously used to label the possessed and diseased Haitians. The use of a Kreyòl word for victims to refer to the infected population anchors La Negrura to Haiti not only geographically but also linguistically. While the use of this word speaks to the majority language of the country and also subtly critiques French as the "official language," suggesting that the European language is a product of colonization, the zombification of the "viktims" at the story's end relates specifically to Haiti and its vodou tradition. Quesada posits the zombies in "Monstro" as a "trans-American phenomenon" and a "byproduct of slave-trade commerce" (295). The emergence of zombies linked to the plantation system presumes the soulless beings as a consequence of the trans-American slave trade, transformed into zombies against their will, often to maintain social order within the plantation system and as a warning and threat to other slaves. In recent decades Hollywood has popularized the vision of reanimated corpses through horror films and recent blockbuster films such as *World War Z* and *28 Days Later* or AMC's hit series *The Walking Dead*. Despite American popular culture's attempt, conscious or not, to whitewash the origins of zombies and the historical roots of the zombie figure, "Monstro" historically references the possessed souls of Haitian slaves, traditionally thought to occur to those who committed suicide while working on the plantation. The act of committing suicide forbade the slaves from returning to Africa in their afterlife, or *lan guinée*. Reading the zombie figure as symbol or metaphor, albeit fragmented, reappropriated, and often misinterpreted, allows readers to explore and problematize the disfiguration of black bodies. The manifestation of zombies in "Monstro" critiques a system of global capitalism in which the citizens and residents of impoverished, third-world countries still undergo a disembodiment of sorts; they are modern-day slaves in a system in which they have no control or authority.

Whereas the representation of zombie-like "viktims" in "Monstro" inherently references the boundaries between the living and the dead, the overall story insists on the constant utilization of the term *border* to refer to both a physical and a geographical demarcation between "us" (the narrator and his friends in the Dominican Republic) and "them" (the infected Haitians). The constant allusion to borders in the story also serves as a foundation on which to dissect the metaphorical boundaries that bind social disasters together on a global scale. The notion of boundaries and borders manifests from the outset; at first onlookers discard La Negrura as a possible international threat because it remains contained within a specific geographical zone and only Haitians appear susceptible. Toward the end of the story, though, the disease's initial "respect" of geopolitical borders cedes: "The blast seemed to have a boner for fusion, respected no kind of boundaries." With this shift, the epidemic morphs into something uncontrollable and undiagnosable: a cohort of World Health Organization doctors enter the quarantine zone and never exit, and unexplained killings and violence begin to erupt within the quarantine zones and in the surrounding areas. As senseless violence ensues, the intensifying situation in Haiti finally merits the attention of what Díaz labels the "Great Powers" and prompts immediate action, including the closing of borders between the two nations of Hispaniola: "The entire country of Haiti was placed under quarantine. All flights in and out cancelled. The border with the D.R. sealed." In Díaz's near-future sf story, the past and present states of the border represent what the border theorist Norma Iglesias calls "floating borders," borders with no fixed significance. Thus, prior to the fictionalized outbreak of La Negrura in Haiti, there were no fixed categories along the border, and thus border spaces were, on a social level, spaces of cultural hybridity. Díaz's apocalyptic, zombie-creating "black mold-fungus" emerges as a concrete hindrance to border porosity on the island of Hispaniola.

Díaz's 2012 reference to a sealed border between the Dominican Republic and Haiti can be read as a precursor to the October 2013 Tribunal Court ruling and the shift in immigration policies in the Dominican Republic, directly targeting generations of Haitian migrants. Other moments in the story also can be read in relation to *la sentencia*. The beginning of "Monstro," for example, describes the early onset of the mysterious disease, and more specifically the moment when those infected individuals in the quarantine zones began to resort to violent acts: "The riots were beginning in the camps and the Haitians in the D.R. were getting deported over a freckle." The sarcastic tone implicit in the idea of an individual being "deported over a freckle" responds to the reality of racial profiling in current immigration policies in the Dominican Republic. At military checkpoints on established roadways in the Dominican Republic—checkpoints that increase in number closer to the border—random reviews of passersby's documentation occur. Buses leaving the border regions (often destined for interior cities of the Dominican Republic such as Santiago) with greater numbers of Haitians and Dominicans of Haitian descent are routinely stopped at these checkpoints. In the Dominican border towns of Pedernales and Dajabón border-patrol agents leisurely cruise the city limits in pick-up trucks and drive anyone profiled as Haitian who is not carrying documentation back to the border for processing. Toward the end of "Monstro," after the "detonation event" occurs, those off island claim that "Port-au-Prince had been destroyed, that Haiti had been destroyed, that thirteen million screaming Haitian refugees were threatening the borders, that Dominican military units had been authorized to meet the *invaders*—the term the gov was now using—with ultimate force" (my emphasis). The term *invaders* here is similar to *in transit,* the crux of the 2013 ruling.[14] Both terms profile transient or undocumented populations and attempt to pinpoint individuals who are in a country illegally. Whereas Díaz's "Monstro" and his postearthquake essay "Apocalypse" both end on a hopeful tone, "Apocalypse" postulates that despite the conflicted history between the Dominican Republic and Haiti, a "shocking reversal of decades of toxic enmity" occurred in the immediate wake of the January 12 earthquake, when "DR was first to come to Haiti's aid."[15] While both the fictional sf story "Monstro" and the nonfictional essay "Apocalypse" offer endings that instill hope, they also serve as wake-up calls for a global audience.

The 2013 Tribunal Court ruling in the Dominican Republic, just three years after the 2010 earthquake and less than a year after the publication of "Monstro," overshadows the collaboration and fraternity that define the relationship between the two countries that make up Hispaniola. The international public outcry following the 2013 decision led to an onslaught from news sources accentuating antithetical, even hostile Haitian-Dominican relations. At the same time, as evidenced by the work of organizations like Reconoci.do and We Are All Dominican, the ruling and its aftermath offer an opportunity for voices on and off the island to challenge the colonial and dictatorial effects of racial discourse both in the Dominican Republic and in the Dominican diaspora. Alanna Lockward writes that there are "reasons to celebrate the TC" (259), suggesting that the consequences of the ruling are not exclusively negative nor have they functioned solely as a hindrance to transnational relations in the Dominican Republic. While Lockward recognizes that academics in the Dominican diaspora have used the ruling as an impetus to form initiatives and organizations that work against the racist vestiges of the Dominican Tribunal Court, she also notes that TC/0168/13 affected her on a personal level, increasing her own feelings of Dominican patriotism: "Desde el TC me solidarizo como nunca con la herencia de esta nacionalidad tan estudiada" (258).

As Quesada notes, "catastrophe stories" like "Monstro" "are meant to inspire people to action" (314). The political pulse of sf, in the context of "Monstro," encourages readers to interpret the zombie-like "viktims" as "both a haunting reminder of our past and a steadfast warning for our future" (314). But this call to activism also problematizes the classification of the narrator and others on the island during the detonation as "time witnesses." The imposed label implicates those on the island, including the narrator, as inactive passersby and mere witnesses to a catastrophic event of global impact. The fictional residents of Hispaniola in Díaz's short story are caught in a specific moment in time and are products of a near-future society in a state of chaos. The fragmentation and distortion of time that guides the sf story, illustrated by the reference to those on the island during the detonation as "time witnesses," aligns "Monstro" with an alternative to the aforementioned social spaces, such as heterotopia or utopia. Richard Robinson instead proposes the term *atopia* for the fragmented, distorted "social spacetime" of postmodernity. Robinson writes that the term *atopia* "suggests an anomalous nowhere space, which does exist, but which evades the taxonomising language of sovereign spatial histories" (6–7). The delineation of atopic spaces confirms that the contemporary realities of "social spacetime" (disoriented and greatly impacted by the effects of processes such as immigration, social and economic inequality, and border disagreements) have created the need for a term that responds to and works within the fragmentation of our contemporary social realities. The model atopia can be defined as the postmodern metropolis, "where the extreme deformation of the social spacetime has gone so far as to generate the imaginary collapse of all distinctions into one impossible distorted continuum" (Gomel 21). In reference to the detonation at the end of "Monstro," Hispaniola is a site no longer adequately described as dystopic. *Dystopia* is a totalizing term that does not address the hybrid nature of borders or an island split into two countries. The term *atopia* better describes Hispaniola in the story's final moments. The use of *atopia* to describe Díaz's vision of Hispaniola in "Monstro" construes the Dominican Republic and Haiti as spaces marked by social fractures and aligns with his argument that the 2010 Haitian earthquake was not a natural disaster but a social disaster.[16] Similarly, *atopia*—"nowhere space"—recalls Díaz's classification of Haiti as a "blind spot," a space people don't want to see: "For most people Haiti has never been more than a blip on a map, a faint disturbance in the force so far removed that what happened there might as well have been happening on another planet" ("Monstro").

Brooklyn as *Kalfou:* Daniel José Older's Urban Fantasy

Like "Monstro," Older's novel *Shadowshaper* fits the sf genre tag. The novel is not set on the geopolitical Dominican-Haitian border but instead centers on the metaphorical border(s) between (Afro-)Latino/a communities in the US diaspora. Exploring the interethnicity of New York City, *Shadowshaper* puts diverse national groups into conversation with one another and draws connections between Caribbean communities other than Haiti and the Dominican Republic in the US diaspora. While the immigratory experience and reality of Dominicans in Puerto Rico and Haitians in the Dominican Republic or the intersections between Puerto Ricans and Dominicans or between Haitians and Dominicans in the US diaspora continue to be of interest to scholars writing on contemporary Caribbean transnational relationships, the solidarities and liaisons between Haiti and the Hispanic Caribbean, in addition to Haiti's connection with its eastern neighbor, also deserve attention. The mulatto Masonic leader of the late nineteenth century, Ramón Emeterio Betances, championed trans-Antillean coalitions with a concerted focus on the social, political, and ideological implications of the events of the Haitian Revolution. Born to Dominican parents in Puerto Rico, Betances identified himself through his writing as an ally of both Haiti and the Dominican Republic, as Jossianna Arroyo asserts in *Writing Secrecy in Caribbean Freemasonry*. For Betances, a radical supporter of Puerto Rico's independence, Haiti's history offered a lesson and model of constitutional and revolutionary history for the Spanish Caribbean. Within Betances's Antillean discursive framework "the Haitian Revolution—feared and erased by most Creole elites in Cuba, Puerto Rico, the Dominican Republic, Venezuela, Colombia, and Brazil—was at the center of this social imaginary" (Arroyo 90). Betances's early works, outlining the central role the events of the Haitian Revolution played in social and political spheres in the Caribbean region and, more broadly, the transnational ties between Haiti and the Hispanic Caribbean, provide a nineteenth-century model of the Antillean linkages between Puerto Rico and Haiti, two communities that Older's *Shadowshaper* also puts into conversation in the contemporary US diaspora.[17]

Beyond the classification as sf, Older's *New York Times* bestseller can be aptly described as young adult (YA) fiction, Afro-Latino/a fantasy, Afrofuturist, and magical realism. The author roots his 2015 novel, with a sequel titled *Shadowhouse Fall* (2017), in the Afro-syncretic practice of shadowshaping. Described in the novel by a shadowshaper as "working with spirits. . . . Some of 'em are the ancestors of us shadowshapers, some are just other folks that passed on and then became spirits. But they're like our protectors, our friends even" (62–63), shadowshaping ties the novel to fantasy or sf, and specifically to Afrofuturism. Afrofuturists traditionally move away from cultural and/or historical recovery and "turn the critical postcolonial gaze toward the future" (Rivera 159). As Lysa M. Rivera asserts, while some Afrofuturist predecessors elected to return to the past in order to (re)write African diasporic experiences, "Afrofuturists use speculative fiction to bring 'black' to the future" (159).[18] Older's *Shadowshaper*, while relying heavily on the importance of ancestry and cultural tradition, envisions a modern or near-future urban landscape in which diverse characters band together to create their own "Universopolis." The term *Universopolis* references José Vasconcelos's foundational *La raza cósmica,* in which the Mexican intellectual campaigns for a superior race founded on the basis of *mestizaje*. His mixed-race utopic vision for the future, written in the wake of the Mexican Revolution, espouses a racial transnational identity meant to unite Latin Americans via the emergence of what Vasconcelos considers a "fifth race." The fictional city Vasconcelos engenders in his ideological essay, Universopolis, becomes a model urban space for racial harmony. Vasconcelos's imagined metropolis borders the Amazon region—"the richest place in the world with treasures of all kinds" (35)—and it is here that he imagines racial synthesis and harmony unfurling. Set in Brooklyn, Older's *Shadowshaper* represents, in a different way, a utopic urbanscape and a signpost for multiracial communities and cultural syncretism.

Situated in the Bedford-Stuyvesant (Bed-Stuy) neighborhood of Brooklyn, *Shadowshaper* boasts a teenage Puerto Rican protagonist named Sierra Santiago. The omniscient narrator introduces Sierra as an artist whose talents are compromised by a threat to the shadowshaping community, to which she is barred entrance until the world of shadowshaping finds itself in grave danger. Sierra, together with her friends and her brother, challenges the threat against the shawdowshaping tradition by rushing to uncover a secret that not only destroys the energy of the spirits with whom shadowshapers connect but also desolates and diminishes the Brooklyn murals that serve as catalysts for the living to connect with the spirit realm. The novel portrays a diverse, inclusive realistic future, one that expands well beyond the traditionally whitewashed genre of science fiction.[19] A constant exploration of the relationship between ancestral lineage and the connections between the living and the dead ground the novel, which is rooted in Afro-Caribbean tradition and spirituality. The true "battle" of *Shadowshaper,* nevertheless, is not limited to the shadowshaping community. Instead, the novel emphasizes modern society's battles against racist ideologies.

Antiracist discourses pervade *Shadowshaper*. The protagonist, Sierra, fights against colorist narratives on a personal level as the "negrita" of her family. Sierra's Tía Rosa, whose "off-hand bigotry" (78) Sierra has attempted to tune out throughout her life, warns her niece about dating a Haitian: "'Oh, Sierra, m'ija, what are we going to do with you. Is he, you know . . .' 'If he's darker than the bottom of your foot, he's no good for you'" (77). Tía Rosa prefaces her racist proverb by saying that she is simply repeating what her old Tía Virginia used to say, implying that racism is passed down through generations. Following the discussion with her Tía Rosa, Sierra remembers all the "stupid comments" she has tried to deflect over the years about her *"wild, nappy* hair" and her skin tone (78). The narrator reveals that "the mirror had never been a comfortable place for Sierra" (78) as the protagonist recalls the way she described herself once to someone in an online chatroom, typing that her skin was "the color of coffee with not enough milk" (79). The words *not enough* resonate uncomfortably with Sierra, "as if imprinted in her forehead: *not enough*" (80). The doubts about being "not enough" connect the protagonist to a wider Latino/a experience and a recurring, often binary theme of not speaking Spanish or English enough, not being black or white enough, and so on. Accentuating this "truth" for Sierra, related to her own self-doubt and feelings of racial inadequacy, the novel also focuses intentionally on certain "truths," or social and cultural realities, confronting contemporary Brooklyn, such as police violence and gentrification. As the novel progresses, Sierra's entrance into the world of shadowshaping and her newfound connection to her ancestors empower her as an Afro–Puerto Rican woman. Through her romantic relationship with Robbie, a teenage Haitian shadowshaper and Sierra's love interest, *Shadowshaper* charts clear liaisons between Haiti and Puerto Rico in the space of the US diaspora, referencing commonalities from the indigenous populations to music and Afro-Caribbean spiritualties.

Robbie is marked from the beginning of the novel as Other within Sierra's Brooklyn bubble, which the reader assumes to be composed of her mostly Puerto Rican friends and family. While the majority of Sierra's friends are not tagged racially or ethnically, Robbie stands for Haitian and African in *Shadowshaper*. The first mention of Robbie is from the mouth of Sierra's bedridden Abuelo Lázaro, who has recently suffered a stroke. Between breaths he tells his granddaughter that the shadowshapers (about whom Sierra knows nothing at the time) are in danger:

> "The boy Robbie will help you. Ask him for help, Sierra. You need help. I can't . . . It's too late." He nodded his head, eyes closing again. "No puedo, m'ija. No puedo."
>
> "Robbie from school?" Sierra said. "Abuelo, how do you even know him?" Robbie was a tall Haitian kid with long locks who had shown up midyear with a goofy grin and wild drawings covering every surface of his clothes, his backpack, his desk. If Sierra had been the kind of girl who gave a damn about boys and their cuteness, Robbie the Walking Mural would find himself somewhere on her top-ten list. (8–9)

This initial description of Robbie immediately marks him as Haitian but also as an artist and someone to whom Sierra is physically attracted. Later the same day, Sierra attends a party with her (Puerto Rican) friends and asks if anyone has seen Robbie. Her friend's reply once again marks Robbie ethnically: "You mean the Cartoon-Covered Haitian Sensation?" (14). Sierra, although drawn to the "Haitian sensation" because of their shared artistic talent, does not completely disagree, assenting, "Robbie has always seemed a little different" (16). Although it is Robbie who introduces Sierra to shadowshaping and helps her hone her skills, it is vital to explore whether the novel racially inscribes this "difference." While the novel's portrayal of Robbie does outwardly mark him as Haitian and as a racial Other, his role is to educate and draw transnational ties between Afro-Caribbean communities, thus diversifying the increasingly gentrified urban space in which the novel is set.

A popular-culture connection to the novel's development of shadowshaping as an art form—Sierra and Robbie first connect through their graffiti-style artistic skills, and the novel opens with Sierra painting a sprawling dragon on the side of a new building that remains vacant, abandoned by money-hungry developers—points to the late Haitian–Puerto Rican American artist and social activist Jean-Michel Basquiat. Known for his neo-expressionist contemporary art, Basquiat made headlines in 2013, when the American rapper Jay Z bought one of his paintings for a reported $4.5 million, and more recently when one of his paintings sold for $110.5 million, the highest selling price ever for an American painting (Boakye). The Brooklyn-born Basquiat's style, with roots in the New York punk scene, eventually found a commercial audience. Beyond his largely posthumous success in the global art market, The New York–based writer and activist Chaédria LaBouvier, referencing the fatal police beating in 1983 of the black artist Michael Stewart, explains the importance of Basquiat's work for the movement against police brutality and the larger Black Lives Matter movement of the early 1980s: "I think Basquiat was aware that this was not just about Michael Stewart or even him, but that there is a history of state violence against the black body." The parallels between Basquiat's art and his social activism mirror the prominent dialogue emerging in Older's *Shadowshaper,* with its social critiques of police brutality and gentrification. Likewise, the New Yorker Basquiat's Haitian and Puerto Rican heritage offers an interesting parallel to the novel's focus on the nexus between Haitian and Puerto Rican communities.

Early in the novel, when Robbie and Sierra first go out together, Robbie takes Sierra to a Haitian music club in Brooklyn. The club, described as run-down but very much alive with music and art (the murals on the wall painted by Robbie himself), is called Club Kalfour. *Kalfour* is never translated in *Shadowshaper*, but in Haitian Kreyòl *kalfour* or *kalfou* loosely translated means "crossroads." Once inside the club, Sierra hears the music and tells Robbie "I don't dance Haitian" (95). Robbie replies by asking her if she can dance salsa, and Sierra agrees to dance. On the dance floor Sierra then proclaims, "It's salsa!" While the musical genre is not named in the novel, it is likely *kompa* or *konpa*, a Haitian musical genre considered similar to a modern merengue or salsa, typical of the Caribbean region. Robbie, confirming that salsa and *kompa* are not the same, responds, "Not exactly, but close enough" (96). This conversation between Robbie and Sierra emphasizes cross-cultural, transnational connections. Sierra's recognition of music she associates with her Puerto Rican, Afro-Caribbean heritage—salsa—in the *kompa* rhythm and dance steps makes possible a reconceptualization of the Caribbean diaspora and the inherent crossover between cultures. While the "fragmentation produced by imperial competition and rivalry during the colonial transaction has left contemporary Caribbean people with a region made up of societies still existing within political, existential, linguistic, and ethnonational borders" (Torres-Saillant, "Hispanic Caribbean Question" 33), the US diaspora makes it possible to envision a more expansive Caribbean "archipelago" and a more global notion of the Caribbean region. The name of the club where this conversation occurs, Kalfour, merits further attention, as the concept of *kalfou*, or "crossroads," is one central to vodou, traditionally referring to the intersection between the living and the dead. Madison Smartt Bell explains the notion of *kalfou* in the following way: "Quantities of time and distance in Haiti are more likely to be recognized and understood in terms of intersections, rather than the lines between them. Historically, the island of Hispaniola is a tremendously important *kalfou*—the crossroads where Europeans, Native Americans, and Africans come together for the first time" (6). Older's Brooklyn can also be interpreted as a *kalfou* of sorts, a (diasporic) cultural crossroads.

Another passage in *Shadowshaper* signaling *kalfou* in a broad sense centers on Sierra's discovery of Robbie's network of tattoos. While observing the tattoos that cover Robbie's body, Sierra points to a grim-faced "Indian" that Robbie instead identifies to Sierra as "Taíno," sharing that "Haiti had Taínos, too" (125–26). Next, Sierra notices "an angry African," and Robbie admits that this body art is generic, since he did not know the tribe from which "his people" hailed. This conversation spurs Robbie to proclaim that his tattoos are his "most sacred mural," his "personal source of power—ancestry" (126).[20] This conversation is educational: Robbie teaches Sierra (and by extension the reader) that Taíno Indians were also indigenous to Haiti, and not just to what is today the Dominican Republic or Puerto Rico. Moreover, the conversation's final nod toward the power of ancestry stresses the significance of ancestral lineage for Sierra too. The novel ends with her discovery that Lucera, the authoritative figure of the shadowshaping world, is her maternal grandmother. Without outwardly naming or referencing *kalfou,* this female figure—whom Sierra knew previously as her Mama Carmen—foregrounds *kalfou* as a guiding concept in *Shadowshaper* when she describes the essence of the Afro-Caribbean practice to her granddaughter: "The true source of shadowshaper magic is in that connection, community, Sierra. We are interdependent" (220).

The relevance of ancestry and community in *Shadowshaper* aligns with the author's public comments on the power of community, and more specifically the power of diverse community. While the interracial, cross-cultural romantic relationship between a Haitian, Robbie, and a Puerto Rican, Sierra, is one example of Older's literary portrayal of a diverse community, Older's comment in an interview that "fantasy is *supposed to be* 'apolitical'—which really means 'toeing the line of mainstream white culture'" is revealing ("Q&A," my emphasis). Noting that fantasy and sf novels are "supposed to be" apolitical, Older drives home the point that there *is* no apolitical book. Instead, fantasy in particular is a "deeply political genre. It's been entrenched in white power, colonialism, and defending this idea of empire instead of telling counter-narratives" ("Q&A").[21] *Shadowshaper* crafts a counternarrative and offers readers a new way to interpret a story and thus visualize the relationships between diverse populations and between and within communities. The syncretic nature of the novel—the Afro-Caribbean religions referenced span Santería, Candomblé, and Lucumí—allows a complicated, nuanced story of teenagers resisting the "norm" and persevering in an increasingly gentrified Brooklyn, where oppression and racism have become the status quo. *Shadowshaper* merits classification as a fantastical story that also confronts real-world issues that readers, especially teens, face on a daily basis.

Moreover, Older connects with his majority millennial readership through his active, public Twitter account and blog, in this way emphasizing the myriad manifestations of culture—from music to literature to a tweet—and encouraging the next generation of diverse writers to push back against a publishing industry that may not always find their perspective or story "relatable." Older attributed recent positive changes in the publishing industry to the rise of social media: "Before, we were prey to those headlines. Now, we can post the headlines" ("Q&A"). Although he does not directly reference the apparent whitewashing of the US publishing industry, the critic Ilan Stavans discusses the process of "mainstreaming" that took place two decades prior to Older in *The Hispanic Condition* (1995), observing that the "new generation uses 'mass media,' the enemy's tools, to infiltrate the system and to promote a revaluation of all things Hispanic" (13). Older "infiltrates the system" not only by utilizing digital tools to engage with a wider public via informal social-media platforms and blogging but also by introducing multi-ethnic, multiracial characters, which enable him to establish a diasporic *kalfou* in his young-adult sf *Shadowshaper*.[22]

Shades of Blue: Haitian and Haitian American Trans-Island Perspectives

Gina Athena Ulysse's *Why Haiti Needs New Narratives: A Post-Quake Chronicle* (2015) begins by delineating what she describes as "two Haitis." Ulysse explains her binary approach to Haiti on the first pages of the book's introduction, "Negotiating My Haiti(s)": "There was the one [Haiti] that, due to migration, was being re-created in the diaspora, and the one in the public sphere that continually clashes with the one in my memory" (xviii). The historian Robin D. G. Kelley also emphasizes the duality of Haiti but differentiates between Haiti as victim and Haiti as triumphant republic:

> There is Haiti the victim, the "broken nation," the failed state, the human tragedy, the basket case. Depending on one's political perspective, Haiti the victim was either undermined by its own immutable backwardness, or destroyed by imperial invasion, occupation, blockades, debt slavery, and U.S.-backed puppet regimes. The other Haiti, of course, is the Haiti of James's magisterial *The Black Jacobins*. This is the Haiti that led the only successful slave revolt in the modern world; the Haiti that showed France and all other incipient bourgeois democracies the meaning of liberty; the Haiti whose African armies defeated every major European power that tried to restore her *ancien régime;* the Haiti that inspired revolutions for freedom and independence throughout the Western Hemisphere. (xiii)

While the diverse representations, literary and otherwise, of Haitians and Haitian Americans add to these dual or multiple perspectives of Haiti, the Dominican Republic also has a stake in the myriad representations of its neighbor country. As Anne Eller writes in her historical study *We*

Dream Together, the histories of Haiti and the Dominican Republic are irrefutably intertwined with respect to their struggles for emancipation and independence. Eller notes: "Symbiotically, Santo Domingo and Saint-Domingue grew together" (4). The Haitian-Dominican border stands for yet another Haiti, a Haiti irreversibly linked to the Dominican Republic, and for a Dominican Republic irreversibly linked to Haiti as well. Évelyne Trouillot's *The Blue of the Island* (2012) and Danticat's *The Farming of Bones,* from a Haitian perspective, also envision Haitian-Dominican third space as an important zone of contact and interaction. Both works describe a Haiti created, much as Ulysse remarks, "due to migration" (that is, they show how characters are impacted by migration or the factors that push them to migrate) but also a Haiti re-created or reenvisioned on the border between the Dominican Republic and Haiti.[23]

Trouillot's *The Blue of the Island* and Danticat's *The Farming of Bones* emphasize the perpetual splitting of the island into parts, while at the same time proposing a history of connectivity. The works share in common a fragmentation by both divergent and convergent histories of colonization, emancipation, and independence, in addition to shifting border policies. They purport multiplex understandings of Haiti that become increasingly varied and complicated as they write Haiti alongside and against the porous border region and delve into the relationship(s) between Haiti and the Dominican Republic. Ulysse's proclamation that "Haiti and Haitians have always been plural to me" (xviii) can be further expanded if and when the Haitian-Dominican border forms part of the pluralities to which Ulysse makes reference.

The Blue of the Island and *The Farming of Bones* allude to multiple Haitis and the unique third space that stands for the Haitian-Dominican border by their complicated, nuanced representations of cross-border movement. The two works bear conscious markings of trans-border migration patterns, as well as the physical and emotional burdens of political and economic displacement. Both Trouillot's play and Danticat's novel showcase migration and demonstrate the movement of Haitians and Dominicans of Haitian descent across the border—both from east to west and from west to east—as integral to the complex understanding of Haiti. Although estimates of the number of individuals of Haitian descent living in the Dominican Republic today vary widely—from half a million to more than a million—beyond (and at times because of) the dehumanizing nature of statistics that stand to reduce the human experience to a number, we often expect writers to "give us the human interest stories that pull us into the concrete lives of individual migrants and their families"

(Lionnet and Jean-François 1223). Stuart Hall addresses migration in the Caribbean region as unavoidable, referring to Caribbean peoples as natural migrants and to Caribbean migration as "the signifier of migration itself—of traveling voyage and return as fate, as destiny" ("Cultural Identity" 234). *The Blue of the Island* traces cross-border movement from west to east, depicting an episode of on-border violence in 2000, and *The Farming of Bones* shows movement from east to west, as characters flee the Dominican border region during the 1937 Massacre. Moreover, both texts speak to a broader historical contextualization of Haitian migration to the Dominican Republic: Trouillot's play considers the political turmoil during and following Jean-Bertrand Aristide's presidency, and Danticat's novel subtly highlights US interventions on both sides of the island in the early twentieth century and the US role in the sugar industry. The fact that both works represent specific, historical instances of Dominican-Haitian border violence reflects a trend in Caribbean literature that Myriam J. A. Chancy identifies as texts' attempting to "make sense of a moment in Caribbean history shared across the border of two independent nation-states" (*Sugar to Revolution* ix).

Trouillot's play *The Blue of the Island*, published originally in French as *Le bleu de l'île*, shifts from imagining a historical figure as two-part to purporting the island of Hispaniola as a uniquely binary space, paradoxically uniting and separating Haiti and the Dominican Republic. The play brings to life the journey of Haitian characters traveling in a truck bed from the small town of Piment, Haiti, to Dajabón, Dominican Republic. Although the intraisland migratory route portrayed in *The Blue of the Island* could easily reference an attempt to cross the Dominican-Haitian border by an anonymous group of prototypical Haitian migrants seeking to improve their economic prospects, Trouillot bases the play on a violent border tragedy that took place in June 2000. The event involved Haitian migrants, natives of Piment, en route to Dajabón. Robert H. McCormick Jr., in his introduction to the English translation of *The Blue of the Island*, describes the historical impulse of the play: "In June 2000, a group of Haitians from the small town of Piment, in the North of Haiti, furtively left for the neighboring republic. The Dominican guards are sometimes paid to let groups of 'clandestines' into the country, but it would seem that on this particular Sunday, apparently after a shift change, the new guards were not informed of the operation. They intercepted the vehicle, fired shots, and killed several of the passengers" (211).

As the play reflects a specific historical reference, what appears anonymized in the work is geographical location, particularly the migrants' whereabouts as they close in on the border and prepare to cross into the Dominican Republic.[24] The actual country name Dominican Republic is never once mentioned in *The Blue of the Island*. Cardinal markers and other descriptive identifiers narrate the movement of the Daihatsu-brand truck on its journey eastward. The cross-island movement from west to east repeatedly appears as a pointed juxtaposition to references to color, particularly blue, in both Haiti and the Dominican Republic; as the truck approaches the Dominican border, the blues are increasingly muted or dull, and it becomes unclear whether the "blue of the island" is a trait shared by both nations. A marked jumbling of possessive statements about the island of Hispaniola ranging from "the island" to "our island" to "your island" accompanies this shift in chromatic descriptors. Regardless of the miscellaneous possessive claims to the island at large, *The Blue of the Island* posits that there are only two possible directions in which to traverse Hispaniola: east toward the Dominican Republic or west toward Haiti. The border-crossing route that frames Trouillot's play proves to be not only a passage over land but also an expedition that uncovers memories and divulges the raw, at times burdensome emotions of the passengers.

Évelyne Trouillot belongs to what Madison Smartt Bell refers to as "Haiti's most fertile literary families" (49). Smartt Bell continues by naming members of her well-published, prolific family tree: "Her uncle is the historian Henock Trouillot, and her siblings the novelist Lyonel Trouillot, anthropologist, historian, and political scientist Michel-Rolph Trouillot, and Creole scholar and children's book author Jocelyne Trouillot" (49). Trouillot is not only a novelist but an author of children's books and a poet. Moreover, Trouillot's literary career offers a sustained focus on the "big mass of enslaved people" (Danticat, "Evelyne Trouillot" 51). For Trouillot, as she told Edwige Danticat in a 2005 interview, the "enslaved" can also be labeled "the 'invisible,' since nobody wanted to pay attention to them" (51). Trouillot mentioned in her interview with Danticat that her literary depictions of the throngs of enslaved men and women are the result of her desire to represent more than the heroes and known historical figures related to the events leading up to the Haitian Revolution; *The Blue of the Island* centers on "invisibles." The characters in the play, "invisibles" leading ordinary lives and facing commonplace third-world problems, all hail from the same small, relatively unknown Haitian village of Piment. The characters offer different, albeit related explanations for traveling to the Dominican Republic, many hoping to return soon to Haiti to (re)establish small businesses. Regardless, their stories—some already linked owing to preexisting familial bonds or friendships—begin to merge, making it difficult for the reader to separate the unique experiences that drove the characters to seek new economic opportunities in the neighboring republic. In this way, the characters under the blue tarp of the truck become integrated into the broader population of Haitians living and working in the Dominican Republic, the Haitian diaspora in which the greatest number of Haitian nationals reside and a country in which Haitians compose the largest ethnic minority. The instance of border violence on which Trouillot bases *The Blue of the Island* not only centers on easily imperceptible characters but also speaks to the invisibility of the border region and border policies; while the June 2000 event may initially have been covered by Haitian and Dominican news sources, it left behind no digital footprint and is one of many forgotten border narratives. This decentering of border histories, as Paulino explains, relates to the Western concept that borders represent "retrograde culture" and impede national progress. He notes, "Like many border regions around the world, the Dominican-Haitian border region emerged as a semiautonomous region far from the centers of power" (4). The sparse documentation of the 2000 border violence confirms the border's position outside the "centers of power" into the twenty-first century.

My analysis of Trouillot's seldom-studied play centers primarily on the color-coded space to which the title alludes—the blue(s) of the island—attempting to answer the following questions: How are the blues of the island described? How do the shades and hues of blue appear altered as the characters journey eastward? To which island or island-nations does the title refer? And, relatedly, is the notion of "island" in the title and within the play cast as a unifying approach to Hispaniola? Thus, much as in previous analyses, I focus on space and the concept of a unique Haitian-Dominican third space.[25]

The play's title openly stresses blue as an important, metaphorical hue within the text. From the first technical notes of *The Blue of the Island*, color, along with notions of shadowing and illumination, emerges on a visual and semantic level. The first sentence of the first stage direction reads: "The twelve passengers are reclining, on their knees or bent over under a blue tarpaulin" (213). The use of the preposition *under* in the stage direction positions the characters within a color hierarchy of sorts, their cramped cover beneath the blue tarp implies that the color itself saturates their experience. In the conversation following this directional note, between the passenger Ronald and his wife, Francine, Trouillot describes Francine as transparent. The play's third stage direction states: "[Ronald] approaches her, but cannot touch her. It is as if she were transparent" (213). This notion of transparency starkly separates the memories of the passengers from the visceral reality in the Daihatsu truck as it barrels east, leaving Piment in the dust, already a distant memory. The fact that the passengers are stuck inside the truck, unable to move freely or see beyond the blue material, which does not allow any light to enter—described as "a tarp you want to punch holes in" (252)—underscores the fact that they speak of and in color but have no viewpoint or sense of direction given their entrapment. Despite the view-obstructing blue sheath, the Haitian migrants making their way to Dajabón do perceive the passing of time, both from subtle shifts in light detected from beneath the tarp and from changes in temperature. One passenger, Ronald, shares that the truck bed is "getting hotter and hotter beneath the rising sun" (245). While other senses have a place in the play, as this example demonstrates, sight (or the lack thereof) permeates the entire work. Specific hues of blue are mentioned throughout the work, which perhaps is not surprising given the color's dominating, encapsulating presence for the passengers en route to the Dominican Republic. Blue, however, also materializes as the color most clearly linked to the island as a whole. Trouillot's use of color in *The Blue of the Island* not only adds descriptive or emotive value to the text but also proves relevant to discussions of nation and race.

Analyzing the manifestations of black and blue in film, literature, and art, Carol Mavor, basing her analysis on Roland Barthes's concept of punctum, writes that color is capable of producing pain and evoking difficult memories. She associates blue, for example, with bruising, labeling it a "sad color" and noting that "if our skin is black, the bruises may not show at all. Invisible pain is often the most impossible to reconcile" (15). Asserting that blue hues may be undetectable on black skin connects to Mavor's assumption that memory is also color-coded as black and blue. Memory, too, bruises, stains, marks, and claims subjects.[26] In a similar way, Trouillot evokes color in *The Blue of the Island* to access the characters' emotional status. Fifi, Ronald's pregnant sister, who is also en route to Dajabón, expresses her desire to exit the truck and arrive in the Dominican Republic. She confesses to her brother what she hopes to see upon emerging from the truck bed: "not that dirty, anemic indigo blue soaked too long in water and bleached in an irregular manner, but the real blue, the one that makes my heart skip" (253). Fifi connects the "real blue" with the ability to make her heart skip. Blue, here, is capable of uplifting spirits and emerges as a signal of the economic opportunities awaiting the Piment passengers on the other side of the border. The hues of blue in the play, and more importantly their subtle transformations, can also be read as precursors to the thwarted border passage and the emotional bruising the trip may entail, especially in reference to the original French title of the play, *Le bleu de l'île*. The French *bleu* and the Haitian Kreyòl *ble* can signify not only the color blue but also bruising.

The connections of the color blue to an emotional response—a sentiment often described as "feeling blue" in English—increases in number as the truck journeys eastward. As the truck approaches Dajabón "the tarp becomes taut, then loose, like a blue monster breathing spasmodically" (257). On the following page, *blue* goes from serving as a modifier for *monster* to describing a blue hell: "The blue inferno doesn't allow for any more tricks" (258). The mention of the "blue inferno" does not make clear whether the inferno exists only under the tarp or instead functions as a moniker for the "blue island" of Hispaniola. Confirming the importance of reading color in the play, other colors also represent misfortune for the passengers. The passenger Violetta signals the meaning of yellow: "I knew this Daihatsu was going to bring us misfortune, with its pooh-yellow color, definitely not a color one can trust, a color of treachery, raw and hard" (253). While *blue* is a constant chromatic descriptor in *The Blue of the Island*, a diverse palette of colors manifests in the play, as Violetta's statement suggests. Often colors are mentioned in conventional terms relating to matter and form, describing anything from "the yellow flesh of a recently picked mango fade" (246) to "grey smoke" (239) or "black shoes with laces" (240). No other color saturates the play as blue does, however, emphasizing the color's ability to "stain" not only memories and skin but also specific geographical spaces.

Blue-black is sometimes used to describe a pigmentation that is a step beyond black on the color scale. Alvarez's *How the García Girls Lost Their Accents* utilizes the terminology to describe a Haitian caretaker of the García family: "Chucha was super wrinkled and Haitian blue-black, not Dominican *café-con-leche* black" (213). While the use of *blue-black* as racial descriptor represents popular vernacular or slang, interpreting the color blue as a racial signifier adds to an analysis of the color's inclusion in Trouillot's *The Blue of the Island*. Mavor writes that "blueness (as in blue eyes) and blackness (as in dark skin) are unequivocally about race" (15), but she does not comment on a possible reading of blue as racially coded. She does hint, however, at the inseparability of the two colors: "Black is not the opposite of blue: it is its lining" (15). If one considers the constant application and multifold uses of *blue* in Trouillot's play, the fact that the color can denote race and wash over or tint the island of Hispaniola is significant. The uses of blue in this way dismantle traditional Dominican negations of blackness by positioning residents on both sides of the border as one, under the same blue sky, possibly under the same "blue-black" skin. Chancy's *From Sugar to Revolution* positions Haitians as interlopers within the Dominican body politic, which "actively resists racial contamination without regard for the fact that it has become synonymous with the Dominican nation as a body *morcelé* ('in pieces') and hybrid" (89). *The Blue of the Island* challenges perceptions of racial contamination by writing the island as one under the "blue of the island" and linking the experiences of Haitians and Dominicans sharing the same land mass. As Fifi says: "So many children to be born under the blue of the island" (263). Through this statement, the female passenger—shot to death at the play's end by Dominican border-patrol agents—assumes the linked destinies of unborn children on both sides of the border. For Fifi, all children born on the island of Hispaniola, regardless of nationality or geography, are born beneath the same blue sky; the character binds together the experiences of the unborn children rather than contrasting them.

The discussion in the truck between the two siblings, Ronald and Fifi, dominates the last few pages of the play. And as the truck approaches Dajabón, the references to the color blue increase. The blue that saturates this final conversation, however, becomes a blue that carries over from Haiti to the Dominican Republic—a blue linked deliberately to both hope and despair. Ronald magnifies the similarities between the eastern and western parts of the island for his sister: "The people seem different, for sure, the language is unknown, but it's the same blue, the same sky. The blue of the island" (252). Cast in a positive light, this first mention of the blue of the island as a whole is juxtaposed to the mention of the blue sky that envelops the island on the final page of the play. "The blue of the island" is at first hopeful and unifying but later, as Ronald shares his final words with his dying sister, signals only opportunities lost and continued poverty and oppression. Ronald tells Fifi: "It seems to me that we wanted to find a solution and we forgot that the blue sky doesn't change crossing the border" (263). The final references in the play to the "blue sky" are confusing. In the final dialogue, the characters mix up Haiti and the Dominican Republic, and it becomes unclear whether the speakers are referring to both sides of the island or the Dominican Republic or Haiti in particular.

Trouillot's careful, conscious employment of color in the play magnifies a complex relation to senses, in particular passengers' visual perceptions of changing landscape as they imagine it from underneath the blue tarp.

The tangential references to the Dominican Republic (the official name of the nation-state is never used), however, attempt to convolute and contradict the shifting border policies and the contested history of Haitian migration to the island's eastern half by dissolving the borderline. This "erasure" also relates to a discussion concerning to which side(s) of the island the Piment passengers express a sense of belonging or a desire to belong. Dajabón, the end destination of the truck, is mentioned in the play (223, 224), but the unidentified link between Dajabón and the Dominican Republic instead posits Dajabón as a border community that stands for a heterogeneous third space, a site of intersection that belongs to both communities. Aside from references to the intended destination, Dajabón, the Dominican Republic appears to be positioned geographically in relation to Haiti. Such references include "across the border" (219), "the other side of the border" (224), "oriented toward the east" (243), and the "eastern part" (243, 246). There are numerous other mentions of cardinal directions that simply posit the two countries as "East" or "West" (226, 230). The allusion to the Dominican Republic as the "other side" or the "East" to Haiti's "West" confirms the geographical intertwinement of the two countries, one as counterpart to the other, while also subtly underlining the presence of an ideological border in the Dominican Republic that sought to perpetuate the border "as a racial line to be defended by state violence" (Paulino 56), especially in reference to the 1937 Massacre and its aftermath.

Another work that does not mention the Dominican Republic by name is Louis-Philippe Dalembert's novel *The Other Side of the Sea* (2014, originally published as *L'autre face de la mer* in 1998). Dalembert's novel, comprising three intercalated stories, begins with "Grannie's Story," narrating the migratory exchanges between the Dominican Republic and Haiti. "Grannie's Story" relays border crossings without formal reference to the Dominican Republic, instead electing to anonymize Haiti's neighbor. The most frequent cognomen for the eastern part of the island in Dalembert's text is the abbreviated Kreyòl phrase *pa'lá*, meaning "over there," further defined in the novel as "the other side of the mountains" (14). Subsequent references to the Dominican Republic follow this pattern. The narrator, "Grannie," remembers her life in the Dominican Republic before fleeing the country during the 1937 Massacre: "What have I retained of the language from over there? ... A few words: 'Calao!' the rare times that I get irritated and 'ta buen' to praise something as a connoisseur, even though I do everything to rid myself of them. I don't remember any others. In school, as was the case for the language of the whites, I refused to study the one from the other side of the mountains" (31). While the reference to "the other side of the mountains" perhaps responds to the popular Haitian proverb describing Haiti's landscape and, metaphorically, the perpetuation or repetition of difficult situations—"Dye mon, gen mon" (Mountains beyond mountains)—the constant allusion to "another" side of the mountains or the "other side" of the mountains decentralizes and depreciates the Dominican Republic in relation to Haiti. Moreover, there are many "sides" in Dalembert's *The Other Side of the Sea,* including the United States and ancestral Africa. Dalembert's allusion to multiple Haitian diasporas challenges the presupposition that the "other" side of Haiti's mountains is always the Dominican Republic, instead pointing to other natural and geographical (and also ideological) borders. Similarly, Trouillot references other migratory routes in *The Blue of the Island,* mentioning Miami as the final destination of Fifi and Ronald's absent father (237).

The pattern of anonymizing the Dominican Republic in both Trouillot's and Dalembert's works also reflects the multitude of "official" names for both Haiti and the Dominican Republic in the countries' long recorded history, spanning precolonial, colonial, and postcolonial times. The historian Graham T. Nessler's study *Islandwide Struggle for Freedom,* for example, offers what Nessler refers to as a "note on geography," which speaks to the confusion around terms for the colonies and, later, independent nations (3–4). This indeterminacy also references Hispaniola's history of shifting borders. Alternatively, the nameless status of the Dominican Republic in both Trouillot's and Dalembert's texts represents a reversal of a similar pattern in Dominican literature to anonymize and dehumanize Haitians, particularly in plantation novels, or *novelas de la caña* (Graciano), such as Marrero Aristy's *Over.* These Haitian- and Haitian American–authored examples, however, catalyze the experience of Haitian characters on and off border while deemphasizing and decentering the Dominican Republic.

Even though Trouillot, like Dalembert, avoids naming the Dominican Republic, the final dialogue of *The Blue of the Island* centers on possessives describing the island as a whole rather than the island as bipartite. Evariste, the most cynical passenger in the truck, confirms that everyone has a reason for crossing, whether it be to search for loved ones or to flee adverse economic conditions. He speaks to the congruity of those under the tarp: "I am not alone in this vehicle" (243). While there is a sense throughout the play that the Piment passengers are all members of an extended family, it is clear that the Dominican Republic and Haiti represent different things for different passengers. The confusion about the island and the quest for its "true blue" chromatic overpowers the final dialogue between Fifi and Ronald:

> FIFI: On which side of the island?
> RONALD: A part of me will stay here with you. With you, with Edgar and your baby who moved today for the first and only time. A part of me will stay here with you forever.
> FIFI: Promise me you won't forget the blue of the island. Promise me to come back from the other side of the island and take care of my daughter and your son. And of your Amadine-to-be . . . (263)

Fifi again reminds Ronald to take care of his "Amadine-to-be," as his wife, in Haiti, is expecting their second child. Ronald responds to his sister with a predisposed return date in mind: "In September, on *our* side of the island" (263, my emphasis). Given that readers learn in the first pages of the play that Ronald left his wife, Amadine, behind in Piment, "*our* side of the island" here can be understood as Haiti. While Fifi dies pleading for her brother to return from the "*other* side of the island" (the Dominican Republic) to take care of their families, she also asks that he not forget "the blue of the island." If she assumes Ronald will stay in the Dominican Republic, this is evidence that Fifi understands "the blue of the island" as exclusively Haitian. Fifi's employment of the phrase "the blue of the island" encourages the reader to interpret the island as one or as one-sided, juxtaposing the "true blue" of Haiti with the "monster blue tarp" or "blue hell" that the truck passengers describe when nearing the Dominican border. The direction Ronald takes as he flees the crime scene confirms this hypothesis of Haiti as representative of the "blue of the island": "Ronald stares at the corpses of his brother-in-law and his sister. One sees him stand up and salute the dead. Then, he heads off toward the West. Gradually, as he advances, the stage becomes blue, more and more blue, almost an unbearable blue" (263).

Trouillot's reference to "an unbearable blue" in this final stage direction contrasts the muted blue of the tarp that the passengers experienced en route to Dajabón. The adjective *unbearable* here refers to a (positively) overwhelming blue as opposed to the intolerable, oppressive blue of the tarpaulin. Ronald leaves the corpses of his family, friends, and neighbors behind (in the East) and is overtaken, saturated, by the blue(s) of Haiti in the West. While the Haitian-Dominican border remains a constant allusion in the play, the characters never cross the border into the Dominican Republic. The positioning of Haiti as plural and the geographical centering of the play on the western side of Hispaniola serves to posit the

Dominican Republic as singular. Trouillot's Dominican Republic, then, is a static one, a never-reached destination, a neighbor country never formally addressed or defined. The reason for this exclusion, however, is not to silence the Dominican Republic in the same way that Michel Rolph-Trouillot establishes the historical silencing of Haiti in *Silencing the Past* or that Sibylle Fischer confirms that the Haitian Revolution has been confined to the margins of history in *Modernity Disavowed: Haiti and the Cultures of Slavery in the Age of Revolution*. Instead, it reflects a recognition of the crucial roles of other key players in reference to Haitian history and reality. A patterned absence, conscious or not, of the Dominican Republic in these Haitian-authored texts likewise speaks to the fact that the centrality of Haiti in Dominican nationalist discourse does not signal the veracity of the inverse; Haitian nationalist discourses instead rely more heavily on France and the United States. J. Michael Dash outlines Haiti's attempt to define itself in the face of a traumatic relationship with the North. In *Haiti and the United States: National Stereotypes and the Literary Imagination,* Dash explores the nationalist Haitian discourses in relation to travel and movement: "The nation as the individual's absolute point of departure, dominated the migrant's experience" (14).[27] The notion of emigration or exile in Haitian literature focuses on migratory movements but expands beyond an eastward trajectory to the Dominican Republic, and Trouillot's anonymous marking of the Dominican Republic alludes to the other transnational communities more deeply rooted in the Haitian national imaginary.

Danticat's novel *The Farming of Bones* gives voice to a different historical moment: the 1937 Massacre of Haitians and Dominicans of Haitian descent. Through a fictional first-person narrator fleeing the Dominican Republic during *el corte,* Danticat highlights the movement from east to west that also cardinally details Ronald's return to Haiti in the final moments of *The Blue of the Island.* While *The Farming of Bones* intercalates the memories of a fictional narrator in testimonial form, a literary portrayal of the Duvalier regime in Danticat's *Breath, Eyes, Memory* (1994) and a critique of the US immigration policies toward Haiti in the late twentieth century in *Krik? Krak!* (1995) and *Brother, I'm Dying* (2007) also confirm Danticat's keenness toward the historical-fiction genre. Danticat, a Haitian American writer who explores many spaces in her writing, challenges the dominant structure of nation-state by considering how Haitians residing in the US diaspora or in the Dominican Republic (in the case of *The Farming of Bones*) reframes the common opposition between concepts of nation and diaspora. If, as Carole Boyce

Davies notes, "diaspora assumes expansiveness and elsewhereness" (37), Danticat's expansive literary corpus allows readers to envision the Haitian diaspora as a moving, mutable arm instead of part of an imaginary spectrum or unmappable, fixed space. Much as Danticat constitutes a voice for the Haitian diaspora, Chancy also posits her as a "witness" for voiceless Haitians ("Recovering History" 109) and asks Danticat in an interview about the attention paid to the "traumas that Haitians, common Haitians, have been enduring throughout history" (109). *The Farming of Bones* "pays attention" to the often neglected (historical) traumas by giving voice to the silenced victims of the 1937 Massacre. In this way, Danticat revives and rewrites historical moments traditionally silenced; she reclaims the history of the massacre as transnational and offers a platform, albeit literary and fictional, from which "actors in the communal dramas shared across the border" (Chancy, *From Sugar to Revolution* xiii) can contribute to and reshape certain historical moments, construing a broader and more inclusive understanding of the event.

In the acknowledgments to *The Farming of Bones,* Danticat pays homage to the work of the Haitian Jacques Stephen Alexis, in particular his novel *General Sun, My Brother* (originally published as *Compère Général Soleil* in 1955): "To Jacques Stephen Alexis, for Compère Général Soleil. One. Always" (312). In her aforementioned interview with Chancy, Danticat further lauds Alexis's multitiered approach to the massacre by situating both Haiti and the Dominican Republic within a broader historical context that includes the US military occupations in both Haiti and the Dominican Republic in the early twentieth century:

> Alexis does an excellent job of showing the role of the U.S. Occupation, what in the book is called the Yankee occupation, in Haitian and Dominican affairs. The whole island was occupied by the United States for nineteen years. Trujillo was a trainee to the United States Marines, the same ones who create the Haitian army that we had until recently. So it's not always black and white. We have to look at the nuances, the crevices in these situations. (121)

Similar to Alexis's complex portrayal of the massacre, Danticat's novel also recognizes the complicity of not only Dominican leaders at the time but also the Haitian presidents Sténio Joseph Vincent and, later, Elie Lescot. She contextualizes the US invasions in both the Dominican Republic and Haiti and argues their monumental role in pushing for cheap foreign labor on the largely US-owned sugar plantations. *The Farming of Bones* considers and emphasizes the "nuances" and "crevices"—the histories easily overlooked or difficult to understand—in reference to the Dominican-Haitian border and the 1937 Massacre. As Reyes-Santos notes, Danticat's novel "remembers not only the massacre but also how Haitians, Dominicans, and Dominicans of Haitian descent have coexisted and shared kinship ties" (134). Reyes-Santos further asserts that *The Farming of Bones* "challenge[s] the Trujillato's attempt to build strict racial distinctions between Dominican and Haitians" (137).

Danticat's novel recounts the unchronological and fragmented memories of Amabelle Désir, a Haitian woman orphaned at a young age after her parents drowned trying to cross the Massacre River and enter the Dominican Republic. Taken in by a Dominican woman, Doña Valencia, and her Spanish father, Amabelle works as a house servant in the Dominican border community that Doña Valencia and her father call home, a place that becomes a home for Amabelle too. To use Eller's term, Danticat imagines a "center island" community that is composed of both Haitian and Dominican landowners as well as individuals who work on the sugar plantations and in other roles within the community. Before the massacre, Alegría is a model third space, a hybrid transcultural site that recognizes and celebrates the commonalities between Haitians and Dominicans. The Haitian Father Romain verbalizes these transnational connections in his sermons in Alegría; Amabelle notes that "he often reminded everyone of common ties: language, foods, history, carnival, songs, tales, and prayers" (73).

The fictional border town at the center of the novel, Alegría, transforms in the wake of the massacre, as do the victims themselves. Amabelle's own body becomes, as she describes it, a map that marks the physical abuses of the massacre and unwillingly recalls the historiographic record of the event. When Amabelle arrives at Cap-Haïtien, Haiti, she reflects on her body, a survivor's body, after the massacre: "Now my flesh was simply a map of scars and bruises, a marred testament" (227). The corporeal body evidences the massacre, while the once-familiar, friendly town of Alegría loses its subsistence; Amabelle's "homecoming" later in the novel renders the town nonexistent: "That she [Doña Valencia] did not recognize me made me feel that I had come back to Alegría and found it had never existed at all" (294). Before the massacre, Alegría was a superfluous and porous border town that in many respects lived up to its name. Although the novel's depiction of the relative peace between Haitians and Dominicans leading up to 1937 finds support from historians such as Turits, Derby, and Paulino, who describe the premassacre border as a porous region with well-established economic and social communities (Paulino 7), Amabelle's memories of the massacre "do not fit within the conventional historical accounts of either the Dominican or Haitian nation-states" (Reyes-Santos 136). The novel portrays the massacre as a memory born of the fictional Amabelle's personal experiences, and her memories rewrite and challenge dominant understandings of the event.

Most pertinent to a discussion about third space and borders in Danticat's novel is the fact that Amabelle's testimonial account of the event suggests resistance in border communities to Trujillo's Dominicanization of the region. As the historian Amelia Hintzen writes: "Rural residents did not view the Haitian presence in the country in the same way as the urban elite did" (36). Hintzen's testament to the fact that rural residents resisted attempts by the central state authorities to control the Haitian immigrant population both prior to and following October 1937 aligns with *The Farming of Bones*'s collaborative vision of the Haitian-Dominican border that counteracts Trujillo's division of the island into two. In the closing pages of the novel, Amabelle returns to the border and the Massacre River, literally submerging herself in the "warm and shallow" October water (310). Not only is it significant that Amabelle returns to the border in October, the month of the massacre's anniversary, but her conscious act of cleansing, as April Shemak notes, "evokes contradictory images," including "the attempted ethnic cleansing of the massacre" (105). Amabelle's obsession with the river, where she has the cabdriver drop her before dawn, stems not only from her final memories of her parents but also from a desire to erase the river, perhaps the border, from memory: "In the coal black darkness of a night like this, unless you are near it, the river ceases to exist" (308). Much as Amabelle imagines Alegría nonexistent or obsolete after the massacre, she also chooses to erase the river border. As Amabelle deluges her body, a physical testament to the massacre, beneath the warm water she reflects on the painful deaths of those whose graves were in the riverbed. In doing so, she posits the river as a gravesite and a reflective border space, a signpost for the transnational history of Hispaniola.

While the river border itself is representative of a shared reality and history between the two nations of Hispaniola, the novel's prioritization of the (fictional) memories of a Haitian woman offers alternative approaches to the 1937 Massacre. As Chancy suggests, the novel encourages healing between the Dominican Republic and Haiti in the massacre's wake, a transnational healing that functions by "sharing lived memory of a time that both nations would rather forget" ("Violence, Nation, and Memory" 144). The novel also serves as a reminder of the two countries' collaborative and fraternal relationship—which existed before the massacre and was not erased in its wake—a relationship that even the racist vestiges of the Trujillo regime could not abolish. In the final sentence of the acknowledgments, Danticat provides a necessary bridge between remembering the past and acknowledging the present. Danticat links the victims of the massacre to Haitian migrants who still face prejudice on the eastern side of Hispaniola today: "And the very last words, last on the page but always first in my memory, must be offered to those who died in the Massacre of 1937, to those who survived to testify, and to the constant struggle of those who still toil in the cane fields" (312). Danticat's final reminder to her readers, then, frames and values the historical echoes of the massacre on both sides of the border.

A Shared Commitment to Place

A relation to place is common to the multigenre works analyzed in this chapter. Díaz, Older, Trouillot, and Danticat utilize what Glissant refers to as "the language of landscape" (*Caribbean Discourse* 145) in order to (re)construct third space, signaling the bilateral history between Haiti and the Dominican Republic as well as between Haiti and the Spanish Caribbean in the space of the diaspora. The authors' commitment to Haitian-Dominican third space, portrayed in both on- and off-border settings, engenders diverse texts that problematize the notions of place and displacement. While the power of the diaspora to uproot Dominicans' previous cultural, racial, and social realities is undeniable, the Latino texts examined at the outset of this chapter reference the ability of the diaspora to transgress both ideological and geographical borders. Díaz's short story "Monstro" approaches third space vis-à-vis an sf border narrative that critiques the anti-Haitian discourse in the Dominican Republic, while Older's novel imagines a literary, diasporic *kalfou* seeking to connect multiethnic communities in Brooklyn. Trouillot's *The Blue of the Island* and Danticat's *The Farming of Bones,* in different ways, offer (Haitian) perspectives on Haitian-Dominican third space and the intraisland migratory movement that defines these hybrid zones of contact.

Numerous Dominican and Dominican American authors have depicted the relationship between Hispaniola's neighboring states in literature. Veloz Maggiolo's "Tipología del tema haitiano" is an attempt to classify these varied literary representations of Haitians. However, there is no Haitian counterpart to Veloz Maggiolo's categorical study, no attempt to catalog the representation of Dominicans in Haitian literature. In the view of many scholars, this is because there is less representation of Dominicans in Haitian literature. As I argue in this chapter, by considering Trouillot's

The Blue of the Island and, briefly, Dalembert's *The Other Side of the Sea*, some Haitian authors instead "write" the Dominican Republic by not writing it at all. In other words, Haitian writers may consciously neglect to outwardly name Hispaniola's eastern half and mention the Dominican Republic only referentially or through the use of cardinal directions and subtle geographical markers. My analysis of the migratory experiences of Haitians at the root of *The Blue of the Island* and *The Other Side of the Sea* identifies their purposeful exclusion of the proper name Dominican Republic in an attempt to dismantle a Caribbean, New World narrative that erases Haiti and the history of the first black republic by instead signaling the global players (other than the Dominican Republic) influential to Haiti's nationalist discourses. Danticat's *The Farming of Bones* also unsilences the past by envisioning female characters as active agents in the (re)making of history.

The Haitian, Haitian American, and Latino texts analyzed in this final chapter posit an understanding of metaphorical and physical borders as intersectional in that they forge links between communities. "Monstro," *Shadowshaper*, *The Blue of the Island,* and *The Farming of Bones*, spanning multiple genres, all offer perspectives on Dominican-Haitian relations that challenge the (false) antipodal narrative between the two neighboring countries. While "Monstro" and *Shadowshaper* turn to the near future and *The Blue of the Island* and *The Farming of Bones* approach historical events from diverse perspectives, all of the works portray Haiti not as singularly odd or ordinary but instead as multiple and evolving.

Conclusion

[A border is] to be related, without translation, to all the "trans"-s that are at work here.
                    —Jacques Derrida, "Living on Border Lines"

    The narratives discussed in *Mapping Hispaniola* examine borders, both metaphorical and physical, in distinct ways. While the geopolitical border between Haiti and the Dominican Republic is a constant in Prestol Castillo's *El Masacre se pasa a pie* and Díaz's "Monstro," other texts emphasize the varying ideological or imaginary borders that can both appear and dissipate as consequences of emigration and assimilation in Hispaniola's diaspora or for Haitians or Dominicans of Haitian descent residing in the Dominican Republic. All of the texts herein share an authorial interest in a relation to place as their common denominator. The Dominican, Haitian, Haitian American, Dominican American, and Puerto Rican American primary texts all deal with third space, theoretically situating on- and off-border sites as counterhegemonic. These transformative and transcultural spaces connect communities and reveal the historically silenced voices of traditionally underrepresented groups such as Haitians and Haitians of Dominican descent in the Dominican Republic and the Dominican diaspora. Third space surfaces as more than a geographical or spatiotemporal foundation for narratives that reenvision past, present, and future relations between Haitians and Dominicans vis-à-vis a relation to the border. Not only does utilizing third-space nomenclature to analyze on- and off-border literature constitute an exploration of postmodern terminology but approaching the Haitian-Dominican border as a unique example of third space designates a discursive practice.

    Prestol Castillo begins *El Masacre se pasa a pie* by referencing his geography class as a young boy. He confirms how foreign the word *Dajabón* sounded to him and how his unknowing teacher interpreted the Dominican-Haitian border communities as nonnative and insignificant. Marcio Veloz Maggiolo offers a hybridized vision of the Dominican-Haitian border in *El hombre del acordeón* and *La vida no tiene nombre*; in these novels the border stands for a "line" or "stripe" that characters cross without contention, and protagonists on both sides of the border envision themselves as part of a broad, transnational and trans-border community. Dominican American authors such as Raquel Cepeda, Junot Díaz, and Julia Alvarez use autobiographical forms of narrative and genre fiction to grapple with the complex concept of the Haitian-Dominican borderlands, inserting the US diaspora as another point of intersection between communities.

Some authors imbed physical maps within their works as attempts to visualize Hispaniola. Alvarez's *A Wedding in Haiti* offers a map plotting her 2009 route to Haiti and return to the Dominican Republic as well as her 2010 route to the Dominican Republic via Port-au-Prince (138). The place names on the map, aside from Santo Domingo, mark only those mentioned in the travelogue-style memoir. Beneath the names of many of the towns and cities, small notes—verbal mementos such as "Back road where we bought dulce en yagua & casave" to "Little hospital with big heart"—remind the reader, and perhaps Alvarez herself, of memorable moments. The map key displays two clear border crossings, and the eastern quarter of the Dominican Republic and the southwestern tip of Haiti are missing.[1] Daniel José Older's *Shadowshaper* makes a textual reference to a map of Hispaniola, a map tattooed on the Haitian character's chest. He confirms that the "strange splotch" just beneath his nipple, described in the novel as a "stain," is Haiti: "See how one side's flat. That's where it borders with the DR" (126). While Alvarez's physical map and Older's illustrative allusion to a map of Hispaniola can be read and interpreted in various ways, both clearly mark and reference the border even when the texts themselves, set both on and off the geophysical border, signal the dividing line as porous and fluid. Figures 2 and 3 in the present volume emphasize the crucial, at times strategic relationship between mapping and literature, as well as the relationship between Haitian and Dominican communities existing both on and off island and on and off border. The title *Mapping Hispaniola* alludes to this visual and geographically informed approach, and my creation and insertion of two maps bolsters analyses centered on literary portrayals of Haitian and Dominican third space.

The opacity of the *raya,* to reference Manuel Rueda's moniker for the dividing line, and the porosity of the Dominican-Haitian frontier—not only the geographical border but also the cultural, religious, linguistic, and social borders—overtly emerges in many of the close readings in *Mapping Hispaniola*. While a spatial relation to Hispaniola marks all of the works analyzed in this project, even anonymous or semianonymous geographical locations—such as the plantation in Ramón Marrero Aristy's *Over* or the fictional town of La Salada in Veloz Maggiolo's *El hombre del acordéon*—appear clearly set on Hispaniola. In this sense the island holds a specific meaning and references a distinct, unique history. Regardless of the allusion to geographical anonymity in some texts, Hispaniola is not just any space but rather "other-space." Foucault's heterotopia remains an ideal framework for classifying both geographical and social spaces, but the unique topologies found in fiction and memoir stretch and expand the concept of "other-space" to include varying literary spatial representations of both Hispaniola and the US-based Haitian and Dominican diasporas.

The literary confrontation of the hegemonic, dominant campaign of *antihatianismo* in the Dominican Republic serves as a metaphorical reconfiguration of the border between the two countries of Hispaniola, allowing for a mutation or negation of the very existence of the *raya* that separates Haiti from the Dominican Republic. Jean-Pierre Boyer, the president of Haiti from 1818 to 1843 and the provocateur behind the 1822–44 Haitian domination of the Dominican Republic, is often remembered for his unified vision of the island. Boyer triumphantly proclaimed in 1822 that Hispaniola was united under one shared government. While Boyer's desire to establish Haitian control over Santo Domingo was well intentioned—his goals included land reform and abolition of slavery in the former Spanish colony—he underestimated the differences between Haiti and Santo Domingo. Thus, his drive to re-create Santo Domingo as Haiti's twin neither championed the individuality of both nations nor fostered camaraderie and solidarity between them. Boyer's attempt to convert Santo Domingo into "another Haiti" failed; instead, the differences between Haiti and the present Dominican Republic were intensified and further pronounced during this time period. As Matibag writes, "The collective memory of the 22-year occupation serves as a historical referent and landmark by which the Dominican national identity sets itself off, politically and psychologically, against the image of the Haitian Other" (101). Further evidence of the distancing effect of the Haitian domination is the origin of Dominican Independence Day. February 27, 1844, the day the Dominican Republic won its independence from Haiti—rather than the day the former colony of Santo Domingo was granted its independence from Spain—is recognized and celebrated as Dominican Independence Day.

The significance behind the Dominican national holiday on February 27 can be understood in part as evidence of the politically charged decision of some Dominicans to position themselves as non-Haitian and to view the two countries of Hispaniola as separate entities, despite the geography that ties them together. While the literary analyses herein highlight the commonalities and the integrative, contrapuntal relationship between Dominicans and Haitians, an alternative understanding of this relationship is not synonymous with a wholeness or totality that binds the two countries together as Boyer attempted to do and failed. As Michaelsen and Johnson assert in their introduction to *Border Theory: The Limits of Cultural Politics*, any explanation of completeness and totality with respect to border spaces is problematic: "If the world begins in completely separate, unlike, anterior cultures, what guarantees or secures the very possibility of wholeness or wellness—completeness and totality?" (13). Although there is no guarantee of "wholeness," as Boyer learned from experience, literature provides an opportunity for a new expression of the border region, an expression that does not confront or clash with the issues of theorizing the border that Michaelsen and Johnson address. Writing the border in fiction, even though the narratives are often rooted in history, allows for a culture of inclusivity to define both geographical and ideological borders that emerge within them. Anzaldúa, too, exposes the tensions inherent in theorizing the crossing of a border, focusing on the fact that border subjects are becoming conscious of the effects of border crossing and the "multiplicity" of borderlands. I propose that literature can do the same for the reader, making one conscious not only of the action of crossing a border but also of the *seres fronterizos, rayanos,* or *nepantler@s* transformed by the act of crossing, whether from Haiti into the Dominican Republic or from Hispaniola to the US diaspora.

The Dominican Juan Bosch referred to Haiti as an "imperial frontier" in an attempt to categorize the country as a space where empires have clashed both with each other and with local and regional populations. Haiti can also be understood as an "imperial frontier" for its ability to capture the attention of a global audience; scholarship focused on Haiti has spiked following the bicentennial anniversary of its independence in 2004 and the 7.0-magnitude earthquake that struck Port-au-Prince and surrounding areas in 2010. Moreover, viewing Haiti as a focal point for Latino/a literature speaks to a literary imperialism of sorts, the country increasing its prominence and range of influence by drawing to its history Latino/a writers such as Julia Alvarez and Junot Díaz, two authors who are further propelled to write about Dominican-Haitian relations as a means of social activism. Moreover, Bosch's use of *frontier* in his definition of Haiti as an "imperial frontier" can be interpreted in multiple ways since the Haitian frontier belongs also to the Dominican Republic. The dividing line between the two countries that marks this frontier, a line that has at different times in Hispaniola's history both shifted and

Conclusion 167

dissolved, has at times disjointed the people living on either side of it. Stuart Hall's essay "Who Needs 'Identity'?" suggests that identity is "constructed within, not outside discourse." Hall further stresses that identity becomes meaningful "through the relation to the Other, the relation to what it is not, to precisely what it lacks, to what has been called the constitutive outside" (4). In the case of Haiti and the Dominican Republic, the relation to the Other—for Dominicans, the Haitian Other—appears accentuated most prominently at the border. The narratives examined in *Mapping Hispaniola*, however, challenge the border's differential status.

Confirming the transnational scope of this study, the analyzed texts move beyond Hispaniola's physical border. This global scope paves the way for future avenues of scholarship. The geographical scope of the study, for example, could expand further to other important Dominican and/or Haitian diasporas. Moreover, the presence of both Haitians and Dominicans on other Caribbean islands such as Cuba and Puerto Rico is relevant to a discussion of Hispaniola beyond its borders. For example, Puerto Rican writers with a connection to the island of Hispaniola include the poet Luis Palés Matos, Mayra Santos Febres, Ana Lydia Vega, and the Cuban Puerto Rican Mayra Montero. Analyzing the works of Haitian and Haitian American writers in addition to Edwidge Danticat and Évelyne Trouillot who use literature to reenvision the relationship between Haiti and the Dominican Republic would be a worthwhile addition to any comparative-literature project focused on Hispaniola. The inclusion of other texts viewing Hispaniola from the outside looking in, as an accompaniment to chapters 3 and 4 focused on Latino/a literature, would help to read the island comparatively alongside and against other Caribbean and Latin American countries.

The history of a colonial presence, US interventions, occupations, tyrannous dictatorships, and shifting border policies in Haiti and the Dominican Republic both parallel and provide a point of comparison to events that define other Latin American countries. The "double effect" on the island of Hispaniola (the fact the history of one side of the island both contrasts with and complements that of the other) intensifies these historical events and their representations in literature. The works analyzed in this volume share similarities with respect to the ways that they portray and reimagine history. Related to this interest in history and the desire to reveal and unsilence what Kamau Brathwaite calls "alter/native historiographies," many of the texts appear fragmented, lacking a traditional organization or structure, and they utilize myriad narrative voices to tell one, complex and multifaceted story. *El Masacre se pasa a pie, El hombre del acordeón,*

How the García Girls Lost Their Accents, and *The Brief Wondrous Life of Oscar Wao* all have multiple narrators. The repeated shift in narrative perspective can be understood as confirmation that the story of Hispaniola is a communal one. This same fragmentation or choppiness also seeks to define the Haitian-Dominican relationship and the border region. The setting on the Dominican-Haitian border, a sustained interest in the *trujillato* or the Haitian Revolution, or a focus on the search for identity that takes place in the diaspora allows a representation of the Haitian subject to form part of the core of these novels, as does the choppy, fragmented organization of the works. *El hombre del acordeón* references this disordered aspect: "No se pretende que todo quede tan en orden como debiera ser. Es como hacer una colcha con retazos de diferentes tipos de tela y de colores como las que hacían las abuelas durante los años nebulosos de la infancia" (11). This patchwork metaphor is representative of the overlapping testimonies recalling Honorio Lora's death, but it is also telling of the border itself and relates to border narrative on a larger scale.

This narrative fragmentation should also be considered for the plurality of voices it engenders. Within the texts analyzed here, Dominican Other(s), including Ramón Vieth in *La vida no tiene nombre* and anonymous Kreyòl speakers in *El Masacre se pasa a pie,* share their perspectives. Dominican Americans, too, are sometimes classified as non-Dominican because their experiences on US soil distance them from islanders. The multiple voices rewriting Hispaniola's history and the relationship between Haitians and Dominicans confront racial and ethnic inconsistencies, and this communitarian perspective—embracing the complexity of the self—is shared by Anzaldúa in her challenge to the Anglo purporting a one-sided, hegemonic narrative: "Admit that Mexico is your double, that she exists in the shadow of this country, that we are irrevocably tied to her. Gringo, accept the doppelgänger in your psyche" (*Borderlands* 86). Not only are there multitudinous narrative voices in many of the works considered in the present here but character traits often blend and coalesce with one another. Non-Haitians, for example, are given stereotypical Haitian traits that pertain to a primitivistic discourse in works such as *Over, La vida no tiene nombre,* and *Oscar Wao*. Dominicans and North Americans are presented as thieves, liars, and violent threats to the societies in which they are embedded. An understanding of the ample historical context of Hispaniola helps the reader to decipher the reasons behind such mixed messages and blending of stereotypes, in large part reflective of censorship during and after the *trujillato,* North American ownership of sugar plantations, and US interventions.

Conclusion   169

The works analyzed in *Mapping Hispaniola* refuse to let the past disappear or to let history establish itself as one-sided. They offer readers new ways of understanding Hispaniola's history by rewriting the Haitian-Dominican relationship from both an on- and an off-border perspective. These authors reposition Haiti and the Dominican Republic on a metaphorical *and* physical map of Hispaniola and offer a more complex and comprehensive geographical understanding of the island. This understanding deemphasizes the border as a cultural, racial and ethnic, and spiritual signifier—a line of demarcation between "us" and "them"—and instead focuses on points of contact between Haiti and the Dominican Republic. A representation of third space provides the common denominator in the analyses that foreground this project, and the various postcolonial understandings of third terms answer to and challenge concepts, or neighboring countries, historically approached as polar opposites. Soja delineates his Thirdspace as "using two opposing categories to open new alternatives" (*Thirdspace* 5), and this notion of third space as a mode of articulation to describe spaces that engender new possibilities and alliances guides my approach to literature written both on and off the geophysical border between the Dominican Republic and Haiti. If borders, in the Foucauldian sense, can be invisible and exist anywhere, the alternate perspectives of the Haitian-Dominican relationship present in the texts examined in *Mapping Hispaniola: Third Space in Dominican and Haitian Literature* construct a trans-border subjectivity that binds the two countries of Hispaniola together, charting the inexorable links of their past, present, and futures.

Notes

Introduction

1. Following the 1937 Haitian Massacre, the infamous Dominican dictator Rafael Leónidas Trujillo Molina, in power from 1930 to 1961, reportedly spoke the words in the epigraph above to a subordinate, referencing the "successful" policing of the Dominican frontier. Turits, *Foundations of Despotism* 165.

2. In addition to Eller's *We Dream Together,* see, e.g., Paulino; García-Peña; and Turits, "A World Destroyed, A Nation Imposed."

3. *Transnational Hispaniola: New Directions in Haitian and Dominican Studies* (2018) expands on the concept of transnational Hispaniola. April J. Mayes and Kiran C. Jayaram note in the introduction to the anthology that the project "encourages analysis of moments of collaboration and convergences of interests among Haitians and Dominicans" (2). Because *Transnational Hispaniola* was published when this book was in the copyediting stage, it was difficult to incorporate the volume more fully into my analyses.

4. Anzaldúa's *Borderlands/La Frontera: The New Mestiza* (1987) is a semi-autobiographical poetical-theoretical text that defies genre and discipline. The work theorizes the US-Mexican border and defines the existence and growth of a "New Mestiza consciousness" that seeks to represent the experience of border subjects, or *fronterizos.* Anzaldúa describes the border shared between the United States and Mexico as "una herida abierta," or an open wound, asserting that from this wound a third world, a "border culture," is created and sustained.

5. The term *heterotopia* was first mentioned in Foucault's 1966 book *Les mots et les choses* (published in 1970 as *The Order of Things*). Foucault informally returned to the idea in a 1966 radio broadcast in which he first spoke of the concept as related to social and cultural spaces, as opposed to explicitly textual space. Foucault defined the term explicitly in a 1967 lecture, "Des espaces autres." This lecture was published in French in *Architecture, mouvement, continuité* in 1984 and, finally, in English as "Of Other Spaces" in *Diacritics* in 1986. For our purposes here, I focus primarily on the published lecture in English.

6. Esther Cuesta, in her article "A modo de testimoniar: Borderlands, Papeles, and U.S. Academia," links Anzaldúa to Foucault by underscoring a foundational relationship central to the works of both: the relationship between power and knowledge. Cuesta notes, "Anzaldúa is, like Foucault, an archeologist of knowledge. She digs for ideas, symbols, and myths in her own historic and mythic past" (166).

7. Paulino's use of the term *zones of contact* to describe "a section of territory beyond the control and regulation of colonial authorities—a contested area" (5) builds on Mary Louise Pratt's term *contact zone,* an earlier example of a poststructuralist model of oppositional or contested space.

8. Accounts of Border of Lights's beginning appear divided. Paulino, one of the event's organizers and cofounders, notes: "With the support of people like Julia Alvarez, Michelle Wucker, Junot Díaz, and Edwidge Danticat, a group of us in the United States founded the organization Borderoflights" (231). While Danticat, Díaz, and Wucker have supported the event through book and monetary donations as well as through taking part in planning-committee phone calls, Alvarez has attended Border of Lights each year since the event's inauguration. Moreover, scholars referencing Border of Lights commonly incorrectly cite dates and/or general information about the event. García-Peña writes the following: "An unofficial collective annual commemoration began in 2013 organized and led by Edward Paulino, a Dominican American historian" (214). Mónica G. Ayuso also references Border of Lights in "Toward Forgiveness and Reconciliation: Three Novels from Haiti."

9. Hashtags began as #borderoflights and most recently have begun to specify the year by utilizing the hashtags #belights2017 or #bol2017.

10. In 2014 President Danilo Medina's administration passed a law in response to TC/0168/13. This law, 169–14, eliminated the retroactive nature of TC/0168/13 in the sense that it allowed for the validation of birth certificates and the restoration of nationality to individuals whose births had been registered in the Dominican Republic between 1929 and 2007. Law 169–14, however, still created many uncertainties and inconsistencies in regard to unregistered births in or informal migration to the Dominican Republic despite creating a special registration procedure for such individuals.

11. The term *antihaitianismo,* meaning "anti-Haitianism," referring to anti-Haitian nationalist sentiment, needs to be contextualized historically to understand its use in the following chapters. As Lauren Derby writes, "Anti-Haitianism must be understood as more than racism as such. It arose initially as consciousness of colonial difference, an identity marked first by language (French versus Spanish; the import of the linguistic ascription of alterity still lingers today), then by a series of derivative collective assertions of differences originating in colonial rivalries between the French and the Spanish. Anti-Haitianism's second layer of meaning stemmed from Saint Domingue's (which later became Haiti) former economic supremacy and colonial grandeur, in stark contrast to the poverty of the Spanish

colony" ("Haitians, Magic, and Money" 495). More broadly, I also use the term *negrophobia* to refer to antiblack sentiment.

12. See Pimentel's December 2016 article in the Dominican newspaper *El acento,* "'¡Diga perejil!'"

13. Quisqueya (also spelled Quisqueia and Kiskeya), meaning "Mother of the Earth," is the Taíno name for Hispaniola.

1. Haitian and Dominican Third Space and the *Trujillato*

1. For more on the differences between *hispanicismo* and *antihaitianismo* (as well as differences between *dominicanidad* and *antihaitianismo*), see Mayes, *Mulatto Republic*.

2. Andrés L. Mateo employs the term *trujillistas teóricos* in *Mito y cultura en la era de Trujillo* to describe the group of intellectuals allowing their hand to be dictated by Trujillo. As Néstor E. Rodríguez confirms, with the definition of this term "Mateo alude a aquellos intelectuales que por su ubicación positiva dentro de la maquinaria estatal ejercían un poder epistémico concreto: el de artificiar y transmitir punto por punto la trayectoria ideológica del régimen trujillista" (*La isla y su envés* 2). In *Dividing Hispaniola,* Paulino instead utilizes the term *guaraguaos,* a Dominicanism meaning "hawk," to refer to the nationalist intellectuals that crystallized the anti-Haitianism of the Trujillo Era.

3. In the context of the Dominican plantation system, the term *cocolo* refers to workers from the English- and Dutch-speaking Antilles. Individuals from these islands began arriving to the Dominican Republic in large numbers in the late nineteenth century when the global demand for sugar increased. *Over* presents *cocolos* as preferable (for North American bosses) to Haitian labor on plantations, largely due to the fact that many spoke English. In general, and outside of the Dominican context, the term *cocolo* is used to describe non-Hispanic African descendants. See Stinchcomb, "Haitians, *Cocolos,* and African Americans," for more on the term in reference to nineteenth- and twentieth-century Dominican literature.

4. See Moya Pons, *La dominación haitiana,* for more on these events.

5. See Paulino, *Dividing Hispaniola;* Candelario, *Black behind the Ears;* Rodríguez, *Escrituras de desencuentro;* and Sagás, *Race and Politics*.

6. Comprehensive biographies of Trujillo confirm Trujillo's genealogy as partly Haitian. Jesús de Galíndez notes that authors "agree" on the identity of Trujillo's parents and grandparents and confirms that his maternal grandmother was Luisa Ercina Chevalier, "of Haitian parentage" (9). An earlier biography written by Robert D. Crassweller shortly following the dictator's assassination asserts the same: "On the maternal side, Trujillo's grandfather was Pedro Molina, a rural Dominican of obscure means but not unfavorable reputation. He married Luisa Erciná Chevalier, the illegitimate daughter of a Haitian Army officer and a Haitian woman, Diyetta Chevalier, who had arrived in Dominican territory during the Haitian occupation" (27).

7. The decline of the sugar estate in the 1920s as a result of plummeting sugar prices led to labor disputes on numerous Dominican plantations. As Mayes confirms, "Sugar-workers organized strikes as early as 1919, demanding higher wages to offset inflation" (102).

8. The Dominican critic Berta Graciano prefers the term *novela de la caña* to refer specifically to a Dominican pattern of literature centered on the sugar plantation.

9. Peña Batlle confirms in *Historia de la cuestión fronteriza dominico-haitiana* that "el pueblo dominicano encontró en Trujillo el cuerpo de su unidad" (197).

10. This 1983 work is a second edition of his 1947 text, *La realidad dominicana: Semblanza de un país y de un régimen.*

11. See Gallego Cuiñas, *Trujillo, el fantasma y sus escritores.*

12. The dance the night before the wedding took place in the home of Manuel Rueda's grandmother (Doña Emiliana in the novel). The house was in its final stages of construction at the time of the wedding, in March 1927. According to the novel, Trujillo requested that the dance be held at "el Club" in Montecristi, but the request was denied by the club (86).

13. In the two other mentions of the Haitian girl, she is described as "la haitiana de los paquetes" (85) and "la haitianita ensimismada" (89).

14. At the time, these newspapers were the most widely distributed in the country, as they remain today. *El Diario* is the principal paper in Santiago, and *El Nuevo Diario* circulates most widely in Santo Domingo.

15. Marrero Aristy also served as editor in chief of *La Nación* and deputy secretary of state and national labor and economy.

16. Marrero Aristy was assassinated by Trujillo in 1959. Marrero Aristy traveled to New York in 1958, where he conspired with anti-Trujillo Dominican exiles. Upon his return to the Dominican Republic in June 1959, the author was involved in a car accident. According to the *Enciclopedia dominicana, Tomo IV* (1968), "Se afirma que fue asesinado personalmente por el tirano" (712).

17. Scholarship centered on the Dominican sugar industry as well as on North American interest in the plantation economy includes Mayes's aforementioned *Mulatto Republic*; Sánchez, *La caña en Santo Domingo*; and Corten, Acosta, and Duarte, *Azúcar y política en la República Dominicana*, among others.

18. Two Dominican writers asserting their blackness around the time when Marrero Aristy wrote were Aída Cartagena Portalatín and Blas Jiménez. See Stinchcomb, *Development of Literary Blackness*, for more on this topic.

19. Trujillo not only controlled the sugar industry by means of political policies and government corruption; he also owned a large number of plantations. His economic investments extended far beyond the sugar industry, and as Moya Pons notes, "Trujillo managed to become the largest saver and investor in the Republic and finally the first great captain of industry in the Dominican Republic" (*Dominican Republic* 362). Reportedly, none of the plantations owned by Trujillo or US citizens were touched during the 1937 Massacre.

20. *Over* has now been printed twenty times, most recently in 2011 by Alfaguara Press.

21. Recent examinations of the novel have gone beyond Sommer's insistence on the absent father figure in her attempt to critique the North American "capitalists who masquerade as fathers at their convenience" ("Populism as Rhetoric" 265). These contemporary analyses of Marrero Aristy's bestseller include García-Peña; Reyes-Santos; Paulino; and Victoriano-Martínez.

22. Moscoso Puello's novel portrays the North American administrators' negotiation of Dominican culture, showing plantation managers to be victims (alongside Dominicans and Haitians) of a capitalist, US-owned system. Regardless of the blanket representation of managers, Haitians, and Dominicans as victims of the plantation's external owners, a hierarchy based on race and class remains intact.

23. García-Peña notes that the novel takes place on a "sugarcane *batey* in the east" (102).

24. In Marrero Aristy's *Over*, the term *cocolo* is used to identify non-Haitian West Indian immigrants in the Dominican Republic. However, the Dominican poet Pedro Mir more recently defined *cocolo* as "any Haitian that crossed the border" (Mota Acosta 6).

25. As mentioned previously, the *cocolo* workforce comprised workers from other Caribbean islands, largely the West Indies. The term *bracero* was used to refer to contracted workers, largely from other neighboring, small islands.

26. Sommer, in her article "Populism as Rhetoric," identifies Daniel as the spoiled "anti-hero" (at the novel's start) who is later converted into a "variation of the romantic independent Husband who plans to repossess his Land, but one who would recognize his own weakness and be available for a stronger leader" (263). Daniel proves capable of thinking and independently advocating for the Haitians, but he is not led to action, not a "leader."

27. Prestol Castillo refers to these hidden notes as "notas de la frontera" (141).

28. Another notable text of Prestol Castillo's is *Pablo Mamá*. This work describes a border war and centers on the protagonist, of debatable ethnicity, who is the leader of the Restoration War and rules in part through his magical powers. This work links to the recurring theme of the Restoration War (1861–65), as well as the Haitian Occupation (1822–44), in Dominican literature.

29. For more on the 1937 Haitian Massacre, see Richard Lee Turits, "Bordering the National: Race, Colonization, and the 1937 Haitian Massacre in the Dominican Frontier," in Turits, *Foundations of Despotism* (2003).

30. For more on Beverley's definition of the Latin American *testimonio*, see his *Testimonio*.

31. Prestol Castillo is not the only author to recall the 1937 Massacre in literary form. Other notable novels portraying the event with roots on the western side of Hispaniola include the Haitian American Edwidge Danticat's *The Farming of Bones;* the Haitian Jacques Stephen Alexis's *General Sun, My Brother;* and the Haitian René Philoctète's *Massacre River*.

32. Fumagalli also notes the author's hesitation to align himself with the dominant Trujillo ideology of the time, noting his "inability and unwillingness to either fully embrace or resolutely reject dominant discourses" (141), Prestol Castillo refusing to take sides publicly.

33. This selective bolding of certain words in the text appears in the first four editions of the novel, published by Taller (1973, January 1974, February 1974, and 1977), as well as in reprints of these editions.

34. Dajabón is the name of both the province itself and the capital city of the province.

35. A mere one year before the massacre, Trujillo solidified a new border agreement, the Trujillo-Vincent Treaty. This treaty formally divided previously anonymous border zones inhabited largely by *rayanos*. The treaty also signaled the increasing influence of Haitian culture in and around the Dominican borderlands. The booming sugar industry (along with the thousands of Haitian workers keeping the sugar mills afloat), the 1936 Trujillo-Vincent Treaty, and the 1937 Massacre represented a triple threat to the country's program for "Dominicanization."

36. Juan Nazario's mixed-race family's situation is the same as Manuelita and Yosefo's. His children are labeled "catizos" (61, *sic*), and the children's linguistic choice confirms this: "Los hijos de Juan Nazario hablen en 'patois'" (60). The Dominican Juan Nazario stops the troops barely in time to save his family of *negros castizos* from slaughter. He screams, "Peidone [*sic*] a estos negros! . . . que son mis hijos! ¡aunque sean mitad haitiano!" (62).

37. In *Paisajes y meditaciones,* unsurprisingly, not once is a Haitian or Haitian Dominican considered on an individual basis or given a name. Instead, Prestol Castillo addresses the group as a collective whole, offering no anecdotal evidence to contradict the Trujillo-authorized discourse in regard to the Haitian subject.

38. The name Jean Pié here could have ties to Juan Bosch's story "Luis Pie" (written in 1942 and published in 1962). "Luis Pie" shows how little value the life of a Haitian *bracero* had in the Dominican countryside. The protagonist, Luis Pie, has an injured foot from work on an *ingenio,* but he is blamed for starting a brush fire in fact ignited by the manager's cigar thrown carelessly from his car. Stories by Ramón Lacay Polanco (*Punto Sur* 1958; South point) and Bosch's story mentioned previously, for example, provide alternatives to the markedly anti-Haitian narratives published in the 1930s and early 1940s, questioning and disputing the unconcealed contempt shown toward the Dominican's neighboring state in earlier literature.

39. Other examples include: "A través de este documento se perfila toda una sociedad perezosa, en la que todos viven de la producción natural de la tierra, llámese bosque o animal" (38) and "El negro de Haití es el africano más auténtico en las Antillas, vale decir, es el tipo negro menos evolucionado" (50).

40. Soulouque was elected president of Haiti in 1847, and two years later, in 1849, he was proclaimed emperor of Haiti. His reign was marked by violence, and although he ordered the Haitian army to invade the Dominican Republic numerous times, all attempts to annex the eastern side of the island failed.

41. The novel refers to Angela Vargas as a "modelo de virtud" (142), expressing the narrator's envy of her ability to openly denounce the regime.

42. Juan Bosch, for example, wrote from exile in Cuba during the greater part of the *trujillato* and published his well-known collections of short stories, *Cuentos escritos en el exilio* (1962; Stories written in exile) and *Más cuentos escritos en el exilio* (1962; More stories written in exile). Bosch also was a politician and historian; he founded the Dominican Revolutionary Party (PRD) and served as the first democratically elected president of the Dominican Republic (for a mere eight months in 1963). His legacy stresses the unbreakable connection between literature and politics in the Dominican Republic. The dictatorship, its control over the sugar industry, "dominicanización" policies, and anti-Haitian ideology were central themes in his writing.

2. A Disappearing Act

1. Torres-Saillant calls Veloz Maggiolo "the most prolific contemporary Dominican writer" ("Marcio Veloz Maggiolo" 322), and Horn refers to Veloz Maggiolo as the "most renowned living Dominican novelist" (51).

2. The Premio Nacional de la Novela, awarded by the Fundación Corripio and the secretary of state for education, was presented to Veloz Maggiolo for both his fiction and his anthropological and archaeological investigations. Considered one of the most prominent Caribbean archaeologists, Veloz Maggiolo has published widely in the area; some of his most well-known articles include "Arqueología prehistórica de Santo Domingo," "Las sociedades arcaicas de Santo Domingo," and "La isla de Santo Domingo antes de Colón." Veloz Maggiolo also received the Premio Nacional de Poesía in 1961 and the Premio Nacional de Cuento in 1981.

3. Other well-known novels by Veloz Maggiolo include, but are not limited to, *Judas, El buen ladrón* (1960), *Ritos de cabaret* (1992), *Trujillo, Villa Francisca y otros fantasmas* (1996), *Nosotros los suicidas* (1965), *Los ángeles de hueso* (1967), *Florbella* (1986), and *El jefe iba descalzo* (1993).

4. *El hombre del acordeón* and *La vida no tiene nombre* are not Veloz Maggiolo's only novels that clearly portray the ties between the two countries of Hispaniola. For example, the author roots *La biografía difusa de Sombra Castañeda* in the Haitian-Dominican folkloric tradition and makes reference to both Taíno and African cultures.

5. Hereafter, I use the English term *Trujillo narrative* to refer to this literary subgenre.

6. Some critics prefer to refer to Trujillo narrative written after 1961 as "(neo)trujillato" narrative. As De Maeseneer notes, "Hasta hoy en día siguen sobreviviendo en la sociedad y la política dominicana estructuras típicas de lo que unos llaman neotrujillismo y otros, autoritarianismo, para usar el término menos connotado con el contexto dominicano" (*Seis ensayos* 20).

7. Latin American literary scholarship often classifies this subgenre of historical narrative, centered on the figure of the dictator, as *literatura del dictador*

or *novela del dictator*. Sharon Keefe Ugalde instead suggests employing the term *narrativa de dictador/dictadura*, this latter classification only addressing novels with a *principal* focus on the figure of the dictator or effects of a given dictatorship (130).

8. Veloz Maggiolo won his first Premio Nacional de la Novela for *Judas*. As González-Cruz writes, one possible reading of the novel views the father of Judas, Simón de Idumea, "como símbolo del tirano y Judas como representación del hombre dominicano, desposeído" (108).

9. As with the literary corpus of the authors considered in chapter 2, not all of Veloz Maggiolo's work is considered openly anti-Trujillo. In fact, in the early 1930s he published an article in the dictator's favor (Gallego Cuiñas 19). Veloz Maggiolo is not the only Dominican writer to praise the dictator during his thirty-one-year reign, as censorship during this period made it difficult to publish anything considered remotely anti-Trujillo.

10. *El hombre del acordeón* states that the capital of La Línea is Montecristi (32).

11. *Nepantla*, as defined in Anzaldúa's "(Un)natural Bridges, (Un)safe Spaces," describes spaces between worlds. It is the physical location that marks the actual crossing itself, the place where one has crossed point A but is yet to enter point B.

12. While the 1937 Massacre of Haitians and Dominicans of Haitian descent is the historical, thematic backdrop of the novel, the geographic one is the Massacre River. The town of La Salada is noted as being nestled on "las orillas del río Masacre" (30).

13. There is no question that Brigadier is indeed a pseudonym for Trujillo. Not only do biographical facts align—the narrator mentions that Brigadier's grandmother was Haitian (14) and notes the date of his death in 1961 (67), for example—but so do the dates of his presidency and his involvement with the 1937 Massacre. Additionally, the middle or second name of Brigadier is Leónidas, and Trujillo's middle name was Leónidas.

14. "No estaba tan delineada" (*Acordeón* 14, my translation).

15. González-Cruz lists other literary devices commonly employed by Veloz Maggiolo: "Entre los recursos técnicos frecuentemente empleados por Veloz Maggiolo, se pueden citar: la invención de palabras, las enumeraciones intensificadores, los espacios en blanco para sugerir silencios significativos, el entrecruzamiento de planos temporales y del fluir de la conciencia de diferentes personajes, la fragmentación del discurso para traducir con fidelidad procesos de asociación de ideas" (110).

16. In the following pages, references to both the border itself *and* the fictional town (La Salada, located within La Línea) will be written as "la L/línea." This dual connotation allows a broader understanding of the border that also includes a metaphorical understanding of the multiplicity of the frontier.

17. The Dominican poet Pedro Mir, in his poem "Las dos patrias," refers to the relationship between the Dominican Republic and Haiti in this way. His

allusion to the "unitarian current" that runs through the island as a whole speaks to a heritage and history that is common to both countries.

18. Music and performance as a crossroads in spaces defined by a physical border has been the subject of study for those interested in the US-Mexican border. See Madrid's *Transnational Encounters;* and Ragland's *Música Norteña.*

19. It is important to note the distinction between *rayanos* and *fronterizos* in the novel. While the term *rayano* traditionally refers to a border inhabitant, the references in *El hombre del acordeón* mark *rayanos* as biracial and biethnic. Page 17 defines *rayanos* as a "mezcla mulata de negros y blancos." While this definition is confusing, as many Dominicans (with no ties to the border region or Haiti) could be considered a "mezcla mulata," page 62 clarifies that the use of the term *rayanos* seems to refer specifically to Dominicans of Haitian descent, noting that the *rayanos* hid in Haiti after 1937 because of the dangerous atmosphere after the massacre. Another quotation points to the *rayanos'* dual religion: "rayanos al fin, creen en ambas religiones" (84). For these reasons, within the context of this novel, *rayano* can be interpreted as a Dominican of Haitian descent or a Haitian living in the Dominican Republic, while *fronterizo* refers to anyone who lives along La Línea, for example, Honorio Lora.

20. See Montenegro, *21 Divisions.*

21. See Fumagalli, *On the Edge* 159, for a more detailed description of the *volanderas.*

22. While rebellion is key to *El hombre del acordeón,* it is important to highlight the literary rebellion of Veloz Maggiolo and his Dominican counterparts. Aída Cartagena Portalatín, in a brief anthology titled *Narradores dominicanos,* points to the rebellion of the younger generation of Dominican writers regarding their response to the traditions of the generations of writers preceding them.

23. Fumagalli writes that Honorio Lora's music "taps into merengue's history of rebellion against central power: before Trujillo's appropriation, the accordion-based merengue typical of the Cibao area had in fact epitomized the country's resistance to North American occupation" (154).

24. The *bachata* musical genre, considered music of the underprivileged and marginalized populations during the *trujillato,* is also linked to resistance to the Trujillo regime, as it was "a cultural reaction to his oppressive regime" and "even listening to *bachata* music can be considered a form of resistance to upper-class hegemony" (Reagan 378).

25. The Dominican folklorist Fradique Lizardo was one of the first to openly claim merengue's African origins. See *La cultura africana en Santo Domingo.*

26. This metaphor repeats in the novel: "El acordeón, que era como su arma de guerra" (33).

27. Page 67, for example, marks Vetemit as "cuentero de profesión." This characterization appears to be in part generational, as Vetemit's own father is also categorized in this way; an "informe" written by Alzaga mentions the death of his father "por bandolero y charlatán" (70).

28. Other twentieth-century Dominican novels, including Marrero Aristy's *Over* and Presto Castillo's *El Masacre se pasa a pie,* portray Haitians as untrustworthy. J. Michael Dash's analysis of Zora Neale Hurston's *Tell My Horse* (1938) reveals this same patterned representation of Haitians in non-Dominican literature. Dash writes that "Hurston's reader is advised that Haitians were compulsive liars" and that the author "sees Haitians as untrustworthy" (59).

29. Veloz Maggiolo does, however, mention *La vida no tiene nombre* as an example of the "integrated Haitian" in his "Tipología del tema haitiano" (30).

30. Veloz Maggiolo's publication following *La vida no tiene nombre, Los ángeles de hueso,* is more commonly regarded as a post-Boom novel. See Candelier, "Marcio Veloz Maggiolo."

31. Horn frames a shift in Dominican letters following the *trujillato* by examining the modernization of Veloz Maggiolo's narrative, notably in *Los ángeles de hueso.*

32. *La vida no tiene nombre* is only Veloz Maggiolo's second novel, following *El buen ladrón* (1960). His first publication was a *poemario* titled *El sol y las cosas* (1957).

33. Another novel for which the 1916 US invasion is a historical framework is Nelly Rosario's *Song of the Water Saints.* This Latino/a text reveals a generational female storyline in which the first-generation character, Graciela, comes of age in Santo Domingo during the first US occupation.

34. For more on the 1916–24 US Military occupation, see Moya Pons, *Dominican Republic* 321–39.

35. "El Cuerno" here refers to Ramón's "illegitimate child" status. He is "un hijo del cuerno," a Dominican Haitian born of an act of sexual assault and infidelity.

36. See Moya Pons, *Dominican Republic.*

37. See Fiallo Billini's "La revolución de abril," for more on the Revolution of 1965.

38. *Judas* and *El buen ladrón,* separate works, were first published together in 1960.

39. The following quote also points to the necessity of reevaluating history after the fall of Trujillo: "El análisis sociopolítico y la reevaluación histórica era una necesidad después de la caída del régimen que había conseguido hacer tergiversar la historia a conveniencia de su propia práctica política" (Alcánta Almánzar 373).

40. For more examples of such comparisons, born of the naturalist tradition, see Candelier 94.

41. Also spelled El Seybo, the province is not to be confused with the macro region in the Dominican Republic, El Cibao (also known for cattle). While the El Seibo region was the site of some sugar plantations in the early 1900s, it has traditionally been known for its cattle farms, as it continues to be today. Ramón describes the region in this way: "La tierra donde vivíamos, muy cerca de El Seibo, estaba dedicado al ganado, porque a mi papá le gustaba eso de la ganadería y vivía metido entre los potreros y las vacas" (13).

42. There are also significant populations of both Japanese and Jewish in the Dominican Republic. These groups arrived as legal immigrants to the country during the *trujillato* as a direct result of Trujillo's plan to "whiten" the country.

43. Ramón first introduces his mother in his testimony as "aquella haitiana llamada Simián . . . mi madre fue sirvienta de la casa durante mucho tiempo" (19). Ramón notes that her biggest "sins" were "el haberme parido y el ser haitiana" (25).

44. See Horn, *Masculinity after Trujillo,* esp. chap. 2, "One Phallus for Another: Post-dictatorship Political and Literary Canons," for an analysis of gendered Trujillo narratives, in particular of Veloz Maggiolo's novels *De abril en adelante* (1975) and *Uña y carne: Memorias de la virilidad* (1999).

45. Gallego Cuiñas utilizes a similar term, *el enemigo que está detrás,* to describe the US government in *De abril en adelante:* "El 'enemigo que está detrás'—en la sombra—es el gobierno Estadounidense, el cual propició la incursión de Trujillo (formando en sus filas durante la intervención de 1916) en el poder y que más tarde dio el beneplácito y la aquiescencia a su modo de gobernar, arrogándose el tirano su apoyo en muchas decisiones" (163).

46. "Pienso en papá y todavía el odio me rezuma en las entrañas" (17).

47. While the goals of the *gavilleros* began as patriotic, to defend the nation against a foreign presence on the island, the rebel forces "terminó degenerándose y convirtiéndose en fuerzas temerías y temibles a los ojos de la población, y a los gavilleros se sumaron todas la banda deseosas de saqueo, sin escrúpulos para violar y matar, para robar y atemorizar, y esos elementos negativos, aunque numérica y militarmente engrosaban el pelotón de combatientes, moralmente desacreditaban al movimiento revolucionario" (Candelier 87).

48. Moya Pons postulates that Boyer's first public decision after official possession of Santo Domingo "fue decretar la abolición de la esclavitud y prometer tierras a todos los libertos para que pudieran dedicarse a vivir de la agricultura" (*La dominación* 35).

49. It should be noted that numerous twentieth-century Dominican poets have also incorporated the Haitian subject in their work, namely, Manuel Rueda, Pedro Mir, Ramón Francisco, and Manuel del Cabral. Often, the Haitian subject penetrates poems by these Dominican nationals as an integrated part of society and an integral part of the Dominican landscape.

50. My decision to consider novels by two male authors reflects twentieth-century publishing trends in the Dominican Republic. While female Dominican authors began to publish more frequently after Trujillo's assassination, the primary genre of expression for Dominican females, especially in the mid- to late twentieth century, has been poetry. Sara V. Rosell confirms this, writing: "La poesía es el género que más impulse la apertura y el desarrollo de la literatura femenina" (36). See her book *La novela de escritoras dominicanas de 1990 a 2007* for more on Dominican women writers. Erika M. Martínez's *Daring to Write* (2016) is a recent anthology of multigenre writing by Dominican women.

3. "Here We Are the Haitians"

1. The play was first performed in April 2014 at the ONE Festival in New York City. Subsequent performances include the People's Theatre Project at the Alianza Dominicana Cultural Center in September 2014; "Border Story Fest: The Dominican Republic and Haiti" at Duke University on March 30, 2016, and performances at numerous universities in the United States, including Rutgers, Brown, and the University of California–Santa Cruz, among others.

2. Vicioso expands on her experience with racial identity in the United States in "Discovering Myself: Un testimonio," an essay in the edited collection *The Afro-Latin@ Reader.* Vicioso, who first arrived in the United States in 1967, depicts her experience with racial classifications as a Brooklyn College student first asserting her *caribeña* identity: "In the United States, there is no space for fine distinctions of race, and one goes from being *trigueño* or *indio* to being 'mulatto' or 'Black' or 'Hispanic.'" Vicioso writes that she "adopted the Black identity as a gesture of solidarity" and that she has since continued to identify herself as a "Black woman" (263).

3. The Dominican American Dr. Rafael Lantigua speaks of the Dominican diaspora in the United States and echoes this same sentiment: "We're the Haitians here" (Mindlin).

4. The term *Latino* itself has proven problematic as it is used to refer to an increasingly diverse population in the United States. Dávila, in *Latino Spin,* points to a contemporary US discourse that too often overethnicizes or de-ethnicizes Latinos/as "whether by presenting them as a threat or as contributors to the 'national community'; by highlighting their growing purchasing power and intrinsic 'values'; or because of their coming of age or eagerness to assimilate" (4–5).

5. Royal Caribbean's website describes the Paradise Cove Escape as a "shore excursion" in Labadee, Haiti, with optional activities ranging from zip lines to jet skiing.

6. The podcast, formerly known as *About Race,* aired on Slate's Panoply network from 2015 to 2017.

7. Cepeda, "So, THIS Happened Last Night at the United Nations."

8. Later attempts of Dominicans on the island to "whiten" their race include the fact that the most commonly used racial classification on the Dominican *cédula* or identity card was *indio/a* (as opposed to *negro/a*) until the Dominican Republic Electoral Law Reform eradicated the category in 2011.

9. Báez also shares this sentiment, highlighting the duality of the Dominican American identity: "Americanness and Dominicanness can hardly be deemed polar extremes since neither is itself homogeneous. Dominicanish resists and combats rigid definitions of culture" (13).

10. This differentiation between "us" and "them"—read as two different groups of Dominicans in the space of the diaspora—is also palpable in Díaz's

This Is How You Lose Her: "Remember the Spanish chick, the one who'd been crying over him at the Yarn Barn? Well, turns out she was actually Dominican. Not Dominican like my brother or me but *Dominican* Dominican. As in fresh-off-the-boat-didn't-have-no-papers-Domincan" (100). Juan Flores approaches the us-and-them dichotomy in the Latino community—a community he marks as one of Benedict Anderson's "imagined communities"—as a constant questioning of who is and who is not Latino/a. He notes, "Beyond the issue of names and labels, and even who is using them, there are differing levels or modes of meaning simultaneously at work in the very act of apprehending and conceptualizing the 'community' and 'identity' in question" (193–94).

11. Flores confirms the rising number of Latinos/as in *From Bomba to Hip-Hop:* "Hispanics are the nation's 'fastest-growing minority,' on course to become the 'largest' minority at some (variously defined) point early in the coming century" (195).

12. A line earlier in the memoir expresses the same sentiment: "When you see a thing, what then is your obligation?" (108).

13. Among the few critical essays on *A Wedding in Haiti* are Ellen Mayock's "Julia Alvarez and Haiti" and Kelly Lyon Johnson's "Both Sides of the Massacre."

14. A subsequent entrance by Alvarez into Haiti, bypassing customs, also appears uncomplicated: "No fees, red tape, endless lines or avoiding all of the above with a bribe" ("Along the Seam of Hispaniola").

15. Yo serves as a constant reminder to the reader that the novel is historical fiction, based on the author's adolescence and adulthood in the United States, namely, New York City, alongside her three sisters. Although the novel's character Yolanda was born in the Dominican Republic and not New York City (as Alvarez was), the connections between the two are still important.

16. In an autobiographical essay titled "A White Woman of Color," Alvarez briefly speaks of her family's maids in the Dominican Republic, alluding to the Haitian ancestry of many. One maid in particular, Misiá, a Haitian, had been "spared from the machetes of the 1937 Massacre when she was taken in and hidden from the prowling *guardias* by the family" (143). The fictional Chucha in *García Girls* shares a biography with Misiá, leading to the assumption that the character of Chucha is based on Misiá.

17. Another nonliterary commemoration of the 1937 Massacre is the Dominican American composer and saxophonist Juan Colon's recent musical composition *The Parsley Massacre.* The original score premiered at the Pregones Theatre in Bronx, NY, performed by the Multicultural Music Center (MCM) orchestra on June 11, 2010.

18. Ana María Belique shared this sentiment at Border of Lights planning meetings with community partners in both 2016 and 2017. Reconoci.do, also known as Movimiento Reconoci.do, a nonprofit based in the Dominican Republic and made up primarily of Dominicans of Haitian descent, advocates for a

multicultural, intercultural Dominican Republic in which the rights of all are respected and guaranteed by national laws. The organization's name, which means "recognized" in English, also plays on the Dominican Republic domain name, *.do*.

19. An organization similar to Reconoci.do and We Are All Dominican is Dominican@s por derecho. According to the group's mission statement, it is "a group of organizations and people who defend the rights of Dominican of foreign descent impacted by the ruling 168-13 dictated by the Constitutional Tribunal (TC) of the Dominican Republic" ("Who We Are"). The majority of the content on the Dominican@s por derecho webpage, which notes that the organization is "presented and recognized by the Dominican State," is in Spanish.

20. The Twitter handle of We Are All Dominican is @Dominicanxs. Their website is wearealldominicannyc.wordpress.com.

21. *Nos cambió la vida* was published by Centro Bonó, in collaboration with Reconoci.do. The book can be accessed from Reconoci.do's blog.

22. In an e-mail of 17 Mar. 2018, González Díaz shared with me the intended audience for the documentary: "La audiencia primaria son las personas dominicanas de ascendencia haitiana. El documental pretende ser al mismo tiempo una forma de honrar su lucha y también de motivar la reorganización del colectivo. Luego me interesa que el documental llegue al público de a pie en RD. Más allá de los grupos sensibilizados, ongs y activistas sociales, quiero que el documental llegue al público dominicano que solo conoce del tema por los medios de comunicación. Así, la estrategia es colocarla en el cine comercial de RD y tiempo después, ofrecerla gratis por youtube. Por último, me interesa que el documental también llegue a la diáspora dominicana, especialmente en los Estados Unidos."

4. Multiple Haitis

1. The four-part series *Black in Latin America* was Gates's eleventh public-television production. The series, which premiered in May 2011, looked at the influence of African descent on Latin America and spotlighted six countries: the Dominican Republic, Haiti, Cuba, Brazil, Mexico, and Peru ("About"). Gates published a book by the same title, *Black in Latin America,* in July 2011.

2. Relatedly, the relationship between Dominicans and Puerto Ricans, especially concerning the large-scale migration of Dominicans to Puerto Rico and the United States after the *trujillato,* is a more frequent and better-documented interest. Jorge Duany, in "Dominican Migration to Puerto Rico," considers the transnational migration from the Dominican Republic to Puerto Rico, as compared with and opposed to the flow of Dominican migrants to the United States. The Puerto Rican Department of Justice reports that 118,999 Dominican legally immigrated to the neighboring island of Puerto Rico from 1966 to 2002, making them the largest foreign population living in Puerto Rico in the twenty first century. For more on the global Dominican migration patterns, see Guarnizo, "Los Dominicanyorks"; Martínez-San Miguel, *Caribe Two Ways;* and Duany, *Los dominicanos en Puerto Rico.*

3. Accepting Hispaniola as a "blind spot" further aligns the island with Foucault's notion of a heterotopic space—a disturbing, transforming, contradictory, easily forgotten space. The first distinction within Foucault's structuralism paradigm is a "crisis heterotopia." A crisis heterotopia is a site defined by a state of crisis, a space that is forbidden to those who have no relation to it, a "blind spot" or void for those whose lives are not rooted in the crises of that space.

4. José Luis Borges and Alfonso Reyes referred to Henríquez Ureña as "maestro de América" (Avome Mba 71).

5. Soledad Álvarez's 1981 book *La magna patria de Pedro Henríquez Ureña* discusses Henríquez Ureña's Americanist platform and his constant reference to the Americas as the Great Motherland (11).

6. Dominican intellectuals asserting Henríquez Ureña's commitment to Dominican culture include Emilio Rodríguez Demorizi, Juan Jacobo de Lara, and Carlos Federico Pérez y Pérez, among others.

7. The first sentence of the novel describes the Dominican-born *fukú*: "They say it came first from Africa, carried in the screams of the enslaved; that it was the death bane of the Tainos, uttered just as one world perished and another began; that it was a demon drawn into Creation through the nightmare door that was cracked open in the Antilles" (1). *Fukú* is also known as "the curse of the new world" since it originated when Columbus arrived in 1492. The grandiose monument to Columbus in the Dominican capital of Santo Domingo, inaugurated in 1992, is "el faro a Colon," considered to this day a cursed lighthouse.

8. This man with no face, also appears in "Ysrael," the first story in Díaz's 1996 *Drown*, this time in the form of a boy. The older brother, Rafa, chases after and physically assaults a teenager in the Dominican Republic who wears a face mask to hide his disfigured face. The narrator describes what he sees when the mask is ripped off: "His left ear was a nub and you could see the thick veined slab of his tongue though a hole in his cheek. He had no lips" (18–19). The faceless man/boy marks Díaz's early interest in science fiction (sf). On one occasion the author expressed his affinity for sf and his literary goals within the genre to become "a Dominican Octavia Butler or a Dominican Samuel Delaney," referencing two canonical sf writers (Danticat, "Junot Díaz" 92).

9. While I mention sf, my intention is a general approach to the expansive genre. I apply the term *science fiction* or *sf* in a general sense, not excluding fantasy or other sub-genre specificities like Afro-futurism.

10. When first published, "Monstro" was dubbed an excerpt to Díaz's next novel. Interestingly, *Oscar Wao* was also first published as a short story in the *New Yorker*, in 2001.

11. Matthew Goodwin expands on the frontier metaphor in sf. Goodwin considers how contemporary sf writers have turned away from the frontier and instead fixated on the concept of borderland as the "new geographic center of virtual reality" (164). He notes the borderland as a hybridizing, as opposed to an expansionist, orientation of the frontier.

12. There are also overt references to a "cure" in *Oscar Wao*. Yunior references Oscar's sf manuscript in progress and labels it "the cure to what ails us" (333), positioning sf as a societal cure. The phrase also points to Díaz's hope that sf will propose models for the future and serve as an ideal mode of (political) critique, an idea shared by Older.

13. See Lavender's *Race in American Science Fiction:* "When race and contagion are placed together with otherhood in sf, they function as metaphor and metonym simultaneously" (120).

14. In September 2013 the Dominican Tribunal Court redefined the term *in transit* in a constitutional clause. This new understanding of the term found that any individual born after 1929 who did not have at least one parent of Dominican nationality was in the country illegally, thus considered "in transit" and unable to obtain birthright citizenship.

15. Díaz prefaces his commentary on the Dominican Republic assistance following the 2010 earthquake by addressing the relationship between the two nations of Hispaniola: "Consider also my people, the Dominicans. In the modern period, few Caribbean populations have been more hostile to Haitians. We are of course neighbors, but what neighbors!"

16. For more on dystopia in sf, see Fitting, "Utopia, Dystopia, and Science Fiction."

17. Chapter 3 of Arroyo's *Writing Secrecy in Caribbean Freemasonry* focuses primarily on Haiti's and the Haitian Revolution's political, historical, and cultural influence on the Spanish Caribbean and on certain US diasporic communities. Arroyo details Betances's inclusive view of blackness, a racial discourse that veered from those of radical thinkers like José Martí and Eugenio María de Hostos, which favored racial equality but erased the history of the first black republic.

18. The term *Afrofuturism,* which first surfaced in American cultural studies, is credited to Mark Dery. See Dery's "Black to the Future: Interviews with Samuel R. Delaney, Greg Tate, and Tricia Rose" and "Black to the Future: Afro-Futurism 1.0."

19. Isiah M. Lavender III labels science fiction "an outwardly white genre" (*Black and Brown Planets* 10). For more on race and science fiction, see Lavender, *Race in American Science Fiction;* Lavender, *Black and Brown Planets;* and Carrington, *Speculative Blackness.* Older has spoken out on numerous occasions about the lack of diversity in sf novels. Recently, he criticized the *Hunger Games* films for portraying Katniss Everdeen, the nonwhite protagonist in the novels, as white (Ford). One active movement supporting the push for diversity in sf and other literary genres is We Need Diverse Books (WNDB; see weneeddiversebooks.org).

20. *Shadowshaper* includes other overt references to cultural differences and similarities between Haiti and other Hispanic-Caribbean nations, including a discussion about people dancing at funerals (160).

21. Older openly speaks about the need for diversity and the constant whitewashing of black characters in young adult literature. In one interview he

references the "mega-aggressions of the publishing industry," which he cites as "an unwelcoming industry for writers of color and their characters" ("Diversity Is Not Enough").

22. The Dominican American Loida Maritza Pérez's *Geographies of Home* (1999), like Older's *Shadowshaper,* is set in Brooklyn and explores negation(s) of blackness and identity crises. Pérez's novel, however, centers its critique of the American dream and the struggle inherent in forming an identity in the diaspora within the family unit. Angie Cruz's *Soledad* (2002), similarly focusing on a twenty-something Dominican American girl grappling with identity, replicates the complex desire to return home in Pérez's novel.

23. In a foreword to *Edwidge Danticat: A Reader's Guide,* Dany Laferrière suggests that for Danticat, too, there are multiple Haitis: "How to reconcile these two worlds? The question was all the more complex in that there are two, maybe three Haitis: the Haiti that she keeps fresh in her memory, the Haiti of her parents who lived with her in Brooklyn, and the country itself that she continued to see on television and in the newspapers, always in great difficulty" (viii).

24. Évelyne Trouillot's 2003 novel *Rosalie l'infâme* is also inspired by a historical account; the novel centers on an Arada midwife who was brought as a slave to colonial Saint Domingue from West Africa.

25. Fumagalli's comprehensive study *On the Edge* also analyzes *The Blue of the Island* and briefly comments the play's use of the color blue. She notes that the "blue of the island" in the play is "the sky that the migrants are not able to see while in transit" (287). Régine Michelle Jean-Charles's essay "'A Border between Geographies of Grief': River Crossings and Crossroads between Haiti and the Dominican Republic" further interprets the color blue in the play as "a metonym for the island, the sea, and the sky" and as "a contradictory color" that functions as an ideal "metaphor for the border between Haiti and the Dominican Republic" (98).

26. The Barbadian poet and scholar Kamau Brathwaite's poetry collection *Black + Blues* (1977) more specifically marks the Caribbean experience by overt, repeated references to these colors. In particular, Brathwaite's poem "Conqueror" addresses the slave revolts in Haiti and touts the victories of Toussaint Louverture and Henri Christophe, both former slaves. "Conqueror" delineates the contrasts between the green of the land and the blue of the sea surrounding Hispaniola: "green growing in green / green glowing against blue" (11).

27. Dash denotes the circular pattern of departure and return in Haitian literary discourse, using the "peasant novel" and Jacques Roumain's *Masters of the Dew* as examples.

Conclusion

1. The Puerto Rican Mayra Montero's novel *Tú, la oscuridad* (1995)—a social-ecological novel about Haiti—also begins with a map. That map, however, displays all of Haiti, the border, and just the westernmost sliver of the Dominican Republic.

Bibliography

"About *Black in Latin America*." *PBS*, 19 and 26 Apr., 3 and 10 May 2011. www.pbs.org/wnet/black-in-latin-america/about/.

Alcánta Almánzar, José. "Narrativa y sociedad en Hispanoamérica." *Revista Iberoamericana* 54, no. 143 (1988): 372–73.

Alexis, Jacques Stephen. *General Sun, My Brother*. Translated by Carrol F. Coates. U of Virginia P, 1999.

Alvarez, Julia. "Along the Seam of Hispaniola." *New York Times*, 30 Nov. 2014, 1L.

———. *How the García Girls Lost Their Accents*. 1991. Reprint, Algonquin Books, 2010.

———. *In the Time of the Butterflies*. Algonquin Books, 1994.

———. "A Promise Kept: A Conversation with Julia Alvarez." Interview by Megan Jeanette Myers. *Afro-Hispanic Review* 30, no. 2 (2011): 169–76.

———. *Something to Declare*. Plume, 1999.

———. *A Wedding in Haiti*. Algonquin Books, 2012.

———. "A White Woman of Color." In *Half and Half: Writers on Growing Up Biracial and Bicultural*, edited by Claudine Chiawei O'Hearn, 139–49. Pantheon Books, 1998.

Álvarez, Soledad. *La magna patria de Pedro Henríquez Ureña*. Editorial Taller, 1981.

———. "*La vida no tiene nombre*: Un relato existencial entre dos tiempos." In Veloz Maggiolo, *La vida no tiene nombre*, 95–101.

Anzaldúa, Gloria. *Borderlands/La Frontera: The New Mestiza*. 2nd ed. Aunt Lute Books, 1999.

———. "(Un)natural Bridges, (Un)safe Spaces." In Keating, *Gloria Anzaldúa Reader*, 243–48.

Aparicio, Frances R. "Latinidad/es." In *Keywords for Latina/o Studies*, edited by Deborah R. Vargas, Nancy Raquel Mirabal, and Lawrence La Fountain-Stokes, 113–17. New York UP, 2017.

Arroyo, Jossianna. *Writing Secrecy in Caribbean Freemasonry.* Palgrave Macmillan, 2013.

Avome Mba, Gisèle. "Reflexiones sobre el pensamiento utópico de Pedro Henríquez Ureña." *Revista pensamiento americano* 1, no. 1 (2008): 69–75.

Ayuso, Mónica G. "Toward Forgiveness and Reconciliation: Three Novels from Haiti." *Journal of Haitian Studies* 22, no. 2 (2016): 83–104.

Báez, Josefina. *Dominicanish.* Alexander Street, 2005.

Balaguer, Joaquín. *La isla al revés: Haití y el destino dominicano.* Fundación José Antonio Caro, 1983.

Barnet, Miguel. *Biografía de un cimarrón.* Academia de Ciencias de Cuba, Instituto de Etnología y Folklore, 1966.

Benítez Rojo, Antonio. *The Repeating Island: The Caribbean and the Postmodern Perspective.* Translated by James E. Maraniss. 2nd ed. Duke UP, 1996.

Bess, Jennifer. "Imploding the Miranda Complex in Julia Alvarez's *How the García Girls Lost Their Accents.*" *College Literature* 34, no. 1 (2007): 78–105.

Beverley, John. *Testimonio: On the Politics of Truth.* U of Minnesota P, 2004.

Bhabha, Homi K. "Interview with Homi Bhabha: The Third Space." By Jonathan Rutherford. In *Identity: Community, Culture, Difference,* edited by Jonathan Rutherford, 207–21. Lawrence & Wishart, 1990.

———. *The Location of Culture.* Routledge, 1993.

Blanco, María del Pilar. "Reading the Novum World: The Literary Geography of Science Fiction in Junot Díaz's *The Brief Wondrous Life of Oscar Wao.*" In *Surveying the American Tropics,* edited by María Cristina Fumagalli, Peter Hulme, and Owen Robinson, 49–74. Liverpool UP, 2013.

Boakye, Bridget. "Meet Haitian–Puerto Rican Artist, Jean-Michel Basquiat, On What Would Have Been His 57th Birthday." *Face 2 Face Africa,* 22 Dec. 2017. face2faceafrica.com/article/meet-haitian-puerto-rican-artist-jean-michel-basquiat-57th-birthday.

Bonó, Pedro Francisco. *Papeles de Pedro F. Bonó, para la historia de las ideas políticas en Santo Domingo.* Edited by Emilio Rodríguez Demorizi. Editora Caribe, 1964.

Bosch, Juan. *Cuentos escritos en el exilio y apuntes sobre el arte de escribir cuentos.* Librería Dominicana, 1962.

———. *Más cuentos escritos en el exilio.* Alfa y Omega, 1962.

Boyce-Davies, Carole. *Black Women, Writing and Identity: Migrations of the Subject.* 1994. Reprint, Routledge, 2002.

Brathwaite, Kamau. *Black + Blues.* Casa de las Américas, 1977.

Brosseau, Marc. *Des romans géographes.* L'Harmattan, 1996.

Butler, Judith. *Bodies That Matter: On the Discursive Limits of "Sex."* Routledge, 1993.

Cabrera, Fernando. "Marcio Veloz Maggiolo y sus boleros para decir la verdad." In *Arqueología de las sombras: La narrativa de Marcio Veloz Maggiolo,* edited

by Fernando Valerio-Holguín, 50–58. Patronato de la Ciudad Colonial de Santo Domingo, 2000.
Cambeira, Alan. *Quisqueya la bella: The Dominican Republic in Historical and Cultural Perspective*. M. E. Sharpe, 1997.
Candelario, Ginetta E. B. *Black behind the Ears: Dominican Racial Identity from Museums to Beauty Shops*. Duke UP, 2007.
Candelier, Bruno Rosario. "Marcio Veloz Maggiolo: La vida no tiene nombre." In Veloz Maggiolo, *La vida no tiene nombre*, 85–95. Originally published in *Coloquio/El Siglo* 4, no. 29 (1989): 8–11.
Carrington, André M. *Speculative Blackness: The Future of Race in Science Fiction*. U of Minnesota P, 2016.
Cartagena Portalatín, Aída, ed. *Narradores dominicanos: Antología*. Monte Avila Editores, 1969.
Cassá, Roberto, Raymundo González, Dante Ortíz, and Genaro Rodríguez. *Actualidad y perspectivas de la cuestión nacional en la República Dominicana*. Alfa y Omega, 1986.
Cepeda, Raquel, ed. *And It Don't Stop: The Best American Hip-Hop Journalism of the Last 25 Years*. Farrar, Straus & Giroux, 2004.
———. *Bird of Paradise: How I Became Latina*. Atria Books, 2013.
———. "From the Author." In *Companion Curriculum to the Book by Raquel Cepeda*, by Karen Robinson. Robert F. Kennedy Center for Justice and Human Rights. djalirancher.com/books/bird-of-paradise-how-i-became-latina/for-educators/#sthash.dVdd6amW.dpbs.
———. "So, THIS Happened Last Night at the United Nations." *Raquel Cepeda* (blog), 26 Nov. 2014. djalirancher.com/2014/11/so-this-happened-last-night-at-the-united-nations/.
Céspedes, Diógenes. *Antología del cuento dominicano*. Editora Manatí, 2000.
Chancy, Myriam J. A. *From Sugar to Revolution: Women's Visions of Haiti, Cuba, and the Dominican Republic*. Wilfrid Laurier UP, 2012.
———. "Violence, Nation, and Memory: Danticat's *The Farming of Bones*." In *Edwidge Danticat: A Reader's Guide*, edited by Martin Munro, 130–46. U of Virginia P, 2010.
Corten, Andrés, Mercedes Acosta, and Isis Duarte. *Azúcar y política en la República Dominicana*. Taller, 1981.
Costa, Marithelma. "*La Llamarada* de Enrique Laguerre: Una novela de tierra." *Actas del XIV Congreso de la Asociación Internacional de Hispanistas* 4 (2004): 125–30.
Crassweller, Robert D. *Trujillo: The Life and Times of a Caribbean Dictator*. Macmillan, 1966.
Cruz, Angie. *Soledad*. Simon & Schuster, 2002.
Cuesta, Esther. "A modo de testimoniar: Borderlands, Papeles, and U.S. Academia." In *Bridging: How Gloria Anzaldúa's Life and Work Transformed Our*

Own, edited by Analouise Keating and Gloria González-López, 158–64. U of Texas Press, 2011.

Dalembert, Louis-Phillipe. *The Other Side of the Sea.* Translated by Robert H. McCormick Jr. U of Virginia P, 2014.

Dalleo, Raphael, and Elena Machado-Sáez. *The Latino/a Canon and the Emergence of Post-Sixties Literature.* Palgrave Macmillan, 2007.

Danticat, Edwidge. *Brother, I'm Dying.* Knopf, 2007.

———. *Claire of the Sea Light.* Knopf, 2013.

———. *Create Dangerously: The Immigrant Artist at Work.* Princeton UP, 2010.

———. "Evelyne Trouillot by Edwidge Danticat." *Bomb Magazine,* 1 Jan. 2005. bombmagazine.org/articles/evelyne-trouillot/.

———. *The Farming of Bones.* 1998. Reprint, Soho, 2014.

———. *Haiti Noir.* Akashic Books, 2011.

———. "Junot Díaz by Edwidge Danticat." *Bomb Magazine,* 1 Oct. 2007. bombmagazine.org/articles/junot-d%C3%ADaz/.

———. *Krik? Krak!* Soho, 1995.

Dash, J. Michael. *Haiti and the United States: National Stereotypes and the Literary Imagination.* Palgrave Macmillan, 1988.

Daut, Marlene L. *Tropics of Haiti: Race and the Literary History of the Haitian Revolution in the Atlantic World, 1789–1865.* Liverpool UP, 2015.

Dávila, Arlene. *Latino Spin: Public Image and the White Washing of Race.* New York UP, 2008.

Davis, James J. "On Black Poetry in the Dominican Republic." *Afro-Hispanic Review* 1, no. 3 (1982): 27–30.

Dayan, Joan. *Haiti, History, and the Gods.* U of California P, 1995.

Dechaine, Robert D. "Bordering the Civic Imaginary: Alienization, Fence Logic, and the Minuteman Civil Defense Corps." *Quarterly Journal of Speech* 95, no. 1 (2009): 43–65.

Deive, Carlos Esteban. "Marcio Veloz Maggiolo o la pasión por el saber." In *Arqueología de las sombras: La narrativa de Marcio Veloz Maggiolo,* edited by Fernando Valerio-Holguín, 59–70. Patronato de la Ciudad Colonial de Santo Domingo, 2000.

Delaney, Samuel R., Greg Tate, and Tricia Rose. "Black to the Future: Interviews with Samuel R. Delaney, Greg Tate, and Tricia Rose." By Mark Dery. *South Atlantic Quarterly* 92, no. 4 (1993): 735–78.

DeLoughrey, Elizabeth. *Routes and Roots: Navigating Caribbean and Pacific Island Literatures.* U of Hawaii P, 2007.

De Maeseneer, Rita. *Encuentro con la narrativa dominicana contemporánea.* Iberoamericana, 2006.

———. *Seis ensayos sobre narrativa dominicana contemporánea.* Banco Central, 2011.

Derby, Lauren. *The Dictator's Seduction: Politics and the Popular Imagination in the Era of Trujillo.* Duke UP, 2009.

———. "Haitians, Magic, and Money: Raza and Society in the Haitian-Dominican Borderlands, 1900 to 1937." *Comparative Studies in Society and History* 36, no. 3 (1994): 488–526.
Derrida, Jacques. "Living on Border Lines." In *Deconstruction and Criticism*, edited by Geoffrey Hartman, 75–176. Continuum, 1984.
Dery, Mark. "Black to the Future: Afro-Futurism 1.0." In *Afro Future Females*, edited by Marleen S. Barr, 6–13. Ohio State UP, 2008.
———. "Black to the Future: Interviews with Samuel R. Delaney, Greg Tate, and Tricia Rose." In *Black to the Future Flame Wars: The Discourse of Cyberculture*, edited by Mark Dery, 179–222. Duke UP, 1994.
Despradel, Lil. "Las etapas del antihaitianismo en la República Dominicana: El papel de los historiadores." In *Política y sociología en Haití y la República Dominicana: Coloquio domínico-haitiano de ciencias sociales*, edited by Gérard Pierre-Charles, 83–108. Universidad Nacional Autónoma de México, 1947.
Díaz, Junot. "Apocalypse: What Disasters Reveal." *Boston Review*, May/June 2011. bostonreview.net/archives/BR36.3/junot_diaz_apocalypse_haiti_earthquake.php.
———. *The Brief Wondrous Life of Oscar Wao*. Riverhead Books, 2007.
———. *Drown*. Riverhead Books, 1996.
———. "Monstro." *New Yorker*, 4 June 2012. www.newyorker.com/magazine/2012/06/04/monstro.
———. *This Is How You Lose Her*. Riverhead Books, 2012.
Di Pietro, Giovanni. "La novella trujillista." In *Quince estudios de novelística dominicana*, 223–34. Editora del Banco Central de la República Dominicana, 2006.
Duany, Jorge. "Dominican Migration to Puerto Rico: A Transnational Perspective." *Centro Journal* 17, no. 1 (2005): 242–69.
———. "Racializing Ethnicity in the Spanish-Speaking Caribbean: A Comparison of Haitians in the Dominican Republic and Dominicans in Puerto Rico." *Latin American and Caribbean Ethnic Studies* 1, no. 2 (2006): 231–48.
Duncan, Ian. "The Provincial or Regional Novel." In *A Companion to the Victorian Novel*, edited by Patrick Brantlinger and William Thesing, 318–35. Oxford UP, 2002.
Eller, Anne. *We Dream Together: Dominican Independence, Haiti, and the Fight for Caribbean Freedom*. Duke UP, 2016.
Enciclopedia dominicana, Tomo IV. Instituto del Libro, 1968.
Fennema, Meindert, and Troetje Loewenthal. *La construcción de raza y nación en la República Dominicana*. Editora Universitaria, 1987.
Ferrer, Ada. *Freedom's Mirror: Cuba and Haiti in the Age of Revolution*. Cambridge UP, 2014.
Fiallo Billini, José Antonio. "La revolución de abril: El ayer para el hoy el para el mañana." *El Desahogo Dominicano*, 7 Apr. 2015. scharboy2009.wordpress.com/2015/04/07/la-revolucion-de-abril-el-ayer-para-el-hoy-y-el-manana/.

Fischer, Sibylle. *Modernity Disavowed: Haiti and the Cultures of Slavery in the Age of Revolution*. Duke UP, 2004.

Fitting, Peter. "Utopia, Dystopia, and Science Fiction." In *The Cambridge Companion to Utopian Literature*, edited by Gregory Claeys, 135–53. Cambridge UP, 2010.

Flores, Juan. *From Bomba to Hip-Hop*. Columbia UP, 2000.

Ford, Ashley C. "Daniel José Older creates female black heroes to make fantasy more real." *Guardian*, 29 June 2015. www.theguardian.com/books/2015/jun/29/daniel-jose-older-black-heroes-ya-science-fiction.

Foucault, Michel. "Of Other Spaces: Utopias and Heterotopias." *Diacritics* 16, no. 1 (1986): 22–27.

———. *The Order of Things*. Pantheon Books, 1970.

Fumagalli, Maria Cristina. *On the Edge: Writing the Border between Haiti and the Dominican Republic*. Liverpool UP, 2015.

Gaffield, Julia. *Haitian Connections in the Atlantic World: Recognition after Revolution*. U of North Carolina P, 2015.

Galíndez, Jesús de. *The Era of Trujillo: Dominican Dictator*. U of Arizona P, 1973.

Gallego Cuiñas, Ana. *Trujillo, el fantasma y sus escritores: Historia de la novela del trujillato*. Mare & Martin, 2006.

Gallegos, Gerardo. "El autor." In *Trujillo: Cara y cruz de su dictadura*, 9–11. Ediciones Iberoamericanas, 1968.

García Canclini, Néstor. *Hybrid Cultures: Strategies for Entering and Leaving Modernity*. Translated by Christopher L. Chiappari and Silvia L. López. U of Minnesota P, 1995.

———. *Imagined Globalization: Latin American in Translation*. Translated by George Yúdice. Duke UP, 2014.

García-Peña, Lorgia. *The Borders of Dominicanidad: Race, Nation, and Archives of Contradiction*. Duke UP, 2016.

Gates, Henry Louis, Jr. *Black in Latin America*. New York UP, 2011.

Geggus, David. "The Sounds and Echoes of Freedom: The Impact of the Haitian Revolution on Latin America." In *Beyond Slavery: the Multifaceted Legacy of Africans in Latin America*, edited by Darién Davis, 19–36. Rowman & Littlefield, 2006.

Gilroy, Paul. *The Black Atlantic*. Harvard UP, 1993.

Glissant, Édouard. *Caribbean Discourse: Selected Essays*. Edited by J. Michael Dash. U of Virginia P, 1999.

———. *Poetics of Relation*. U of Michigan P, 2010.

———. *Traité du tout-monde*. Gallimard, 1997.

Gomel, Alana. *Narrative Space and Time: Representing Impossible Topologies in Literature*. Routledge, 2014.

Gonzalez, Juan. *Harvest of Empire: A History of Latinos in America*. Penguin Books, 2011.

González-Cruz, Luis F. "Desde el absurdo: La narrativa de Marcio Veloz Maggiolo." In *Arqueología de las sombras: La narrativa de Marcio Veloz Maggiolo,* edited by Fernando Valerio-Holguín, 105–14. Patronato de la Ciudad Colonial de Santo Domingo, 2000.

Goodwin, Matthew. "Virtual Reality at the Border of Migration, Race, and Labor." In Lavender, *Black and Brown Planets,* 163–76.

Graciano, Berta. *La novela de la caña: Estética e ideología.* Alfa & Omega, 1990.

Grieco, Elizabeth. "The Foreign Born from the Dominican Republic in the United States." *Migration Policy Institute,* 11 Oct. 2004. www.migrationpolicy.org/article/foreign-born-dominican-republic-united-states.

Grullón, Iván. *La matanza de los haitianos en "El Masacre se pasa a pie" y "Mi compadre el General Sol."* Editora Universitaria, 1989.

Guarnizo, Luis E. "Los Dominicanyorks: The Making of a Binational Society." *Annals of the American Academy of Political and Social Science,* 1994, 70–86.

Guzmán, Pablo "Yoruba." "Before People Called Me a Spic, They Called me a Nigger." In *The Afro-Latin@ Reader,* edited by Miriam Jiménez Roman and Juan Flores, 235–43. Duke UP, 2010.

Hall, Stuart. "Cultural Identity and Diaspora." In *Identity: Community, Culture, and Difference,* edited by Jonathan Rutherford, 222–37. Lawrence & Wishart, 1990.

———. "Who Needs 'Identity'?" In *Identity: A Reader,* edited by Paul du Gay, Jessica Evans, and Peter Redman, 15–30. Sage, 2000.

Hasta la Raíz. Dir. Juan Carlos González Díaz. Patio Común, 2017.

Henríquez Ureña, Pedro. "La cultura y las letras coloniales en Santo Domingo." In *Obra dominicana,* edited by José Chez Checo, 199–279. Sociedad Dominicana de Bibliófilos, 1988.

———. "La utopía de América." *Antología del ensayo,* 1925. www.ensayistas.org/antologia/XXA/h%20urena/.

Herrera Rodríguez, Rafael Darío. *Montecristi entre campeches y bananos.* Academia Dominicana de la Historia, 2006.

Hintzen, Amelia M. "Cultivating Resistance: Haitian-Dominican Communities and the Dominican Sugar Industry, 1915–1990." PhD diss., University of Miami, 2016.

Horn, Maja. *Masculinity after Trujillo: The Politics of Gender in Dominican Literature.* U of Florida P, 2014.

Howard, David. *Coloring the Nation: Race and Ethnicity in the Dominican Republic.* L. Rienner, 2001.

Jean-Charles, Régine Michelle. "'A Border between Geographies of Grief': River Crossings and Crossroads between Haiti and the Dominican Republic." In *Transnational Hispaniola: New Directions in Haitian and Dominican Studies,* edited by April J. Mayes and Kiran C. Jayaram, 81–103. U of Florida P, 2018.

Keating, AnaLouise, ed. *The Gloria Anzaldúa Reader.* Duke UP, 2009.

———. "Risking the Vision, Transforming the Divides: Nepantlera Perspectives on Academic Boundaries, Identities, and Lives." In *Bridging: How Gloria Anzaldúa's Life and Work Transformed Our Own,* edited by Analouise Keating and Gloria González-López, 142–52. U of Texas P, 2011.

Keating, AnaLouise, and Gloria González-López. "Building Bridges, Transforming Loss, Shaping New Dialogues: Anzalduán Studies for the Twenty-First Century." In *Bridging: How Gloria Anzaldúa's Life and Work Transformed Our Own,* edited by Analouise Keating and Gloria González-López, 1–16. U of Texas P, 2011.

Keefe Ugalde, Sharon. "Veloz Maggiolo y la narrativa de dictador/dictadura: Perspectivas dominicanas e innovaciones." *Revista Iberoamericana* 54, no. 142 (1988): 129–50.

Kelley, Robin D. G. Foreword to Ulysse, *Why Haiti Needs New Narratives,* xiii–xvi.

LaBouvier, Chaédria. "How Basquiat challenged police brutality through his art." Interview by Ted Stansfield. *Dazed,* 18 Nov. 2016. www.dazeddigital.com/artsandculture/article/33756/1/how-basquiat-challenged-police-brutality-through-his-art.

Lacay Polanco, Ramón. *Punto Sur.* 1958.

Laferrière, Dany. "Foreword: A Heart of Serenity in the Storm." In *Edwidge Danticat: A Reader's Guide,* edited by Martin Munro, vii–viii. U of Virginia P, 2010.

Larsen, Neil. "¿Cómo narrar el trujillato?" *Revista Iberoamericana* 54, nos. 1–2 (1988): 89–98.

Lavender, Isiah, III, ed. *Black and Brown Planets: The Politics of Race in Science Fiction.* UP of Mississippi, 2014.

———. *Race in American Science Fiction.* Indiana UP, 2011.

Legrand, Catherine C. "Informal Resistance on a Dominican Sugar Plantation during the Trujillo Dictatorship." *Hispanic American Historical Review* 75, no. 4 (1995): 555–96.

Legros, Ayanna. "As a Haitian-American Woman, I Know I'm Afro-Latina but It's Time For You to Acknowledge It, Too." *Fierce* (blog), 5 June 2018. https://fierce.wearemitu.com/identities/why-i-haitian-woman-identify-as-afro-latina-and-my-sisters-should-too/.

Leyshon, Cressida. "This Week in Fiction: Junot Díaz." *New Yorker,* 27 May 2002. www.newyorker.com/books/page-turner/this-week-in-fiction-junot-daz-3.

Lionnet, Françoise, and Emmanuel Bruno Jean-François. "Literary Routes: Migration, Islands, and the Creative Economy." *PMLA* 131, no. 5 (2016): 1222–38.

Lipsitz, George. *Footsteps in the Dark: The Hidden Histories of Popular Music.* U of Minnesota P, 2007.

Lizardo, Fradique. *La cultura africana en Santo Domingo.* Taller, 1979.

Lockward, Alanna. *Un Haití dominicano tatuajes fantasmas y narrativas bilaterales*. Editorial Santuario, 2014.
López-Calvo, Ignacio. *"God and Trujillo": Literary and Cultural Representations of the Dominican Dictator*. UP of Florida, 2005.
Luis, William. *Dance between Two Cultures*. Vanderbilt UP, 1997.
———. *Literary Bondage: Slavery in Cuban Narrative*. U of Texas P, 1990.
Lyon Johnson, Kelli. "Both Sides of the Massacre: Collective Memory and Narrative on Hispaniola." *Mosaic: A Journal for the Interdisciplinary Study of Literature* 36, no. 2 (2003): 75–91.
Madrid, Alejandro L. *Transnational Encounters: Music and Performance at the U.S.-Mexico Border*. Oxford UP, 2011.
Marrero Aristy, Ramón. "El libertador." In Céspedes, *Antología del cuento dominicano*, 105–16.
———. *Over*. 19th ed. Librería Dominicana, 1998.
———. *La República Dominicana: Origen y destino del pueblo cristiano más antiguo de América: Vol. II*. Editora del Caribe, 1958.
Martínez, Erika M., ed. *Daring to Write: Contemporary Narratives by Dominican Women*. U of Georgia P, 2016.
Martínez, Samuel. "Not a Cockfight: Rethinking Haitian-Dominican Relations." *Latin American Perspectives* 30, no. 3 (2003): 80–101.
Martínez-San Miguel, Yolanda. *Caribe Two Ways: Cultura de la migración en el Caribe insular hispánico*. Callejón, 2003.
———. *Coloniality of Diasporas: Rethinking Intra-colonial Migrations in a Pan-Caribbean Context*. Palgrave Macmillan, 2014.
Mateo, Andrés L. *Mito y cultura en la era de Trujillo*. Editora Manatí, 2004.
Matibag, Eugenio. *Haitian-Dominican Counterpoint: Nation, Race and State on Hispaniola*. Palgrave Macmillan, 2003.
Mavor, Carol. *Black and Blue: The Bruised Passion of "Camera Lucida," "La Jetée," "Sans soleil," and "Hiroshima mon amour."* Duke UP, 2012.
Mayes, April J. *The Mulatto Republic*. UP of Florida, 2014.
Mayes, April J., and Kiran C. Jayaram. "Transnational Hispaniola: An Introduction." In *Transnational Hispaniola: New Directions in Haitian and Dominican Studies*, edited by April J. Mayes and Kiran C. Jayaram, 1–19. U of Florida P, 2018.
Mayock, Ellen. "Julia Alvarez and Haiti: Transgressing Imposed Borders in *In the Time of the Butterflies, A Wedding in Haiti*, and Protests against Ruling 0168-13." *Journal of International Women's Studies* 17, no. 3 (2016): 80–90.
McCormick, Robert H., Jr. "An Introduction to 'The Blue of the Island.'" *Journal of Haitian Studies* 18, no. 2 (2012): 210–12.
Medrano, Marianela. "El Corte." *Black Scholar* 45, no. 2 (2015): 67–68.
Menton, Seymour. *Latin America's New Historical Novel*. U of Texas P, 1993.

Michaelsen, Scott, and David E. Johnson. "Border Secrets: An Introduction." In *Border Theory: The Limits of Cultural Politics*, edited by Scott Michaelsen and David E. Johnson, 1–6. U of Minnesota P, 1997.

Miller, T. S. "Preternatural Narration and the Lens of Genre Fiction in Junot Díaz's *The Brief Wondrous Life of Oscar Wao*." *Science Fiction Studies* 38, no. 1 (2011): 92–114.

Mindlin, Alex. "An Island Rift, Repaired a World Away." *New York Times*, 27 Nov. 2005. www.nytimes.com/2005/11/27/nyregion/thecity/an-island-rift-repaired-a-world-away.html.

Mir, Pedro. *Las dos patrias de Santo Domingo*. ECD, 1975.

Montenegro, Carlos Antonio. *The 21 Divisions: Dominican Voodoo*. Indio Products, 2009.

Montero, Mayra. *Tú, la oscuridad*. Tusquets, 1995.

Moraga, Cherie, and Gloria Anzaldúa. *This Bridge Called My Back: Writings by Radical Women of Color*. Kitchen Table, Women of Color P, 1983.

Moretti, Franco. *Graphs, Maps, Trees: Abstract Models for a Literary History*. Verso, 2005.

Morris-Suzuki, Tessa. *The Past within Us: Media, Memory, History*. Verso, 2005.

Moscoso Puello, Francisco Eujenio. *Cañas y bueyes*. 1935. Reprint, Letra Gráfica, 2015.

Mota Acosta, Julio César. *Los cocolos in Santo Domingo*. La Gaviota, 1977.

Moya Pons, Frank. *La dominación haitiana, 1822–1844*. Universidad Católica Madre y Maestra, 1972.

———. *The Dominican Republic: A National History*. Markus Wiener Publishers, 1998.

———. *El pasado dominicano*. Fundación J. A. Caro Alvarez, 1986.

Nessler, Graham T. *An Islandwide Struggle for Freedom: Revolution, Emancipation, and Reenslavement in Hispaniola, 1789–1809*. U of North Carolina P, 2016.

Nieves, Myrna. *El caribe: Paraíso y paradoja*. Instituto de Cultura Puertorriqueña, 2012.

Nos cambió la vida. Centro Bonó, 2017.

Núñez, Manuel. *Ocaso de la nación dominicana*. 2nd ed. Letra Gráfica, 2001.

Older, Daniel José. "Diversity Is Not Enough: Race, Power, Publishing." *BuzzFeed*, 14 Apr. 2014. www.buzzfeed.com/danieljoseolder/diversity-is-not-enough.

———. "Q&A: Urban Fantasy Counter-Narrative; Daniel José Older on 'Shadowshaper.'" Interview by Shelley Díaz. *School Library Journal*, 16 June 2015.

———. *Shadowshaper*. Scholastic, 2015.

Paulino, Edward. *Dividing Hispaniola: The Dominican Republic's Border Campaign against Haiti, 1930–1961*. U of Pittsburgh P, 2016.

Peña Batlle, Manuel Arturo. *Historia de la cuestión fronteriza dominico-haitiana*. Impresora Dominicana, 1946.

Pérez, Loida Martiza. *Geographies of Home*. Viking, 1999.

Pérez Firmat, Gustavo. *Life on the Hyphen.* U of Texas P, 1994.
Philoctète, René. *Massacre River.* New Directions, 2008.
Piatti, Barbara. *Die Geographie der Literatur.* Wallstein, 2008.
Pimentel, Kharla. "'¡Diga perejil!,' mujer fue montada en guagua de migración al ser confundida por haitiana." *El acento,* 17 Dec. 2016. acento.com.do/2016/actualidad/8411262-diga-perejil-mujer-fue-montada-guagua-migracion-al-confundida-haitiana/.
Pratt, Mary Louise. "Arts of the Contact Zone." *Profession,* 1991, 33–41.
Prestol Castillo, Freddy. *El Masacre se pasa a pie.* 4th ed. Editora Taller, 1977.
———. *Pablo Mamá.* Editora Taller, 1985.
———. *Paisajes y meditaciones de una frontera.* Editorial Cosmopolita, 1943.
Price-Mars, Jean. *La República de Haití y la República Dominicana: Diversos aspectos de un problema histórico, geográfico y etnológico.* 3rd ed. Sociedad Dominicana de Bibliofilos, 1995.
Quesada, Sarah. "A Planetary Warning? The Multilayered Caribbean Zombie in 'Monstro.'" In *Junot Díaz and the Decolonial Imagination,* edited by Monica Hanna, Jennifer Harford Vargas, and José David Saldívar, 291–318. Duke UP, 2016.
"Quick Facts." United States Census Bureau. Accessed 15 Sept. 2016. www.census.gov/quickfacts/fact/table/US/PST045217.
Ragland, Cathy. *Música Norteña: Mexican Migrants Creating a Nation between Nations.* Temple UP, 2009.
Ramírez, Dixa. *Colonial Phantoms: Belonging and Refusal in the Dominican Americas, from the 19th Century to the Present.* New York UP, 2018.
Reagan, Patricia. "Insolent Origins and Contemporary Dilemmas." In *Sounds of Resistance,* edited by Eunice Rojas and Lindsay Michie, 373–96. Praeger, 2013.
Reuschel, Anne-Kathrin, and Lorenz Hurni. "Mapping Literature: Visualisation of Spatial Uncertainty in Fiction." *Cartographic Journal* 48, no. 4 (2011): 293–308.
Reyes-Santos, Alaí. *Our Caribbean Kin: Race and Nation in the Neoliberal Antilles.* Rutgers UP, 2015.
Rivera, Lysa M. "*Mestizaje* and Heterotopia in Ernest Hogan's *High Aztech.*" In Lavender, *Black and Brown Planets,* 146–62.
Robinson, Richard. *Narratives of the European Border: A History of Nowhere.* Palgrave Macmillan, 2007.
Rodríguez, Emilio Jorge. *Haiti and Trans-Caribbean Literary Identity.* House of Nehesi, 2011.
Rodríguez, Néstor E. *Escrituras de desencuentro en la República Dominicana.* Siglo Veintiuno Editores, 2005.
———. *La isla y su envés: Representaciones de lo nacional en el ensayo dominicano contemporáneo.* Instituto de Cultura Puertorriqueña, 2003.
Rodríguez Demorizi, Emilio. *Invasiones haitianas de 1801, 1805 y 1822.* Editora del Caribe, 1955.

Rodríguez-Henríquez, Rafael. *Fuentes de la imaginación histórica en la narrativa de Marcio Veloz Maggiolo.* Edwin Mellen, 2010.

Rondón, Pura. *Estudios críticos de la literatura dominicana contemporánea.* Ediciones Librería La Trinitaria, 2005.

Rosario, Nelly. *Song of the Water Saints.* Parthenon Books, 2002.

Rosell, Sara V. *La novela de escritoras dominicanas de 1990 a 2007.* Edwin Mellen, 2007.

Roth, Wendy. *Race Migrations: Latinos and the Cultural Transformation of Race.* Stanford UP, 2012.

Rueda, Manuel. *Bienvenida y la noche: Crónicas de Montecristi.* Fundación Cultural Dominicana, 1994.

———. *Imágenes del dominicano.* Banco Central de la República Dominicana, 1998.

———. *Las metamorfosis de Makandal.* Banco Central de la República Dominicana, 1998.

Sagás, Ernesto. *Race and Politics in the Dominican Republic.* UP of Florida, 2000.

San Miguel, Pedro. *The Imagined Island: History, Identity, and Utopia in Hispaniola.* U of North Carolina P, 2005.

Sánchez, Juan J. *La caña en Santo Domingo.* Ediciones Taller, 1976.

Sánchez-Valverde, Antonio. *Idea del valor de la Isla Española y utilidades que de ella puede sacar su monarquía.* Impresora de P. Marin, 1785.

Sandoval, Chela. *Methodology of the Oppressed: Theory Out of Bounds.* U of Minnesota P, 2000.

Shemak, April. "Re-Membering Hispaniola: Edwidge Danticat's *The Farming of Bones.*" *Modern Fiction Studies* 48, no. 1 (2002): 83–112.

"Shore Excursions: A Paradise Cove Escape and Haitian Village Experience." Royal Caribbean International. www.royalcaribbean.com/shoreExcursions/product/detail/view.do?sourcePage=shorexByPort&ProductCode=QLB0&DestinationCode=.

Shorris, Earl. *Latinos: A Biography of a People.* Avon Books, 1992.

Simmons, Kimberly Eison. *Reconstructing Racial Identity and the African Past in the Dominican Republic.* UP of Florida, 2009.

Smartt Bell, Madison. *Toussaint Louverture: A Biography.* Pantheon Books, 2007.

Soja, Edward J. *Thirdspace: Journeys to Los Angeles and Other Real-and-Imagined Places.* Blackwell, 1996.

———. "Thirdspace: Toward a New Consciousness of Space and Spatiality." In *Communicating in the Third Space,* edited by Karin Ikas and Gerhard Wagner, 49–61. Routledge, 2009.

Sommer, Doris. *Foundational Fictions: The National Romances of Latin America.* 1984. Reprint, U of California P, 1991.

———. *One Master for Another.* UP of America, 1983.

———. "Populism as Rhetoric: The Case of the Dominican Republic." *Boundary* 11, nos. 1–2 (1982–83): 253–70.
Sontag, Susan. *On Photography*. Penguin, 1979.
Spivak, Gayatri Chakravorty. "*Can the Subaltern Speak?*" In *Marxism and the Interpretation of Culture*, edited by Cary Nelson and Lawrence Grossberg, 271–313. U of Illinois P, 1988.
Stavans, Ilan. *The Hispanic Condition: The Future Power of a People*. Harper, 2001.
Stinchcomb, Dawn F. *The Development of Literary Blackness in the Dominican Republic*. UP of Florida, 2004.
———. "Haitians, *Cocolos*, and African Americans: Early Authors of Contemporary Afro-Dominican Literature." *Journal of Caribbean Literatures* 4, no. 1 (2005): 39–48.
Tavares, Juan Tomás. "Con la mueite en la mano hata ei machete gritó." *Acento*, 2 Oct. 2017. https://acento.com.do/2017/opinion/8496711-la-mueite-la-mano-hata-ei-machete-grito/.
Théodat, Jean-Marie. *Haïti–République Dominicaine: Une île pour deux 1804–1916*. Karthala, 2013.
Torres-Saillant, Silvio. "Dominican Blackness and the Modern World." In *Perspectives on Las Américas: A Reader in Culture, History, and Representation*, edited by Matthew C. Gutmann, Féliz E. Rodríguez, Lynn Stephen, and Patricia Zavella, 274–90. Blackwell, 2003.
———. "The Hispanic Caribbean Question: On Geographies of Knowledge and Interlaced Human Landscapes." *Small Axe* 20, no. 3 (2016): 32–48.
———. *Introduction to Dominican Blackness*. 2nd ed. CUNY Dominican Studies Institute, 2010.
———. "Marcio Veloz Maggiolo (13 August 1936)." In *Modern Latin American Fiction Writers: Second Series*, edited by William Luis and Ann González, 321–24. Gale, 1994.
———. "The Tribulations of Blackness: Stages in Dominican Racial Identity." *Latin American Perspectives* 25, no. 2 (1998): 126–46.
———. "Visions of Dominicanness in the United States." In *Borderless Borders: U.S. Latinos, Latin Americans, and the Paradox of Interdependence*, edited by Frank Bonilla, Edwin Meléndez, Rebecca Morales, and María de los Angeles Torres, 139–52. Temple UP, 1998.
Trouillot, Évelyne. *The Blue of the Island*. Translated by Robert H. McCormick Jr. *Journal of Haitian Studies* 18, no. 2 (2012): 213–64.
———. *Rosalie l'infâme*. Dapper, 2003.
Trouillot, Michel-Rolph. "The Odd and the Ordinary: Haiti, the Caribbean, and the World." *Cimarron: New Perspectives on the Caribbean* 2, no. 3 (1990): 3–12.
———. *Silencing the Past: Power and the Production of History*. Beacon, 1997.

Turits, Richard Lee. *Foundations of Despotism: Peasants, the Trujillo Regime, and Modernity in Dominican History.* Stanford UP, 2003.

———. "A World Destroyed, A Nation Imposed: The 1937 Haitian Massacre in the Dominican Republic." *Hispanic American Historical Review* 82, no. 3 (2002): 589–635.

Ulysse, Gina Athena. *Why Haiti Needs New Narratives: A Post-Quake Chronicle.* Wesleyan UP, 2015.

Valdez, Juan R. *Tracing Dominican Identity: The Writings of Pedro Henríquez Ureña.* Palgrave Macmillan, 2011.

Valerio-Holguín, Fernando. "Primitive Borders: Cultural Identity and Ethnic Cleansing in the Dominican Republic." Translated by Scott Cooper. In *Returning Gaze: Primitivism and Identity in Latin America,* edited by Erik Camayd-Freixas and José Eduardo González, 75–88. U of Arizona P, 2000.

———. "La reinterpretación del trujillato: *En el tiempo de las mariposas* de Julia Alvarez." *El Siglo,* 2 Mar. 2001, 2E.

Vasconcelos, José. *The Cosmic Race/La Raza Cósmica.* 3rd ed. Espasa-Calpe Mexicana, 1966.

Vega, Bernardo. *Trujillo y Haití.* Fundación Cultural Dominicana, 1995.

———. "Variaciones en el uso del antihaitianismo durante la era de Trujillo." *Listín diario,* 24 Oct. 1995, 1.

Veloz Maggiolo, Marcio. *Los ángeles de hueso.* Arte y Cine, 1967.

———. "Apuntes sobre autoctonía y etnicidad." *Boletín de Antropología Americana,* no. 10 (1984): 53–58.

———. *La biografía difusa de Sombra Castañeda.* Editora Taller, 1984.

———. *De abril en adelante.* Taller, 1975.

———. "Entrevista con Marcio Veloz Maggiolo." By Rita De Maeseneer. *Cielonaranja,* 7 Apr. 2003.

———. *El hombre del acordeón.* Ediciones Siruela, 2003.

———. *Judas, El buen ladrón.* 2nd ed. Librería Dominicana, 1962.

———. "Tipología del tema haitiano en la literatura dominicana." *El pequeño universo de la facultad de Humanidades* 3 (1972): 12–55. Reprinted in *Sobre cultura dominicana . . . y otras culturas: Ensayos,* by Marcio Veloz Maggiolo. Editora Alfa y Omega, 1977.

———. *La vida no tiene nombre: Novela de la Ocupación.* 1965. Reprint, Letra Gráfica, 2013.

Vicioso, Sherezada "Chiqui." "Discovering Myself: Un Testimonio." In *The Afro-Latin@ Reader,* edited by Miriam Jiménez Roman and Juan Flores, 262–65. Duke UP, 2010.

Victoriano-Martínez, Ramón Antonio. *Rayanos y Dominicanyorks: La dominicanidad del siglo XXI.* Nuevo Siglo, 2014.

"Vision and Mission Statement." We Are All Dominican. https://weareall dominicannyc.wordpress.com/.

"The 'White People Do Journalism Like This' Episode." *Our National Conversation about Conversations about Race,* 19 Nov. 2014. Panoply. www.showaboutrace.com/episode-015/.

"Who We Are." Dominican@s por derecho. https://dominicanosxderecho.wordpress.com/quienessomos.

Wright, Micah. "An Epidemic of Negrophobia: Blackness and the Legacy of the US Occupation of the Dominican Republic." *Black Scholar* 45, no. 2 (2015): 21–33.

Wucker, Michele. "A Creative Outpour Inspired by a Massacre." *Huffington Post,* 6 Oct. 2016. www.huffingtonpost.com/entry/a-creative-outpour-inspired-by-a-massacre_us_57f66250e4b087a29a5487f6.

Wynter, Sylvia. "Beyond Miranda's Meanings: Un/silencing the 'Demonic Ground' of Caliban's 'Woman.'" In *Out of the Kumbla: Caribbean Women and Literature,* edited by Carole Boyce Davies and Elaine Savory Fido, 355–72. Africa World, 1990.

Zeller, Neici. *Discursos y espacios femeninos en República Dominicana, 1880–1961.* Letra Gráfica, 2012.

Index

Italicized page numbers refer to illustrations.

activism in response to Tribunal Court ruling TC/0168/13 (2013), 119–21, 138
African Americans collaborating with Hispanic/Latino communities, 102–3
Afrofuturism, 140, 186n18
Alexis, Jacques Stephen: *General Sun, My Brother,* 158, 175n31
Algarín, Miguel, 105
alterity. *See* Otherness
Alvarez, Julia: autobiographical forms of narrative and genre fiction used by, 164; background of, 104–5; Border of Lights and, 7, 172n8; compared to Prestol Castillo, 114–15; *How the García Girls Lost Their Accents,* 116–18, 152, 168, 183nn15–16; literary imperialism of Haiti and, 166; Massacre (1937) and, 115–17; in *New York Times* travel section (2013), 114; social justice and, 120; "A White Woman of Color," 183n16. *See also Wedding in Haiti, A*
Álvarez, Soledad, 89, 185n5
AmeRícan, 105
ancestry, 16, 33, 108, 110, 112, 140–42, 145
Ángel Asturias, Miguel: *El Señor Presidente,* 66
anonymous or ambiguous geographical locations: border zones as, 2, 176n35; La Salada as fictional place in Veloz Maggiolo's *El hombre del acordeón,* 72; Marrero Aristy's *Over* and, 21–22, 31, 35–37, 43–44, 62; Prestol Castillo's *El Masacre se pasa a pie* and, 48, 62; in Trouillot's *The Blue of the Island,* 148–49, 153–55, 157, 161–62
anti-Haitianism (*antihaitianismo*): acceptance as state ideology of Dominican Republic, 15, 22, 165; alternates to narratives of, 31, 35, 41–44, 46, 55, 61–62, 176n38; Cepeda referencing, 108–9, 112–13; defined, 172n11; diaspora challenging, 120; Díaz's story "Monstro" and, 161; difference from hispanism (*hispanicismo*), 173n1; in Dominican Republic of today, 9, 14, 172n11; in Dominican writing, 13, 19, 27–28; fostered in early nationalist writings, 27–28; *Hasta la Raíz* documentary and, 122; literature written in resistance to, 4; Prestol Castillo's writing and, 13, 27–28, 58. *See also trujillato* ideology
Anzaldúa, Gloria: on border confusion and clash of voices, 56, 168; *Borderlands/La Frontera: The New Mestiza,* 6, 109–10, 171n4; breaking down borders to achieve *una cultura mestiza,* 113; Foucault and, 172n6; *nepantla* (ideological Border) concept of, 3, 4, 6, 68, 71, 90, 166, 178n11; Soja and, 6
Aparicio, Frances R., 18
Aristide, Jean-Bertrand, 148
Arroyo, Jossianna: *Writing Secrecy in Caribbean Freemasonry,* 140, 186n17
Ayuso, Mónica G., 172n8
Azuela, Mariano: *Los de abajo,* 95

Index

Báez, Josefina: *Dominicanish* (performance text), 105, 110, 182n9
Balaguer, Joaquín: anti-Haitian sentiment and, 13, 15, 38, 41; *La isla al revés: Haití y el destino dominicano*, 27; power of, 47; Prestol Castillo and, 58; primitive ideology of, 55; rise to power, 89; in Rueda, 30
Barnet, Miguel: *Biografía de un cimarrón* (with Montejo), 47
Barthes, Roland, 151
Basquiat, Jean-Michel, 143
Belique, Ana María, 119, 183–84n18
Bello, Andrés, 128
Benítez Rojo, Antonio, 18, 36, 41
Betances, Ramón Emeterio, 140, 186n17
Beverley, John, 47
Bhabha, Homi K., and third space, 3, 6–7, 63, 65, 74
Billini, Fiallo, 89
Bird of Paradise: How I Became Latina (Cepeda), 17, 99–101, 106–13, 122–24; diaspora's ability to soften us-them mentality, 112, 123–24; ethnic/racial identity of author and her desire to trace her ancestry, 101, 106–7, 108, 110, 112; "fantasy island" as nickname for Dominican Republic, 107; insider/outsider perspective of, 100, 123; memoir of author's childhood in New York City and in Dominican Republic, 106, 164; third space recognized by, 106, 123; as *"us-moir"* instead of *"me-moir,"* 122–23, 124
Black Lives Matter movement, 143
blackness: Betances's view of, 186n17; criticism of Dominicans for negating, 108, 109; Díaz's writings and, 130–31, 133–34; Marrero Aristy's *Over* and, 35; Paulino's *Eddie's Perejil* and, 101–2; *trujillato* discourse on, 132; US administration's effect and, 43. *See also* anti-Haitianism; racial and ethnic identities; racism
Black Panther Party, 102–3
Blanco, María del Pilar, 132–33
Blue of the Island, The (Trouillot, play), 17, 127, 147–57; bruising associated with color, 151–52; color-coded space and, 150–53, 156, 187n25; cross-border movement resulting from on-border violence (2000), 148–50, 154, 156, 161; Dominican Republic references as anonymous in, 148–49, 153–55, 157, 161–62; fragmentation of island coexisting with connectivity, 147, 162; geographical anonymity in, 148–49, 155; invisibility and transparency of passengers versus visceral experience of entrapment in, 149–50, 151; migration routes in, 155, 161–62; multiple Haitis in, 147, 162; third space and, 161–62
Bonó, Pedro Francisco, 26–27
border between Dominican Republic and Haiti: anonymous border zones of, 176n35; *antihatianismo* as negation of, 165; construed as stateless or different country from Dominican Republic and Haiti, 2, 3, 5, 12, 147; crossing requirements of the two sides, 115, 183n14; diminishing significance of, 2, 166–67; erasure and invisibility of, 150, 154; fluidity of, 5, 13, 63, 123, 130, 136, 164; imperial frontier of Haiti and, 166–67; patchwork of writing mimicking chaos of border region, 73, 168; premassacre, 28–30, 159. *See also* Dominicanization of border regions; Haitian Massacre (1937); third space
Border of Lights, 1, 7–9, *11*, 120, 172nn8–9, 183n18
borders: border culture, 171n4; heterotopia in relation to border dichotomy, 74; ideological, 3–7, 16, 68, 154, 155, 163, 166; imaginary, 163; multiplication of cultures as result of, 78; physical and ideological, as sites of disruption, 3, 166; porous nature of, 5, 136–37. *See also* border between Dominican Republic and Haiti; third space
Borges, José Luis, 185n4
Bosch, Juan, 35, 61, 88, 103, 166, 177n42; "Luis Pié," 97, 176n38
Boyce, Carol, 157–58
Boyer, Jean-Pierre, 22, 26, 59, 96, 165, 166, 181n48
Brathwaite, Kamau, 167, 187n26
Brosseau, Marc, 44
Butler, Judith: *Bodies That Matter*, 3

Cabral, Manuel del, 181n49
Cabrera, Fernando, 73
Caribbean cultural influence, extent of, 18
Caribbean scholarship, 72, 126, 166, 174n8, 174n17
Carpentier, Alejo, 87; *El recurso del método*, 66
Cartagena Portalatín, Aída, 61, 174n18, 179n22
Cassá, Roberto, 2
Catholic religion, 76
censorship, 42, 47, 62, 168, 178n9
center-island areas, 2, 5, 12, 159
Centro Montalvo, 8
Cepeda, Raquel: autobiographical forms of narrative and genre fiction used by, 164; background of, 104–5, 108; social justice and, 120. See also *Bird of Paradise*
Céspedes, Diógenes, 57–58; *Antología del cuento dominicano*, 33
Chancy, Myriam J. A., 9, 148, 158, 160; *From Sugar to Revolution*, 153
Christophe, Henri, 187n26
collaborative relations between Haiti and Dominican Republic, 3, 12
Colon, Juan, 183n17
colonial period: European language and, 136; French and Spanish colonies, 22; multiple terms used for colonies, 155; racial prejudices of, 22; rivalries of the French and Spanish, 172n11. See also Saint Domingue; Santo Domingo
Columbus, Christopher, 22, 129, 185n7
Crassweller, Robert D., 173n6
Cruz, Angie, 187n22
Cuba, Dominican and Haitian diasporas in, 125, 167, 177n42
Cuban Americans, 103, 106
Cuesta, Esther, 172n6

D'Acalá, Diego: *La frontera*, 97
Dajabón (Dominican Republic): ambiguity of name, 176n34; commemoration of 1937 Massacre, 1, 8, *11*; Prestol Castillo as magistrate of, 47, 58; in Prestol Castillo's *El Masacre*, 48–54, 56–58; in Trouillot's play *The Blue of the Island*, 148, 154; in Veloz Maggiolo's *El hombre del acordeón*, 72–73

Dalembert, Louis-Philippe: *The Other Side of the Sea*, 154–55, 162
Dalleo, Raphael, 121
Danticat, Edwidge: Border of Lights and, 172n8; on diaspora, 157–58; historical-fictional writing of, 130, 157–58; interview by Chancy, 9, 158; on lack of memorials to 1937 Massacre, 9; living memory and, 9, 10; multiple Haitis for, 147, 162, 187n23; on presentation of Haiti as "atypical" nation, 125; Trouillot (Évelyne) interview by (2005), 149. Works: *Breath, Eyes, Memory*, 157; *Brother, I'm Dying*, 157; *Claire of the Sea Light*, 99; *Create Dangerously: The Immigrant Artist at Work*, 125; *Krik? Krak!*, 157. See also *Farming of Bones, The*
Dash, J. Michael, 180n28, 187n27; *Haiti and the United States: National Stereotypes and the Literary Imagination*, 157
Daut, Marlene: *Tropics of Haiti*, 12
Dávila, Arlene, 182n4
Dayan, Joan, 71
Deive, Carlos Esteban, 64
Deleuze, Gilles, 36
De Maeseneer, Rita, 65, 70, 78, 96, 177n6
Derby, Lauren, 62, 159, 172n11
Derrida, Jacques, 163
Dery, Mark, 186n18
Diario, El, 32, 174n14
diaspora: ability to soften us-them mentality, 112, 123–24; anti-Haitianism and, 120; Cepeda and Alvarez working to educate and activate, 120; commemoration of 1937 Massacre, coming together with border communities for, 8; Dalembert's recognition of multiple Haitian diasporas, 155; Danticat on, 157–58; discrimination against the new arrivals, 111; Dominican American women envisioning effect on Haitian-Dominican past and future, 16, 106; future areas of study on, 167; geographic locations of Haitian Americans and Dominican Americans, 104, *105*, 123; heterotopia of Foucault and, 165; interethnic communities created by, 2, 18, 103, 126, 127, 139; Pérez's *Geographies of Home* and American dream of, 187; racial

diaspora (*continued*)
ideology and racial privilege, understanding of, 102–6; reconceptualization of Dominican-Haitian relationship in, 111–12, 164; re-creation of Haiti in, 146; third space recognized in, 106, 123, 161; transnational relations in US diaspora of Caribbean nations, 140; US diasporic representations of Haitianness by Dominican American women, 16; writers from, insider/outsider viewpoint of, 99–100. See also *Bird of Paradise*; Dominican Americans; *Wedding in Haiti, A*

Díaz, Junot: autobiographical forms of narrative and genre fiction used by, 164; Border of Lights and, 172n8; on Dominican assistance following Haiti 2010 earthquake, 186n15; hopeful endings in works of, 138; literary imperialism of Haiti and, 166; representation of Haitians by, 130–39; writing from Latino perspective on Haiti, 125–26. Works: "Apocalypse" (essay), 113, 134, 138; *The Brief Wondrous Life of Oscar Wao*, 130, 131–34, 168, 186n12; *Drown* (short stories), 130–31, 185n8; *This Is How You Lose Her* (short stories), 130–31, 182–83n10. See also "Monstro"

Di Pietro, Giovanni, 66
discrimination. See anti-Haitianism; racism; *trujillato* ideology
domincanyorks (off-island Dominicans), 105, 110–11
Dominican American literature, 1, 3–5, 14–19, 97, 99, 101–8; on relationship between Haiti and Dominican Republic, 5. See also Alvarez, Julia; *Bird of Paradise*; Cepeda, Raquel; Díaz, Junot; *Wedding in Haiti, A*
Dominican Americans: duality of identity, 182n9; jealousy of more assimilated people, 111; newcomer status compared to other Hispanic Caribbean groups, 103–4; as political exiles during Trujillo era, 103. See also diaspora
Dominican anti-Haitian ideology. See anti-Haitianism
dominicanidad (Dominicanness), 3, 23, 25, 34, 96, 109, 130
Dominican Independence Day, 165

Dominicanization of border regions, 23, 34, 46, 115, 159, 176n35
Dominican literature: early interpretations of Dominican racial imaginary, 26; obsession with the past, 65; post-Trujillo, 16; on relationship between Haiti and Dominican Republic, 5; terminology to describe historical narratives, 66. See also Marrero Aristy, Ramon; *Masacre se pasa a pie, El*; *Over*; Prestol Castillo, Freddy; Veloz Maggiolo, Marcio; *vida no tiene nombre, La*
Dominican Republic: civil war following Trujillo era, 88–89; "fantasy island" as nickname for, 107; founding of, 22, 165; as ground zero in Díaz's science fiction, 133; Haitians considered as untrustworthy in, 38–39, 53–54, 82–83, 175n24; international public response to TC/0168/13, 138; Law 169-14 in response to TC/0168/13, 172n10; Medina's response (Law 169-14) to TC/0168/13 (2013), 172n10; national spirit, disturbance in, 62; need to recognize irreversible link with Haiti, 116, 147; omission from historical anthologies of the Caribbean, 19; plan to "whiten" population, 181n42, 182n8; sugar industry in, 25; superiority to and separateness from Haitians, 2, 22–23, 27, 165; Tribunal Court ruling TC/0168/13 (2013), 10, 12, 14, 16–17, 91, 116, 119–22, 138, 184n19. See also Haitian Dominicans; Haitian Massacre (1937); Trujillo era
Dominican Revolutionary Party (PRD), 88, 177n42
Dominican@s por derecho, 184n19
double attitude to describe relationship between Haitians to Haitians and Dominicans to Dominicans, 85
Duany, Jorge, 111, 184n2
Duncan, Ian, 50

Eichner, Bill (husband of Alvarez), 115
Eller, Anne, 2, 5, 24, 159; *We Dream Together*, 146–47
erasure of national identity and of border, 2, 62, 72, 74, 75, 150, 154
Espaillat, Arturo: *Trujillo: Anatomía de un dictador*, 90

ethnic identity. *See* racial and ethnic identities

Farming of Bones, The (Danticat), 17, 127, 157–62, 175n31; breaking silence and (re)making history in, 157, 158, 162, 163; fragmentation of island coexisting with connectivity, 147, 162; Haitian Massacre (1937) and, 148, 157, 158–61; Massacre River in, 159, 160; movement from east to west to return to Haiti in, 157, 161; multiple Haitis in, 147, 162; third space and, 159, 160, 161

Faustino, Sarmiento, Domingo, 128

Ferrer, Ada, 17, 125, 126, 127

Fischer, Sibylle: *Modernity Disavowed: Haiti and the Cultures of Slavery in the Age of Revolution*, 157

Flores, Juan, 183nn10–11

Foucault, Michel: on anxiety-ridden nature of space, 128; Anzaldúa and, 172n6; "Des espaces autres" (lecture), 171n5; dualism in understanding heterotopia, 74; *Les mots et les choses* (published later as *The Order of Things*), 171n5; "Of Other Spaces: Utopias and Heterotopias," 5, 134, 171n5; Soja and, 6. *See also* heterotopia of Foucault

fragmentation, literary, 45, 73, 123, 139, 159, 167–68

Francisco, Ramón, 181n49

frontier metaphor, 70, 133, 164, 185n11; imperial frontier of Haiti, 166–67

fukú (curse of the new world), 132–33, 185n7

Fumagalli, Maria Cristina, 65, 75, 81, 176n32, 179n23; *On the Edge: Writing the Border between Haiti and the Dominican Republic*, 4, 28, 187n25

Gaffield, Julia: *Haitian Connections: Recognition after Revolution in the Atlantic World*, 126

Galíndez, Jesús de, 173n6

Gallego Cuiñas, Ana, 65, 90, 94, 181n45; *Trujillo, el fantasma y sus escritores*, 66

García Canclini, Néstor, 91

García Márquez, Gabriel: *El otoño del patriarca*, 66

García-Peña, Lorgia: Border of Lights and, 172n8; *The Borders of Dominicanidad:* *Race, Nation, and Archives of Contradiction*, 4, 18–19; on Dominican nationalist text during Trujillo era, 46; on Marrero Aristy's *Over*, 175n21, 175n23; on Prestol Castillo's *El Masacre*, 49; on Trujillismo requirements for writers, 31

Gates, Henry Louis: *Black in Latin America* television series, 126, 184n1

Geggus, David, 126

gender: Dominican American women envisioning diaspora's effect on Haitian-Dominican past and future, 106; female characters of Danticat as agents to (re)make history by breaking silence, 162; gendered Trujillo narratives, 181n44; gender violence revealed in *Nos cambió la vida* testimonies, 121; inequality in United States, 131; masculinity and, 13, 131; novels versus poetry by women writers, 181n50; in Veloz Maggiolo's *La vida no tiene nombre*, 93

genocide. *See* Haitian Massacre (1937)

geography and geospace, 2, 15–16, 48–49, 72. *See also* anonymous or ambiguous geographical locations; border between Dominican Republic and Haiti; borders; center-island areas; maps; third space

Gilroy, Paul, 18

Glissant, Édouard: Caribbean unity of Caribbean character, 18, 36; on interrelations of places, 127, 161; *Poetics of Relation*, 118; *Traité du tout-monde*, 127

Gonzalez, Juan, 102–3

González-Cruz, Luis F., 79, 87–88, 178n8, 178n15

González Díaz, Juan Carlos, 121, 184n22

Goodwin, Matthew, 185n11

Graciano, Berta, 35, 174n8

Grullón, Iván, 46

Guattari, Félix, 36

Guzmán, Pablo Yoruba, 103

Haiti: as apocalyptic dystopia in Díaz's "Monstro," 127–28, 133, 134, 139; difference between Haiti as victim and Haiti as triumphant republic, 146; dystropic depiction of, 17; earthquake (2010), effect of, 116, 120, 134; as "imperial frontier" in language of Juan Bosch, 166; independence of (1804), 22,

Haiti (continued)
126; Latin American scholarship and, 126, 166; multiple Haitis of Haitian and Haitian American perspectives, 146–61; nationalist discourses linked to France and United States, 157, 162; need to recognize irreversible link with Dominican Republic, 116, 147; peculiarity of, 125; as site of first slave revolt, 19, 125; situating in historical and cultural context, 18, 163. *See also* Saint Domingue; *and individual authors and titles*

Haitian American–authored texts, 5, 17–19. *See also* Danticat, Edwidge; *Farming of Bones, The*

Haitian Dominicans: anonymity and, 57, 132; contribution to Dominican Republic, 67; denial of Dominican citizenship by TC/0168/13 Tribunal Court ruling, 10, 12, 14, 16–17, 91, 100, 116, 119–22, 138, 184n19; largest ethnic minority in Dominican Republic, 150; as members of Dominican society, 65, 181n49; migration of, 147–57, 166; representations of, 163; speaking Spanish, 56. *See also* Haitian Massacre; Kreyòl

haitianidad (Haitianness), 3, 96, 130

Haitian literature: representation of Dominicans in, 19, 161–62. See also *Blue of the Island, The;* Trouillot, Évelyne

Haitian Massacre (1937), 7–10, 175n29; Alvarez's writings and, 115–17; anti-Haitianism linked to, 15, 23, 34–35; Anzaldúa on fears of both foreigners and white elites leading up to, 71; commemorative activities and plaque, 1, 8–10, 11, 183n17; Danticat's *The Farming of Bones* and, 148, 157, 158–61; Díaz's *The Brief Wondrous Life of Oscar Wao* and, 132; historical inaccuracy in reporting of, 9–10; literary retelling of, 175n31; mural and its vandalization, 9; Paulino's *Eddie's Perejil* and, 100, 119; Prestol Castillo's *El Masacre* and, 45–47, 52, 54–62; Rueda's writings and, 30; sugar plantations and, 174n19; Veloz Maggiolo's *El hombre del acordeón* and, 71–72, 78–81, 85, 178n12. See also *Farming of Bones, The*

Haitian Occupation (1822–1844), 24, 26, 27, 96, 175n28

Haitian Revolution (1791–1804), 12, 18–19, 24, 27, 59, 149

Hall, Stuart, 148, 167

Hasta la Raíz (2017 documentary), 120–22, 124, 184n22

Henríquez Ureña, Pedro, 5, 128–30, 185nn4–6; *Obra dominicana*, 129; "La utopía de América" (lecture), 128

Herrera Rodríguez, Rafael Darío, 29

heterotopia of Foucault: anonymity of, 36; articulation of border and, 3, 74; crisis heterotopia, 134, 185n3; Díaz's story "Monstro" and, 134; expanding in Caribbean literature of Hispaniola and diasporas, 165; functioning like mirrors, 44–45; Hispaniola considered in terms of, 5–6, 185n3; history of, 171n5; social and cultural space, interpretation of, 4–5; third space and, 130

Heureaux, Ulises "Lilís," 34, 129

Hintzen, Amelia, 160

Hispaniola: binary space of, 148; communal history of, best told through multiple narrators, 167–68; connection with other Caribbean countries, 18–19; Dominican reenvisioning of history of, 14–15, 19; as ground zero in Díaz's science fiction, 133; Haitian literature on history of, 17; heterotopic nature of, 5–6, 185n3; Otherness of, 5; Quisqueya (Taíno name), use of, 17, 173n13; unifications of, 22–23, 24, 59, 96, 165, 166; as utopia, 107. *See also* colonial period

Hispanism (*hispanicismo*), 21, 26; difference from anti-Haitianism, 173n1

historical fiction, 66–67, 177–78n7

hombre del acordeón, El (Veloz Maggiolo), 16, 67–86; accordion as synonymous with weaponry in, 80–81; as alternate, fictional rendering of historical events, 81–82, 178n13; answering the silence following the genocide, 85–86; changing real names of places to fictionalize geography in, 72; choice of work for analysis, 98; complexity of border region and border without boundaries, 64–65, 73, 163; criticism of Trujillo regime in, 79, 80; *Dominicanization of border regions,*

23, 34, 46, 115, 159, 176n35; erasure of national identity and of border in, 72, 74, 75; flashbacks, use of, 73–74; geographical ambiguity in, 67–68, 72; Haitian Massacre (1937) and, 71–72, 78–81, 85, 178n12; Hispanicizing of Haitian last names in, 82, 84, 85; hybridization in, 74, 81; identity, flexibility of, 83–84; impossibility of "una historia simple" in, 82–86, 95; in-between spaces in, 71, 74, 85; life after death and magical cemetery in, 76–77, 84; La Línea's representation in, 67–68, 71–75, 77–78, 81, 84–86, 163–64, 178n16; literary devices employed in, 72, 73, 178n15; Massacre River and, 1, 8, 59, 68, 70, 159, 160, 178n12; multiple narrators in, 167–68; music and resistance in, 75, 78–82, 84, 86; *nepantla* concept and setting of book, 68, 71; normalizing border experience by telling experiences of both Dominicans and Haitians, 72, 163–64; patchwork of writing mimicking chaos of border region in, 73, 168; *rayanos* (Haitian Dominicans) versus *fronterizos* (border dwellers) in, 71, 75, 79–83, 85, 179n19; La Salada as fictional town in, 67–68, 70, 72–75, 77–78, 82, 84, 85, 165; third space and, 65, 82; untrustworthy narrator in, 82–83; vodou religion and ritual in, 76, 81
hooks, bell, 6
Horn, Maja: on Dominican masculinity, 131; on gender discourse in Dominican Republic and diaspora, 106; *Masculinity after Trujillo: The Politics of Gender in Dominican Literature*, 4; on *trujillato* ideology and narrative, 13–14, 66–67; US presence and imperialism in Dominican Republic, effect of, 23; on Veloz Maggiolo, 177n1, 180n31
Hostos, Eugenio María de, 186n17
Howard, David, 40, 60
Hurni, Lorenz, 72
Hurston, Zora Neale, 180n28
hybridization, 6, 56, 74, 81, 176n36; borders as spaces of cultural hybridity, 137; fluid identity and, 109, 111

identity: Dominican identity in light of US imperialism, 23; flexibility in Veloz Maggiolo's *El hombre del acordeón*, 83–84; Hall on identity as internal construct, 167; Henríquez Ureña's rethinking Dominican national identity, 128; non-Haitians with stereotypical Haitian traits, 168; reconstruction and reevaluation of, 3. *See also* anti-Haitianism; racial and ethnic identities
ideological borders, 3–7, 16, 68, 154, 155, 163, 166
Iglesias, Norma, 137
in-between spaces, 2, 6, 8, 30, 68, 71, 74, 85, 110
Indiana Rodríguez, Rita: *La mucama de Omicunlé*, 98
insider/outsider perspective, 99–100, 103, 123
intellectuals: as nationalist followers of Trujillo, 15, 21, 25–27, 33, 34, 173n2; post-Trujillo, 89
interethnic communities, 2, 18, 103, 126, 127, 139

Jacmel (Haiti), 50
Jayaram, Kiran C., 171n2
Jean-Charles, Régine Michelle, 187n25
Jiménez, Blas, 174n18
Johnson, David E., 78, 166

Keating, AnaLouise, 68
Kelley, Robin D. G., 146
Knapp, Henry S., 87
Kreyòl: speakers' inability to pronounce *perejil*, 14, 45, 51, 56, 118, 119; speech remnants of Haitian Dominicans, 154–55, 168; *viktims* in Díaz's story "Monstro," 135–36

LaBouvier, Chaédria, 143
Lacay Polanco, Ramón, 61, 176n38
Laferrière, Dany, 187n23
Lantigua, Rafael, 182n3
Larsen, Neil, 65, 66
Lavender, Isiah, 135, 186n13, 186n19
Lefebvre, Henri, 7
Legrand, Catherine C., 33–34
Legros, Ayanna, 126
Lescot, Elie, 158
Lipsitz, George, 80
Lizardo, Fradique, 179n25

Llaviera, Tato, 105
Lockward, Alanna, 138; *Marassá y la nada*, 98
Louverture, Touissant, 58–59, 187n26

Machado Sáez, Elena, 121
Manzanillo, 72, 84
maps, 187n1; Alvarez's use of, 164; challenging in metaphorical and physical ways, 13, 164; diaspora locations of Haitian Americans and Dominican Americans, 104, 105, 123, 164; locations in Prestol Castillo's *El Masacre se pasa a pie*, 49, 51, 164
Marrero Aristy, Ramón: assassination of, 32, 174n16; background of, 32–33, 174nn15–16; critique of US imperialistic practices by, 32; failure to follow anti-Haitianism of earlier writers, 13, 27–28, 32; intellectuals preceding, 25–27; as National Salary Committee director, 32, 33; *La República Dominicana: Origen y destino del pueblo cristiano más antiguo de América*, 31–32, 62; Trujillo era and pro-Trujillo writing as necessity for, 25, 33; white planters in, 33. See also *Over*
Martí, José, 116, 128, 186n17
Martínez, Erika M., 181n50
Martínez-San Miguel, Yolanda: *Coloniality of Diasporas*, 18
masacre del perejil, la (Parsley Massacre). See Haitian Massacre (1937)
Masacre se pasa a pie, El (Prestol Castillo), 15–16, 45–63; as alternate antinationalist text, 46, 55, 61–62; bolded place names in, 48–51, 49, 176n33; border communities in geography of Dominican Republic and, 163; border space and, 21, 48–50, 163; compared to Marrero Aristy's *Over*, 48, 55, 61–63; compared to *Paisajes y meditaciones*, 60; fight for survival in, 53; genocide effects in, 54–55, 58–59; geographical ambiguity in, 22, 48, 62; Haitian characters in, 25, 50–54, 60; Haitian Dominicans' language choice in, 56, 168; Haitians depicted as untrustworthy in, 53–54, 175n24, 180n28; hybridization and racial mixing in, 56; lack of anonymity of Haitians and Haitian Dominicans in, 57; literary success of, 61; Louverture appearing in dream sequence in, 58–59; multiple narrators in, 167–68; as novel versus *testimonio*, 46–47, 53, 83, 175n30; primitivism and muddling of elitism in, 55, 57–58, 60, 61; publication delayed until after Trujillo's death, 62; repeating official Trujillo discourse in, 57, 60, 61
Massacre. See Haitian Massacre (1937)
Massacre River, 1, 8, 59, 68, 70, 159, 160, 178n12
Mateo, Andrés L., 173n2
Matibag, Eugenio, 78, 165
Matos Díaz, Eduardo: *Quiénes y por qué eliminaron a Trujillo*, 90
Mavor, Carol, 151–52
Mayes, April J., 34, 171n2, 174n7
McCormick, Robert H., Jr., 148
Medina, Danilo, 172n10
Medrano, Marianela: "El corte" (poem), 107
Mélida García: *Oro, sulfuro y muerte*, 97–98
Menton, Seymour, 87
mestizaje and *mestizos* (mixed offspring), 22, 26, 110, 113, 129, 141
Meyreles Soler, Rafael: *Así mataron a Trujillo*, 90
Michaelsen, Scott, 78, 166
migration: border-crossing stories, 147–57, 166; in Caribbean region, 148, 184n2; from Haiti, 25, 147; Haitian nationalist discourses linked to, 157. See also diaspora
Miller, T. S., 132–33
Mir, Pedro, 175n24, 178–79n17, 181n49
"Monstro" (Díaz short story), 17, 126, 127–30, 133–39; Alvarez's *A Wedding in Haiti* and, 113; apocalyptic dystopia in Haiti and, 127–28, 133, 134, 139; border imagery and quarantine zones in, 136–37, 163; Dominican American young adult as narrator in, 133–34; Haitian earthquake (2010) and, 134; hopeful ending in, 138; intersection of Haiti and Dominican Republic in, 161–63; La Negrura as plague in, 134–35; originally called excerpt from future novel, 185n10; third space and, 161; *viktims* in, 135–36, 138; zombies linked to plantation system in, 136

Monte Cristi (port town of Dominican Republic), 22; ethnic divide in, 28–30; in Prestol Castillo's *El Masacre*, 50; in Veloz Maggiolo's *El hombre del acordeón*, 72

Montejo, Esteban: *Biografía de un cimarrón* (with Barnet), 47

Montero, Mayra, 167, 187n1

Montes de Oca, Favio Ramón: *Trujillo y los secretos de su hija rayana*, 98

Mora Serrano, Manuel: *Juego de dominó*, 97

Moretti, Franco: *Graphs, Maps, Trees: Abstract Models for a Literary History*, 16, 50

Morris-Suzuki, Tessa, 67

Moscoso Puello, Francisco Eujenio: *Cañas y bueyes*, 35, 62, 175n22

Movimiento Reconoci.do. *See* Reconoci.do

Moya Pons, Frank, 174n19, 181n48

MUDHA (Movimiento de Muhjeres Dominico-Haitianas), 8

music: *bachata* genre, linked to resistance, 80, 179n24; fusing of two cultures in, 75, 77, 80, 86, 179n18, 179n25; Haitian Massacre commemoration by Juan Colon, 183n17; Older's *Shadowshaper* and, 144; Trujillo's appropriation of merengue as propaganda, 80, 179n23; in Veloz Maggiolo's *El hombre del acordeón*, 75, 78–82, 84, 86

nationness, notion of, 63

negrophobia. *See* racism

Nessler, Graham T.: *Islandwide Struggle for Freedom*, 155

New York: Cepeda's *Bird of Paradise* and, 106; Dominicans living in, 102, 107; Haitian and Dominican populations sharing space in, 104, *105*, 123; Latin Americans mistaken as "Blacks who happen to speak Spanish" in, 103; Vicioso's diasporic experience and, 122; We Are All Dominican (members residing in NYC), 120

Nos cambió la vida (testimonies published by Reconoci.do), 121, 122, 184n21

novela histórica as literary subgenre, 87

El Nuevo Diario, 32, 174n14

Núñez, Manuel: *Ocaso de la nación dominicana*, 105

Nuyorícan, 105

off-border space, 4, 6, 12, 16, 25, 31, 68, 91, 163, 169; Cepeda's *Bird of Paradise* and, 122; as ideological liminal zones, 90; third space as, 7, 21–22, 30, 31, 44

Older, Daniel José: fictional portrayal of Haiti by, 130; on lack of diversity in science fiction novels, 186n19, 186–87n21; *Shadowhouse Fall* (sequel to *Shadowshaper*), 140; Twitter account of, 145–46; writing from Latino perspective on Haiti, 125–26. *See also Shadowshaper*

on- and off-border texts, 5–6, 10, 12–19, 63, 161, 163, 169; Cepeda's *Bird of Paradise* versus Alvarez's *A Wedding in Haiti*, 122–24; Trouillot's play *The Blue of the Island* and on-border violence (2000), 148; Veloz Maggiolo's *La vida no tiene nombre*, 90–93. *See also* off-border space

Operation Bootstrap, 103

Otherness: colonial difference and, 172n11; Dominicans in United States associating themselves with, 102; foreign, 15, 68; of Haitian-based religion, 76; Haitians in Dominican Republic and, 81, 102, 165, 167–68; Hispaniola as space of, 5; identity in relationship to, 167; Oliver's *Shadowshaper* and, 142–43; racial, 14, 23, 143; in US diaspora, 131; in Veloz Maggiolo's *La vida no tiene nombre*, 98

Ouanaminthe (Haiti), 1, 8, 50, 72, 76, 81

Our National Conversation about Conversations about Race (podcast), 108, 182n6

Over (Marrero Aristy), 15, 31–45; as alternate to anti-Haitian ideology, 31, 35, 41–44, 61; autobiographical nature of, 33; censorship and, 42, 62; *cocolo*s in, 36, 173n3, 175n24; compared to Prestol Castillo's *El Masacre se pasa a pie*, 48, 55, 61–63; depersonalizing of Haitian laborers in, 37, 40, 155; geographical anonymity in, 21–22, 31, 36, 43–44, 62, 164; Haitian laborers' role in, 36–40, 44; Haitians depicted as untrustworthy in, 38–39, 175n24, 180n28; heterotopia and, 44–45; hunger trope in, 41; illiteracy and language barriers in, 38; links

Over (Marrero Aristy) *(continued)*
with other Caribbean cultures, 36; literary success of, 31, 61, 175n20; moral compass of, 40–41; non-Haitians with stereotypical Haitian traits in, 168; off-border third space and, 21–22, 30, 31, 44; as plantation novel, 25, 31; term "over," meaning of, 40–41; Trujillo ideology and, 46, 61; US imperialism as negative actor in, 30, 31, 35, 40–43, 62

Palés Matos, Luis, 167
Pan-Caribbean context, 18
Parsley Massacre (*la masacre del perejil*). *See* Haitian Massacre (1937)
Partido Reformista, 89
Partido Revolucionario Domincano (PRD), 88, 177n42
Paulino, Edward: backlands and, 5; Border of Lights and, 172n8; *Dividing Hispaniola*, 173n2; on Dominican separateness from Haiti and anti-Haitianism, 22, 23; *Eddie's Perejil* (play), 100–101, 119, 182n1; Haitian Massacre (1937) and, 100; on lack of documentation on border violence, 150; on Marrero Aristy's *Over*, 175n21; on Monte Cristi's proximity to the border, 28; on premassacre border's communities, 159; understanding of racial privilege, 100–101; zones of contact and, 5, 172n7
Peña Batlle, Manuel Arturo, 13, 15, 27, 41, 55–56, 58, 174n9
Pérez, Loida Maritza, 187n22
Pérez Firmat, Gustavo: *Life on the Hyphen*, 14, 105–6
Philoctète, René: *Massacre River*, 175n31
photography, use of, 114
Piatti, Barbara, 48–49
Pierre, Sonia, 7, 100, 120
Pietri, Pedro, 105
plantations. *See* sugar plantations
Pratt, Mary Louise, 172n7
PRD (Dominican Revolutionary Party), 88, 177n42
Premio Nacional de la Novela, 64, 177n2, 178n8
Prestol Castillo, Freddy: anti-Haitian sentiment and, 13, 27–28, 58; compared to Alvarez, 114–15; Haitian Massacre (1937) and, 45–47; as magistrate of Dajabón, 47, 58; *Pablo Mamá*, 175n28; *Paisajes y meditaciones de una frontera*, 45, 52, 58–60, 62, 114–15, 176n37; Peña Batlle quoted by, 58; refusal to take political sides, 176n32; Trujillo era and espousal of Trujillo-authorized discourse, 25, 58, 176n37. *See also Masacre se pasa a pie, El*
Price-Mar, Jean, 85; *La República de Haití y la República Dominicana*, 35
primitivism, 55, 57–58, 60, 61
provincial novel, 50
Puerto Rican American literature, 17–18, 127. *See also Shadowshaper*
Puerto Rico and Puerto Ricans: Betances and, 140; Dominicans and, 111, 167, 184n2; Haitians and, 17, 167; Martí on need for Cuba to work with, 116; migration to United States, 17–18, 103

Quesada, Sarah, 135–36, 138
Quisqueya (Taíno name for Hispaniola), 17, 118, 173n13

racial and ethnic identities: Alvarez's search for self-identity, 104–5; binational or hyphenated identity, 105–6, 108, 110; blue-black color as racially coded, 152–53; Bonó and Balaguer on common interests of, 26–27; Cepeda's search for self-identity, 104–5, 109; contemporary reenvisioning of, 19; diaspora's effect on, 102–6, 112; Dominican authors asserting, 174n18; of Dominicans, 24, 102–5, 131; fluidity of, 109, 111, 131, 168; of Haitians, 24; Hispanic/Latino as part of US schema, 101, 182n4, 183n11; *mulataje* (new racial category) in Dominican Republic, 110; non-Haitians with stereotypical Haitian traits, 168; prior to eighteenth century, 26; racial empowerment, 103; of Trujillo, 23, 173n6; US schema lacking fine distinctions of, 101, 182n2; us-them dichotomy, 13, 111, 112, 123–24, 169, 183n10. *See also* blackness; *mestizaje* and *mestizos*; Otherness
racism: Cepeda's experiences with, 108–9; of colonial period, 22, 95–96; Díaz's story "Invierno" and, 131; Henríquez Ureña, racial profiling of, 129; infectious disease metaphor for, 135, 186n13;

Marrero Aristy's *Over* and, 42–43; negrophobia, 14, 19, 108, 173n11; *Nos cambió la vida* testimonies revealing experiences of, 121; Older's *Shadowshaper* and, 141, 145; Paulino's understanding of racial privilege, 100–101; Puerto Ricans and African Americans expressing toward each other, 103; of sugar plantations, 175n22; of Tribunal Court ruling TC/0168/13 (2013), 10, 12, 14, 16–17, 91, 116, 119–22, 138, 184n19. *See also* anti-Haitianism; blackness; Kreyòl; Otherness

Ramírez, Dixa, 2, 72; *Colonial Phantoms: Belonging and Refusal in the Dominican Americas, from the 19th Century to the Present*, 4

Ramos, Daniel, 11

raya (the dividing line), 73, 81, 95, 164, 165

reciprocal influence and interdependence, 4, 13, 36, 72; cultural convergence in border spaces, 74–75, 168

Reconoci.do, 8, 119, 120, 138, 183–84n18; *Nos cambió la vida* (published testimonies), 121, 122, 184n21

religion: Afro-Caribbean religions in United States, 127; in border region, 75–77, 84; of *rayanos*, 179n19. *See also* vodou belief

Restoration War (1861–65), 175n28

Reuschel, Anne-Kathrin, 72

Reyes, Alfonso, 185n4

Reyes-Santos, Alaí, 3, 31, 34, 159, 175n21

Rivera, Lisa M., 140

Roa Bastos, Augusto: *Yo el Supremo*, 66

Robinson, Richard, 139

Rodríguez, Néstor E., 173n2

Rodríguez-Henríquez, Rafael, 67, 77, 78–79; *Fuentes de la imaginación histórica*, 87

Roethke, Theodore, 134

Rosario, Nelly, 180n33

Rosell, Sara V., 181n50

Roth, Wendy: *Race Migrations: Latinos and the Cultural Transformation of Race*, 101

Roumain, Jacques, 187n27

Rueda, Manuel, 181n49; *Bienvenida y la noche: Crónicas de Montecristi*, 22, 28–30; *Imágenes del dominicano*, 28; *Las metamorfosis de Makandal*, 28, 30;

premassacre Haitian-Dominican border and, 28–30; rat metaphor in, 30; *raya* (the dividing line), use of term by, 164; Trujillo characterization in, 30

Saint Domingue (French colony): abolition of slavery in, 18; compared to poverty of Santo Domingo, 172–73n11; compared to Santo Domingo, 24; economic growth of, 22, 26; mistaken scholarship confusing with Santo Domingo, 72; slavery in, 24; symbiotic relationship with Santo Domingo, 147. *See also* Haiti

Sánchez-Valverde, Antonio, 27; *Idea del valor de la Isla Española y utilidades que de ella puede sacar su monarquía*, 26

Sandoval, Chela, 6

San Miguel, Pedro, 26

Santiago de la Cruz (Dominican Republic), 51

Santo Domingo: authors participating in *Nos cambió la vida* from, 121; Boyer's desire to unify with Haiti, 96, 165; compared to Saint Domingue, 24; economic potential of, 26; as first colony to import African slaves, 19, 22; as first official colony of the Americas, 19, 22; mistaken scholarship confusing with Saint Domingue, 72; in Prestol Castillo's *El Masacre*, 50; racial mixing of indigenous and Spanish population in, 26; racism of colonial period in, 22; symbiotic relationship with Saint-Domingue, 147. *See also* Dominican Republic

Santos Febres, Mayra, 167

science fiction, 185nn8–11, 186nn12–13. *See also* Díaz, Junot; "Monstro"; *Shadowshaper*

Seibo, El (Dominican province), 68, 91–93, 96, 121, 180n41

sentencia, la. See Dominican Republic, Tribunal Court ruling (TC/0168/13)

Shadowshaper (Older), 17, 139–46; Afrofuturism and, 140; classified as science fiction and young adult fiction, 140, 145; envisioning intercommunity relationships, 145, 162, 186n20; Hispaniola map tattoo in, 164; interethnicity of New York City in, 126, 127, 139, 161; *kalfou* (crossroads) in vodou as intersection between living and dead, 144–46,

Shadowshaper (Older) (*continued*) 161; multiple Haitis of, 162; music in, 144; racism as norm in, 142, 145; relevance of ancestry and community in, 140–42, 145; rooted in Afro-Caribbean tradition and spirituality, 141; teenage Puerto Rican narrator of, 141; third space and border in, 161, 164; Universopolis and, 141
Shemak, April, 160
silence and (re)making history, 15, 54, 85, 119, 157, 158, 162, 163
Simmons, Kimberly Eison, 110; *Reconstructing Racial Identity and the African Past in the Dominican Republic*, 84
slavery, 22, 24, 96, 136, 149, 165; differences between Saint Domingue and Santo Domingo and, 24; in Dominican Republic, 31; Santo Domingo as first colony to import African slaves, 19; site of first slave revolt, 19, 125; slave revolts, 18, 19, 33, 125, 146, 187n26
Smartt Bell, Madison, 144, 149
social justice, 120–21
social media, 8, 145–46. See also Twitter
Soja, Edward W.: *Thirdspace: Journeys to Los Angeles and Other Real-and-Imagined Places*, 6–7, 169
Sommer, Doris, 31, 41, 46, 54, 55, 60, 175n21, 175n26
Sontag, Susan: *On Photography*, 114
Soulouque, Faustin, 59, 176n40
statelessness of Dominican Haitians. See Tribunal Court ruling (TC/0168/13)
Stavans, Ilan, 146
Stewart, Michael, 143
Stinchcomb, Dawn F., 173n3, 174n18
sugar plantations, 21, 24; ambiguous space of, 62; cane sugar as main export from both Haiti and Dominican Republic, 25; *cocolo*, meaning of, 21, 25, 36, 173n3, 175nn24–25; denationalization policy of Dominican Republic and, 62; depressed sugar market and labor unrest, 32, 33, 174n7; Haitian Massacre and, 174n19; international workforce as contract laborers on, 62; literature and scholarship centered on, 174n8, 174n17; in Marrero Aristy's *Over*, 35–36; migration from, 25; in Trujillo era, 35, 174n19; US management of, during occupation, 30, 40, 148, 175n22

Taíno (Dominican Republic's indigenous population), 22, 24, 26, 108, 144
Tavares, Juan Tomás, 9–10
testimonial narratives, 46–47, 53, 65, 175n30
Théodat, Jean Marie: *Haïti-République Dominicaine: Une île pour deux, 1804–1916*, 2–3
third space: Bhabha's concept of, 3, 6–7, 63, 65, 74; border between Haiti and Dominican Republic as, 3, 5, 12, 147, 161, 163; Cepeda's *Bird of Paradise* and, 106, 123; as common denominator of primary texts, 163; Danticat's *Farming of Bones* and, 159, 160, 161; diaspora and, 106, 123, 161; Díaz's story "Monstro" and, 161; fluidity of, 6–7; horizontal hierarchies and, 18; Latino/a authors treating Haiti as weird in, 17; as off-border space, 7, 21–22, 30, 31, 44; Older's *Shadowshaper* and, 161, 164; Soja's concept of, 6–7, 169; Trouillot's *The Blue of the Island* and, 161–62; Veloz Maggiolo's novels creating, 65, 74, 82
Torres-Saillant, Silvio, 31, 33, 34, 102, 177n1
transnational relations: between Haiti and Dominican Republic, 3, 18, 22, 140, 171n3; between Puerto Rico and Dominican Republic, 140; in US diaspora of Caribbean nations, 140
Treaty of Basilea (1795), 22
Tribunal Court ruling TC/0168/13 (2013), 10, 12, 14, 16–17, 91, 116, 119–22, 138, 184n19; activism in response to, 119–21, 138; Law 169-14 in response to, 172n10
Trouillot, Évelyne: interview by Danticat (2005), 149; literary family of, 149; *Rosalie l'infâme*, 187n24. See also *Blue of the Island, The*
Trouillot, Michel-Rolph, 17, 81–82; brother of Évelyne, 149; "The Odd and the Ordinary: Haiti, the Caribbean, and the World" (article), 125; *Silencing the Past*, 157

trujillato ideology, 13–14; border politics and, 115; Díaz's *Oscar Wao* and, 132; Dominican novels focusing on (Trujillo narratives), 65–66, 177nn5–6; Marrero Aristy's *Over* on, 61; Prestol Castillo's *El Masacre* on, 61; racism and anti-Haitian sentiment of, 21, 23–24, 27, 84, 160–61; requirements for writers under, 31

trujillistas teóricos, los, 21

Trujillo Molina, Rafael Leónidas: assassination of and post-Trujillo era, 16, 88–90; on border strengthening, 1, 19, 171n1; as Brigadier in Veloz Maggiolo's *El hombre del acordeón*, 70–72, 80, 83–84, 178n13; Díaz's *Oscar Wao* and, 132, 133; exaggerating Haitian-Dominican animosity, 13–15; faceless man in Díaz's *Oscar Wao* representing victims of, 132; family background of, 23, 173n6; Marrero Aristy and, 31; musical appropriation by, 80, 179n23; plan to "whiten" Dominican Republic, 181n42; premassacre portrayal of, 22; rebellion plots against, 118; sugar industry and, 41, 174n19; US military occupation and, 43, 158; Veloz Maggiolo's *La vida no tiene nombre* and, 93–94. See also *trujillato* ideology; Trujillo era

Trujillo era (1930–61), 12, 14, 16, 28–30; censorship and, 42, 47, 62, 168, 178n9; nationalist intellectuals of, 15, 21, 25–27, 173n2; sugar plantations in, 35; Veloz Maggiolo's literary approach to, 65, 89, 98. See also Haitian Massacre (1937)

Trujillo-Vincent Treaty (1936), 34, 53, 176n35

Turits, Richard Lee, 159

Twitter, 8, 120, 145–46

Ugalde, Sharon Keefe, 178n7

Ulysse, Gina Athena, 17; "Loving Haiti beyond the Mystique" (essay), 125; *Why Haiti Needs New Narratives: A Post-Quake Chronicle*, 99, 146, 147

United States: gender inequality in, 131; Haitian nationalist discourse linked to, 157, 162; Hispanic Caribbean migration to, 103; Hispanic/Latino as part of racial schema in, 101; imperialism of, 23; Mexican border with, 4, 171n4; racial ideology and Dominican migration to, 102–6; role of space for diaspora member, in revisiting country of origin, 17; transnational relations in US diaspora of Caribbean nations with, 140; zombie figures in popular culture of, 136. See also diaspora; US military intervention (1965)

US military intervention (1916–24), 12, 16, 180n34; Alexis's multitiered approach to 1937 Massacre including, 158; Dominican Republic, 23, 30; rebellion against, 93–94; Rosario's novel on, 180n33; in Rueda's writings, 30; Trujillo and, 43, 158

US military intervention (1965), 12, 16

utopia: *atopia* as substitute for, 139; Henríquez Ureña's Latin America as "American Utopia," 129–30; versus heterotopia, 5; Hispaniola as, 107; locating Haiti in America's utopia, 128–30

Valdez, Juan R.: *Tracing Dominican Identity: The Writings of Pedro Henríquez Ureña*, 129

Valerio-Holguín, Fernando, 98

Vargas, Angela, 51, 177n41

Vasconcelos, José, 128; *La raza cósmica*, 141

Vega, Ana Lydia, 167

Vega, Bernardo, 46

Veloz Maggiolo, Marcio, 64–67; background of, 64; called "most prolific contemporary Dominican writer," 177n1; censorship and, 178n9; on Haitian Dominican subject during Trujillo regime, 67, 86; literary devices employed by, 72, 73, 178n15; in literary rebellion of Dominican authors, 179n22; *literatura compadecida* and, 41; on physical border and cross sections of national communities, 62, 177n4; reenvisioning of Dominican history by, 65, 86, 180n39; Trujillo narratives by, 66–67, 89–90, 178n9. Works: *Los ángeles de hueso*, 89, 177n3, 180nn30–31; "Apuntes sobre autoctonía y etnicidad," 69; *El buen ladrón*, 89, 177n3, 180n32, 180n38; *De abril en adelante*, 65, 94;

Veloz Maggiolo, Marcio (*continued*)
Judas, 67, 89, 177n3, 178n8, 180n38;
Nosotros los suicidas, 89, 177n3;
"Tipología del tema haitiano," 41, 85, 97, 161, 180n29. See also *hombre del acordeón, El*; *vida no tiene nombre, La*
Vicioso, Chiqui, 101, 122, 182n2
Victoriano-Martínez, Ramón Antonio, 56–57, 60, 175n21; *Rayanos y Dominicanyorks: La dominicanidad del siglo XXI*, 4
vida no tiene nombre, La (Veloz Maggiolo), 16, 86–98, 180n32; absurd reality merging with fiction in, 87–88, 91, 95; as alternate, fictional rendering of historical events, 95; anti-Haitian jargon and racism in, 92, 95–96; choice of work for analysis, 98; citizenship rights of Haitian Dominicans and, 91; compared to *El hombre del acordeón*, 95; complexity of border region and, 64–65, 163–64; Dominican Other narration in, 65, 87, 89–90, 168; gendered discourse in, 93; guerrilla rebellion against US occupation (1916–1924) as subject of, 86–87, 94; Haitian Dominicans in, 65, 96–97; in-between spaces of inland geography in, 68–69; non-Haitians with stereotypical Haitian traits in, 168; on- and off-border setting of, 90–93, 163–64; as part of Latin American Boom novels, 86, 95, 180n32; rebellion in, 93–97; second US occupation (1965) and, 88; El Seibo province as setting of, 91–93, 96; Trujillo's role in, 89–90, 93–94

Vincent, Sténio Joseph, 158
vodou belief, 71, 75–76, 81, 84, 97, 136, 144

We Are All Dominican, 17, 120–22, 124, 138, 184n20
Wedding in Haiti, A (Alvarez), 17, 99–101, 113–19; bearing witness as part of "seeing" in, 113–14; Díaz's "Monstro" and, 113; failure to garner critical attention, 115, 183n13; geographic locations of Haitian Americans and Dominican Americans, 104, *105*; Haitian history and suffering woven into, 113, 116, 118–19; Haitian Massacre (1937) and, 115, 116; insider/outsider perspective of, 100, 103; maps used in, 164; photographs in, 114; post-earthquake Haiti and, 116, 120; racial identifications and, 101; setting on Hispaniola, along border, and in Haiti, 106, 113, 122, 123, 164; as "*us-moir*" instead of "*me-moir,*" 115, 122, 124
We Need Diverse Books, 186n19
whiteness, 24, 27, 34, 35, 43, 101, 109, 135, 181n42, 182n8. *See also* racial and ethnic identities
Wright, Micah, 43
Wucker, Michele, 7, 172n8
Wynter, Sylvia, 106

Young Lords Party (Puerto Rican), 102–3
Yspaniola (organization), 8

Zeller, Neici, 106
zones of contact, 5, 7, 12, 74, 169

RECENT BOOKS IN THE NEW WORLD STUDIES SERIES

Stanka Radović, *Locating the Destitute: Space and Identity in Caribbean Fiction*

Nicole N. Aljoe and Ian Finseth, editors, *Journeys of the Slave Narrative in the Early Americas*

Stephen M. Park, *The Pan American Imagination: Contested Visions of the Hemisphere in Twentieth-Century Literature*

Maurice St. Pierre, *Eric Williams and the Anticolonial Tradition: The Making of a Diasporan Intellectual*

Elena Machado Sáez, *Market Aesthetics: The Purchase of the Past in Caribbean Diasporic Fiction*

Martin Munro, *Tropical Apocalypse: Haiti and the Caribbean End Times*

Jeannine Murray-Román, *Performance and Personhood in Caribbean Literature: From Alexis to the Digital Age*

Anke Birkenmaier, *The Spectre of Races: Latin American Anthropology and Literature between the Wars*

John Patrick Leary, *A Cultural History of Underdevelopment: Latin America in the U.S. Imagination*

Raphael Dalleo, *American Imperialism's Undead: The Occupation of Haiti and the Rise of Caribbean Anticolonialism*

Emily Sahakian, *Staging Creolization: Women's Theater and Performance from the French Caribbean*

Candace Ward, *Crossing the Line: Early Creole Novels and Anglophone Caribbean Culture in the Age of Emancipation*

Ana Rodríguez Navas, *Idle Talk, Deadly Talk: The Uses of Gossip in Caribbean Literature*

Nadège T. Clitandre, *Edwidge Danticat: The Haitian Diasporic Imaginary*

Charlotte Rogers, *Mourning El Dorado: Literature and Extractivism in the Contemporary American Tropics*

Megan Jeanette Myers, *Mapping Hispaniola: Third Space in Dominican and Haitian Literature*

www.ingramcontent.com/pod-product-compliance
Lightning Source LLC
Chambersburg PA
CBHW030825230426
43667CB00008B/1385